BARRON'S

NEW JERSEY GRADE 7

ELA/LITERACY TEST

Joseph S. Pizzo

About the Author

Joseph S. Pizzo teaches 7th grade language arts at the Black River Middle School in Chester, NJ. An adjunct professor at Union County College and Centenary College, he is an accomplished writer, poet, workshop presenter, and voice-over provider. An original member of Ch. 9's A+ for Teacher's Hall of Fame, he is a former co-director of NJCTE and a board member for NJAMLE, NJ Schools to Watch, and Scholastic's National Teacher Advisory Board. Mr. Pizzo is also a WMGQ-FM Teacher Who Makes Magic and served as an announcer for the 2014 Summer Special Olympics at Princeton University.

© Copyright 2015 by Barron's Educational Series, Inc.

All rights reserved.
No part of this publication may be reproduced or distributed in any form or by any means without the written permission of the copyright owner.

All inquiries should be addressed to:
Barron's Educational Series, Inc.
250 Wireless Boulevard
Hauppauge, NY 11788
www.barronseduc.com

ISBN: 978-1-4380-0559-1

Library of Congress Catalog Card No.: 2014949913

Date of Manufacture: January 2015
Manufactured by: B11R11

Printed in the United States of America
9 8 7 6 5 4 3 2 1

10% POST-CONSUMER WASTE
Paper contains a minimum of 10% post-consumer waste (PCW). Paper used in this book was derived from certified, sustainable forestlands.

Contents

Introduction: Overview of PARCC Grade 7   **1**

Chapter 1
Writing an Argumentative Essay   **5**

- Compositional Risk   5
- Insight   9
- Major Task: Write an Argumentative Essay   10
- Ten-Step Strategic Plan for Success   16
- Independent Writing Practice   40

Chapter 2
Writing a Speculative Essay   **45**

- What Is a Speculative Essay?   45
- Creating a Story Plan   46
- Ten-Step Strategic Plan for Success   47
- Independent Writing Practice   64

Chapter 3
Reading: Literature and Informational Text   **69**

- Test Changes   69
- Major Task 1: Answer Questions Based on Literature—Literary Analysis   72
- Skills Practice—Warm-up Exercises   72
- Major Task 2: Answer Questions Based on Paired Passages—Research   86
- Major Task 3: Writing Clear, Thorough Essays Based on Reading Passages   93

Chapter 4
Reading: Informational (Everyday) Text   **143**

- What Is Everyday Reading?   143
- Major Task: Answer Questions Based on Informational Text   144
- Practice for Target Skills   145

Chapter 5
Writing — 189

- Grammar Guide: Using Grammar Correctly in Your Writing — 189
- Practice for Target Skills — 189

Answers and Explanations for Practice Exercises for Chapters 1–5 — 229

Chapter 6
Practice Test—Performance-Based Assessment — 275

- Answers — 301

Chapter 7
Practice Test—End-of-Year Assessment — 313

- Answers — 328

Appendix A
Sample Graphic Organizer and Organization Chart for Writing — 333

- Argumentative Essay Flow Chart — 333
- Speculative Writing Organization Sheet — 335

Appendix B
Grade 7 English Language Arts Common Core Standards — 337

Index — 345

Introduction: Overview of PARCC Grade 7

As you prepare to take your New Jersey Grade 7 ELA/Literacy Test, you probably have questions. Before we begin preparing for the test, let's try to answer some common questions that you may have.

What Is the NJ PARCC Test?

The PARCC (Partnership for Assessment of Readiness for College and Careers) is a test given by the State of New Jersey to all of New Jersey's public school students. In grade 7, the two areas being tested are language arts and math. The curriculum that you are following in school is based on the Common Core state standards (CCSS), which is much more demanding than the prior Core Curriculum content standards (CCCS).

Is the PARCC Test Required?

The State of New Jersey requires all students to take the test so it can be determined whether you are learning the proper skills in your classroom each year. If you happen to do poorly, then your school will get you extra help so you can learn all your skills and get a better score on the next year's test.

When and How Is the PARCC Given?

The NJ PARCC is broken up into two exams. The PBA (Performance-Based Assessment), which is given after approximately 75% of the school year, and the EOY (End-of-Year Test) that is administered after 90% of the school year. Both exams are mainly comprised of reading passages; both literary and informational, multiple-choice questions, and writing responses by way of essays. The PARCC is given on the computer, so you should be familiar with technology and how to input information. As you answer the (TECR) Technology Enhanced Constructed Response questions, you will be asked to select multiple answers to demonstrate that you know which choices are the most important or in what order the choices have occurred. For some of the (PCR) Prose-Constructed Response questions and (EBS) Evidence-Based Selection questions, you may be asked to read two to three passages of text and then view a video before responding to multiple-choice questions and writing responses. For more information about the types of questions and what they may look like on screen, please see below. Each type of question has a detailed explanation of what you might be asked to do, either select an answer, select multiple-answers, drag and drop, or highlight.

2 · New Jersey Grade 7 ELA/Literacy Test

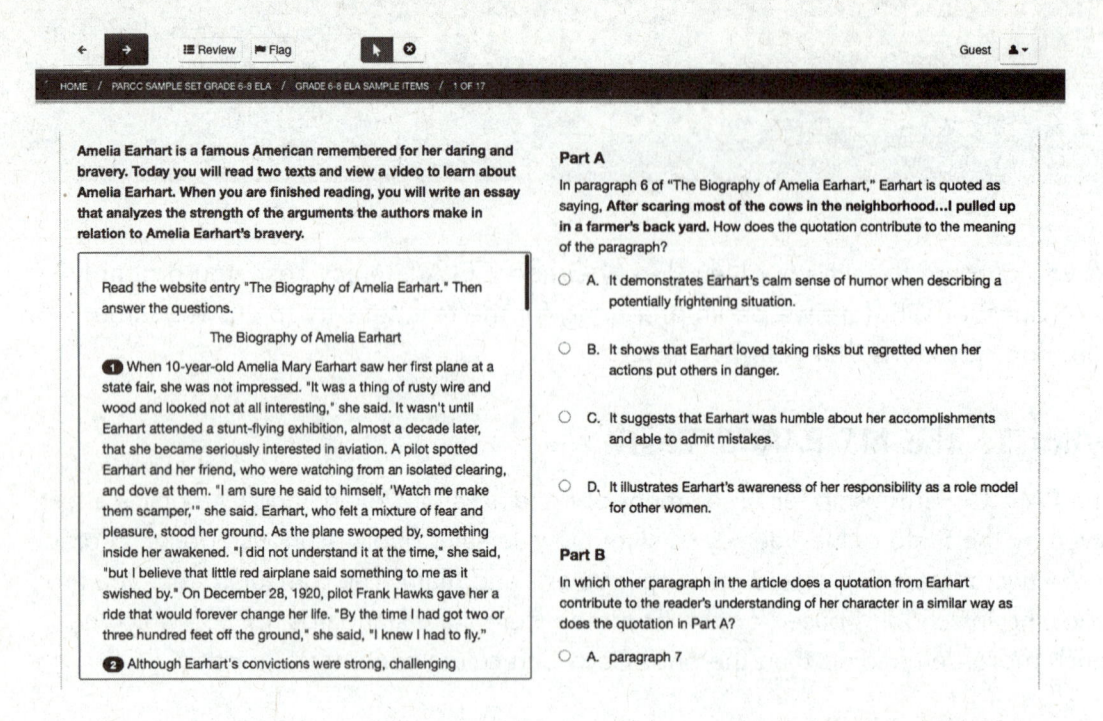

Amelia Earhart is a famous American remembered for her daring and bravery. Today you will read two texts and view a video to learn about Amelia Earhart. When you are finished reading, you will write an essay that analyzes the strength of the arguments the authors make in relation to Amelia Earhart's bravery.

Read the website entry "The Biography of Amelia Earhart." Then answer the questions.

The Biography of Amelia Earhart

1 When 10-year-old Amelia Mary Earhart saw her first plane at a state fair, she was not impressed. "It was a thing of rusty wire and wood and looked not at all interesting," she said. It wasn't until Earhart attended a stunt-flying exhibition, almost a decade later, that she became seriously interested in aviation. A pilot spotted Earhart and her friend, who were watching from an isolated clearing, and dove at them. "I am sure he said to himself, 'Watch me make them scamper,'" she said. Earhart, who felt a mixture of fear and pleasure, stood her ground. As the plane swooped by, something inside her awakened. "I did not understand it at the time," she said, "but I believe that little red airplane said something to me as it swished by." On December 28, 1920, pilot Frank Hawks gave her a ride that would forever change her life. "By the time I had got two or three hundred feet off the ground," she said, "I knew I had to fly."

2 Although Earhart's convictions were strong, challenging

Part A
In paragraph 6 of "The Biography of Amelia Earhart," Earhart is quoted as saying, **After scaring most of the cows in the neighborhood…I pulled up in a farmer's back yard.** How does the quotation contribute to the meaning of the paragraph?

○ A. It demonstrates Earhart's calm sense of humor when describing a potentially frightening situation.

○ B. It shows that Earhart loved taking risks but regretted when her actions put others in danger.

○ C. It suggests that Earhart was humble about her accomplishments and able to admit mistakes.

○ D. It illustrates Earhart's awareness of her responsibility as a role model for other women.

Part B
In which other paragraph in the article does a quotation from Earhart contribute to the reader's understanding of her character in a similar way as does the quotation in Part A?

○ A. paragraph 7

Only part of the passage that you see in these examples is visible. You will need to scroll down on the computer to read the whole passage.

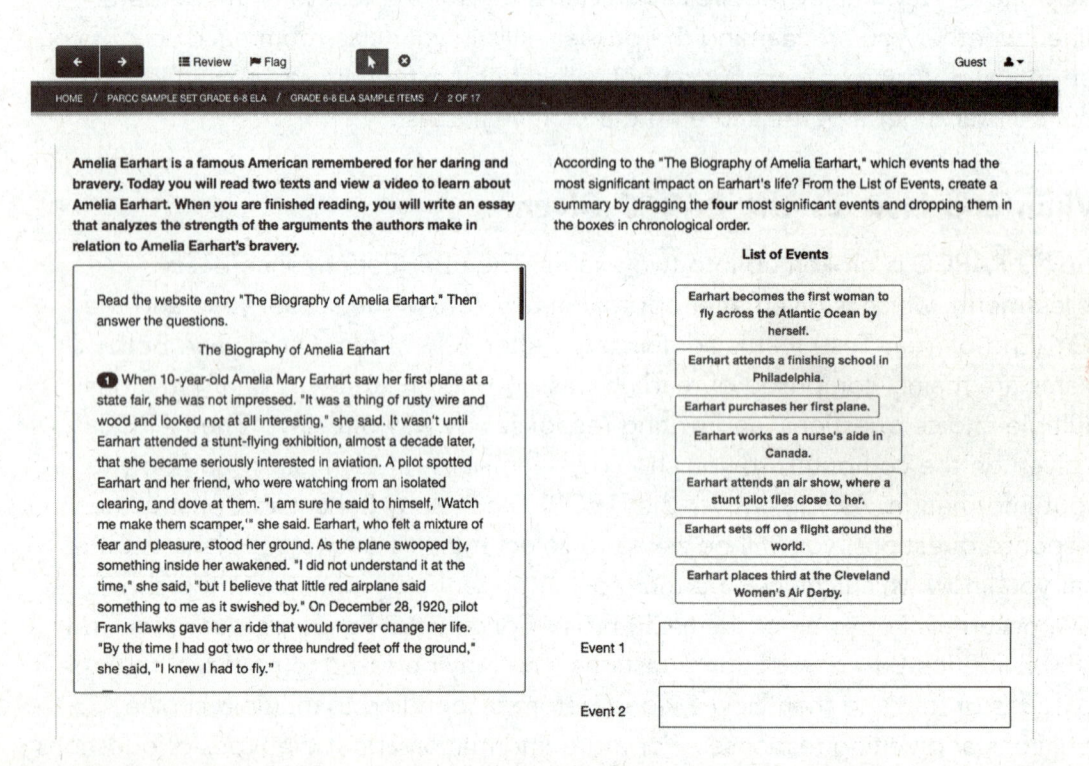

Amelia Earhart is a famous American remembered for her daring and bravery. Today you will read two texts and view a video to learn about Amelia Earhart. When you are finished reading, you will write an essay that analyzes the strength of the arguments the authors make in relation to Amelia Earhart's bravery.

Read the website entry "The Biography of Amelia Earhart." Then answer the questions.

The Biography of Amelia Earhart

1 When 10-year-old Amelia Mary Earhart saw her first plane at a state fair, she was not impressed. "It was a thing of rusty wire and wood and looked not at all interesting," she said. It wasn't until Earhart attended a stunt-flying exhibition, almost a decade later, that she became seriously interested in aviation. A pilot spotted Earhart and her friend, who were watching from an isolated clearing, and dove at them. "I am sure he said to himself, 'Watch me make them scamper,'" she said. Earhart, who felt a mixture of fear and pleasure, stood her ground. As the plane swooped by, something inside her awakened. "I did not understand it at the time," she said, "but I believe that little red airplane said something to me as it swished by." On December 28, 1920, pilot Frank Hawks gave her a ride that would forever change her life. "By the time I had got two or three hundred feet off the ground," she said, "I knew I had to fly."

According to the "The Biography of Amelia Earhart," which events had the most significant impact on Earhart's life? From the List of Events, create a summary by dragging the **four** most significant events and dropping them in the boxes in chronological order.

List of Events

| Earhart becomes the first woman to fly across the Atlantic Ocean by herself. |
| Earhart attends a finishing school in Philadelphia. |
| Earhart purchases her first plane. |
| Earhart works as a nurse's aide in Canada. |
| Earhart attends an air show, where a stunt pilot flies close to her. |
| Earhart sets off on a flight around the world. |
| Earhart places third at the Cleveland Women's Air Derby. |

Event 1 [   ]

Event 2 [   ]

Some questions give you more than four answer choices and require you to click on each correct answer choice or drag them into answer boxes.

Screen 1 (6 of 17)

Amelia Earhart is a famous American remembered for her daring and bravery. Today you will read two texts and view a video to learn about Amelia Earhart. When you are finished reading, you will write an essay that analyzes the strength of the arguments the authors make in relation to Amelia Earhart's bravery.

Read the article "Earhart's Final Resting Place Believed Found." Then answer the questions.

Earhart's Final Resting Place Believed Found

by Rossella Lorenzi

1 Legendary aviatrix Amelia Earhart most likely died on an uninhabited tropical island in the southwestern Pacific republic of Kiribati, according to researchers at The International Group for Historic Aircraft Recovery (TIGHAR).

2 Tall, slender, blonde and brave, Earhart disappeared while flying over the Pacific Ocean on July 2, 1937 in a record attempt to fly around the world at the equator. Her final resting place has long been a mystery.

3 For years, Richard Gillespie, TIGHAR's executive director and author of the book "*Finding Amelia*," and his crew have been searching the Nikumaroro island for evidence of Earhart. A tiny coral atoll, Nikumaroro was some 300 miles southeast of Earhart's

Part A

Below are three claims that could be made based on the article "Earhart's Final Resting Place Believed Found."

Claims	Earhart and Noonan lived as castaways on Nikumaroro Island.
	Earhart and Noonan's plane crashed into the Pacific Ocean.
	People don't really know for certain where Earhart and Noonan died.

Select the claim that is supported by the **most** relevant and sufficient evidence within the article "Earhart's Final Resting Place Believed Found." The claim you select will be highlighted in yellow.

Part B

Select evidence from the article that **best** supports the answer in Part A. Drag **two** sentences from the list and drop them into the Evidence box.

"A tiny coral atoll, Nikumaroro was some 300 miles southeast of Earhart's target destination, Howland Island." (paragraph 3)

"Although she did not succeed in her around-the-world expedition, Earhart flew off into the legend just after her final radio transmission." (paragraph 10)

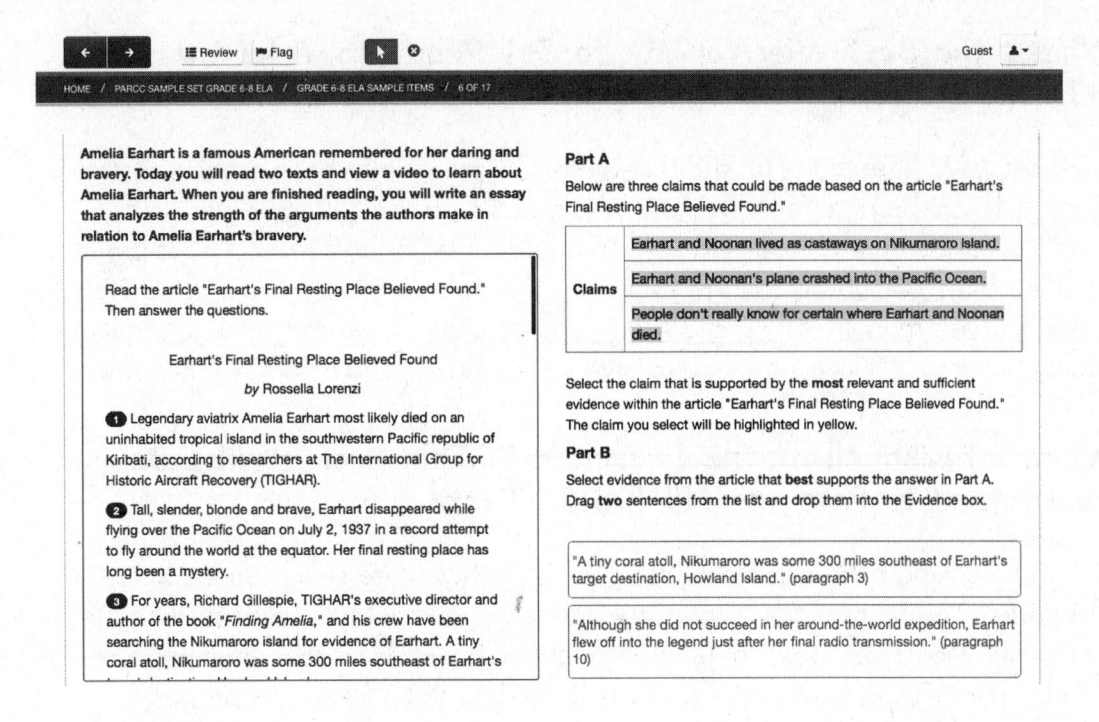

Some essays require you to draw specific information from multiple resources to make specific references.

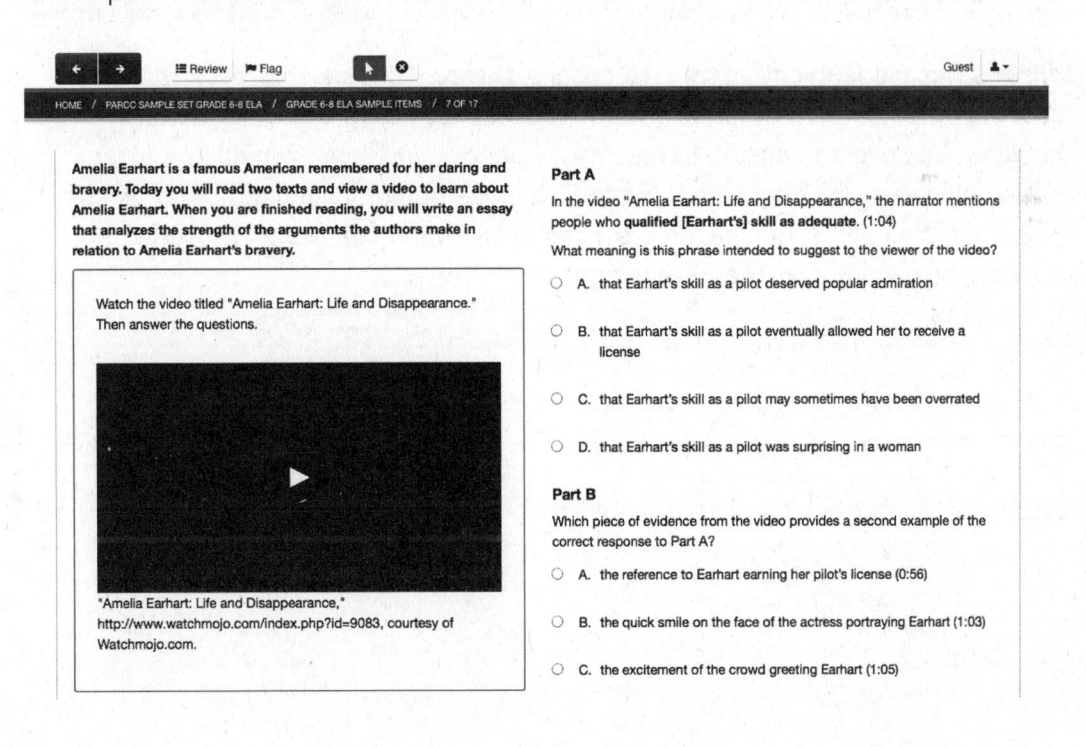

Screen 2 (7 of 17)

Amelia Earhart is a famous American remembered for her daring and bravery. Today you will read two texts and view a video to learn about Amelia Earhart. When you are finished reading, you will write an essay that analyzes the strength of the arguments the authors make in relation to Amelia Earhart's bravery.

Watch the video titled "Amelia Earhart: Life and Disappearance." Then answer the questions.

"Amelia Earhart: Life and Disappearance,"
http://www.watchmojo.com/index.php?id=9083, courtesy of Watchmojo.com.

Part A

In the video "Amelia Earhart: Life and Disappearance," the narrator mentions people who **qualified [Earhart's] skill as adequate**. (1:04)

What meaning is this phrase intended to suggest to the viewer of the video?

○ A. that Earhart's skill as a pilot deserved popular admiration

○ B. that Earhart's skill as a pilot eventually allowed her to receive a license

○ C. that Earhart's skill as a pilot may sometimes have been overrated

○ D. that Earhart's skill as a pilot was surprising in a woman

Part B

Which piece of evidence from the video provides a second example of the correct response to Part A?

○ A. the reference to Earhart earning her pilot's license (0:56)

○ B. the quick smile on the face of the actress portraying Earhart (1:03)

○ C. the excitement of the crowd greeting Earhart (1:05)

What's the Best Way for Me to Get Ready to Take the NJ PARCC Test?

The best way to get ready for the test is basic. Make sure to be in a positive state of mind as you prepare for the test. Emphasize the phrase "I'm going to do my best" rather than the phrase "I'm so worried about taking this test." About a week before the test, try not to change your daily routine too much. Have a good, healthy breakfast each morning and avoid sugary snacks. Stay away from caffeinated and/or sugary beverages. Finally, be sure to give your mind a good workout every day.

When I Finish All of the Exercises in This Book, Will I Be Guaranteed to Pass the NJ PARCC Test?

Unfortunately, no book can make that guarantee. If you are serious and you complete all of the sections in this book carefully, your chances to do well on the test should increase. Please remember to review any sections that you find to be difficult ones. The only way to learn is to study the right information properly.

IMPORTANT NOTE

Barron's has made every effort to ensure the content of this book is accurate as of press time, but the PARCC Assessments are constantly changing. Be sure to consult *https://www.parcconline.org/* for all the latest testing information. Regardless of the changes being announced after press time, this book will still provide a strong framework for seventh-grade students preparing for the assessment.

Writing An Argumentative Essay

CHAPTER 1

COMPOSITIONAL RISK

How Using Compositional Risk Can Help You Write Argumentatively

A compositional risk is meant to grab the reader's attention. Sometimes called a "hook" or a "teaser," a compositional risk gets your reader interested in your message. It is a first impression that your reader gets about your essay and its level of interest. You may even want to think of a compositional risk as doing the same job that a friendly handshake or a warm greeting does: giving your reader a good reason to listen to that which you are saying.

If you fail to include a compositional risk, the highest grade your essay can receive is a grade of 2 out of 4. The top grades of 3 and 4 represent "Advanced Proficient" scores while a 2 represents a "Proficient" score. The lack of insight in your essay will likely do the same. The use of a compositional risk does not automatically ensure that your essay will receive a grade of a 3 or a 4. It gives you a chance to receive a 4 if your essay is outstanding and has an effective compositional risk. Your essay will receive a 3 if your essay is outstanding, but your attempt at writing a strong compositional risk is weak instead.

Types of Compositional Risks

There are different types of compositional risks. For example, one of the most common is the rhetorical question. A *rhetorical question* is one that does not require an answer. In an essay about friendship, the rhetorical question raised may ask "When you think of the most important things in your life, could you possibly imagine anything more important than friendship?"

Telling a Brief Story: Good Idea or Bad Idea?

A brief story (known as an anecdote) is a good way to begin an essay about friendship. For example, you may describe the time that you were locked out of your house during a rain storm and your best friend who lives next door invited you to come into his/her house, change into some dry clothes, and have lunch while you waited for your mom or dad to come home. Be sure to keep this anecdote

5

brief since you can easily lose your effectiveness if your story replaces the idea of friendship as the theme of your piece. Furthermore, the NJ PARCC is a timed test that is much more challenging than the NJASK was. Therefore, spending too much time on your introduction will serve only to reduce the time you have to spend on developing the body of your writing piece.

Using Imagination

Is it a good strategy to let my reader use his/her imagination? To do so, try a similar compositional risk simply known as "What if?" In an essay about friendship, you may wish to ask your reader to "Think about the people who mean the most to you in your life. Think about the people who help you to celebrate the good times while comforting you during the difficult times. Think about the people who help to make your life special. Your family members are very important to you, and so are your friends. Moreover, that special friend who listens to all your complaints and worries and who gives you the best advice can be almost as important as your own family."

Notice that the phrase "Think about" was repeated for dramatic effect. That's actually another compositional risk known as parallelism, which is another way of using repetition for effect. Rev. Dr. Martin Luther King, Jr. used this technique effectively when he gave his "I Have a Dream" speech and repeated the speech's title many times for effect as he presented his speech. Let the reader see what you want the reader to see by showing good story development and not neglecting specific details.

Paint a Word Picture

Painting a word picture, also known as "using vivid imagery," is a good idea for most essays unless you are being required to cite facts and procedures for an explanation of the steps in a math problem or explain steps in a laboratory report, for example. Anyway, the use of vivid imagery in a language arts essay tells your reader that you are demonstrating complex thinking. This type of thinking usually translates to effective writing. For example, your essay about friendship might mention the sound of the rain that was falling, the way the rain drops were cascading down your hair, or even the distinctive aroma of the dampness as the rain fell. These details add depth to the essay you are writing about being caught in the rain and then "waited for your mom or dad to come home."

Using References

Using a reference from a book or play, known as a literary allusion, is also a good way to incorporate a compositional risk. For example, mentioning the importance of the friendship that Dorothy in *The Wonderful Wizard of Oz* formed with the Tin Man, the Scarecrow, and the Cowardly Lion is an example of a literary allusion. You may consider making a reference to a popular song, TV show, or movie, but these as not as powerful as a literary reference is. Besides, the audience you are writing for is an audience of English teachers who are evaluating your writing. It is a wiser choice to refer to something with which the evaluators are already familiar. When using a literary allusion, be sure to use it correctly and assign credit to the correct individuals. For example, it was Shakespeare's Macbeth who said "Fair is foul, and foul is fair."

Using Quotations

Using a quote would definitely impress an English teacher. However, you may not use any outside sources to look up a quote to use during the test. Remember, you don't know what the topics are ahead of time. Even so, you may want to memorize up to five different quotes that each refer to a common situation or emotion: friendship, tolerance, happiness, courage, and perseverance are some possibilities. For your essay dealing with friendship, you may wish to use one of these following quotes:

> "My best friend is the one who brings out the best in me." (Henry Ford)
>
> "It is the mark of an educated man to be able to entertain a thought without accepting it." (Aristotle)
>
> "The best way to cheer yourself up is to try to cheer somebody else up." (Mark Twain)
>
> "Without courage, all other virtues lose their meaning." (Winston Churchill)
>
> "Fall seven times, stand up eight." (Japanese Proverb)

Please be aware that citing the words of a Shakespearean character can be effective, but be sure you are assigning the quote to the correct character. For example, "This above all: to thine own self be true" is an appropriate quote when writing about individualism. However, you must be sure that you credit Polonius and not Hamlet for speaking the quote.

Interesting Facts and Compositional Risk

An interesting fact can make an effective compositional risk—as long as you can remember it accurately. I would suggest that you use a fact that you are sure is true. For example, mentioning the celebration of Friendship Day in the United States is a fact that is easy to remember. However, remembering the names of all the actors who star in the series *Friends* is not only difficult, but also not particularly relevant information for your essay. Also, remember that there is no access either to the Internet or reference books to research your idea while you are taking the NJ PARCC.

Humor as a Compositional Risk

Most writers will tell you that humor is one of the most difficult emotions to capture in writing. Therefore, unless you are considered by adults to be naturally funny, you may wish to avoid using humor as a compositional risk. Moreover, never use humor that is achieved at the expense of someone else. Jokes about people's physical traits or shortcomings are never a good idea to include in your essay. They are simply rude and unacceptable.

Startling Statements

A startling statement might work in an essay in which you are trying to get the reader to react to the shock of what you are stating. If you are going to cite the lives of heroes like Mahatma Ghandi, Mother Teresa, and Rev. Dr. Martin Luther King, Jr. as individuals whose lives exceeded the boundaries of friendship as they demonstrated their heroism on behalf of all individuals, then a startling statement would be appropriate for an essay about friendship. Nevertheless, you may be better served by using a quote or an allusion that is a bit less shocking.

More Compositional Risks

Yes, there are more compositional risks. For example, some writers will use statistics, brief scenarios, or even sarcasm (which is risky if not done properly and with constraint). I would avoid using sarcasm since it usually is not taken well by a serious audience. However, the compositional risks that we have discussed are very common ones that I have seen students like you use successfully over the years. Moreover, they are easy to remember and reasonably easy to learn to use.

INSIGHT

The term insight refers to the personal thoughts that you, the writer, bring to the topic you are covering. For example, in the essay about friendship, you may conclude that "A life without good friends is an empty life indeed." You may also observe that "The ability to make friends is the direct result of the ability to be a friend." Conclusions like these represent insight since they require you, as the writer, to bring some of your own personal thoughts and learning to your essay. In effect, you make a personal connection and demonstrate your thinking process when you connect the text to another part of the text (a character's earlier actions connected to his/her later actions), to yourself (your experience with a similar situation), or to the world (those experiences and situations that are considered to be common to most of us). This type of writing also demonstrates a sophistication that you are bringing to your essay. There is careful thought that is supporting your ideas, and that is critical for your writing to achieve success.

Please understand that your insight represents either the significance of your remarks or a life lesson being taught. This so-called significance is sometimes known as "So what?" or "Why do I need to know this?" It is the reason for the reader to invest time into listening to your essay. Your thoughts, while they may be wonderfully constructed, also need to have significance for your reader to invest time and energy in your piece. Otherwise, your writing is simply formula writing that could be produced by anyone at any time. Unless your writing contains insight, it will never be taken seriously nor will it be considered to be outstanding.

Insights may be made throughout your essay. Nonetheless, be sure to include at least one insight in your final paragraph. Otherwise, the evaluator who reads your essay will not assign you the top score possible, 4. In fact, your chance at receiving a score of 3 is also weakened.

Argumentative vs. Persuasive: Know the Difference

Before we begin exploring ways to write an argumentative essay effectively, let's compare it to the typical persuasive essay. The framework for each essay is quite similar. The opening paragraph in each includes a compositional risk and an overview of the essay's main points. Nonetheless, the persuasive essay has three main points in the three body paragraphs, whereas the argumentative one has two main points in the two body paragraphs. The reason is a simple one. The argumentative essay includes the strongest opposing viewpoint and a counter-argument to disprove it.

The structure of the body of both the persuasive and the argumentative essays includes the strongest supporting point in paragraph two and the second strongest supporting point in paragraph three. It is in the fourth paragraph where the structure differs. In a persuasive essay, this third body paragraph (fourth paragraph overall) features the third strongest supporting point. On the other hand, the argumentative essay states the strongest point of the opposing view and then demonstrates the major way to counter (disprove) this argument. The final paragraph in both essays is summative, featuring the main points stated in the three body paragraphs. Before the insight is included, however, the argumentative essay also recounts the opposition's major argument and the stated counter to the argument.

We are going to address the way to create an argumentative essay since this is considered to be a more difficult task. Evaluators are more likely to assign a higher score to a writer who not only proves a point, but who also counters the opposition's major point as well.

MAJOR TASK: WRITE AN ARGUMENTATIVE ESSAY

One type of major essay writing you will do for the NJ PARCC ELA/Literacy Test for Grade 7 is argumentative writing. Your essay needs to be five paragraphs long, well planned, and well written. Let's look at some of the ways that you can write an essay to impress those who will be scoring your writing.

On the actual NJ PARCC, you may be given a situation and asked to compare the information in a fiction passage with that in a non-fiction passage or video. Remember to add direct references ("quotes") when completing this type of research task.

Use this section to get yourself prepared for the text-based writing. These skills will establish a foundation needed for "research" questions.

Plan Effectively to Write Effectively

Prewriting is a strategy that you're probably using in your language arts class. The key is planning. To write effectively, every writer needs first to plan effectively. Good planning allows you, the writer, to collect your thoughts before you write them down on paper.

Let's do a brief exercise to get ready for the test. First, let's look at the writing prompt and then at the plans that two students have written before writing their own essays.

Writing an Argumentative Essay • 11

Strategic Practice

Write an essay that convinces your classmates to listen to either your favorite music or musical group. Make a writing plan for your essay before you begin writing.

In the space provided, write down the type of music you like best and list three main reasons for your choice.

My favorite type of music is _Pop_

I like this music because:

1. _It really gets me into it_
2. _The beat is really great to get lost into_
3. _The best songs that are hit are mostly Pop_

Now, check your answers as you read through Ronnie's and Billie's answers. See how your answers compare to theirs.

Ronnie's Plan

My favorite type of music is hip hop.

I like this music because:

1. It's awesome!
2. It really gives me a rush.
3. It's great to listen to.

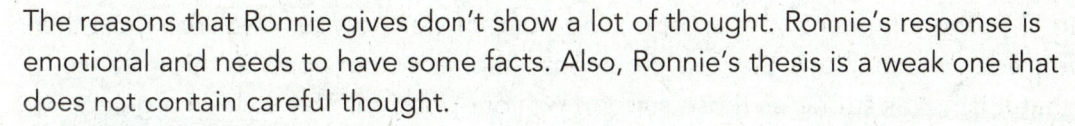

The reasons that Ronnie gives don't show a lot of thought. Ronnie's response is emotional and needs to have some facts. Also, Ronnie's thesis is a weak one that does not contain careful thought.

==Good argumentative essays use facts rather than emotions to convince the reader. Without good facts, these emotions can't support an opinion.==

Let's look at Billie's plan next to see if his reasons are better ones.

Billie's Plan

Hip hop music is the best music for my generation to listen to.

I like this music because:

1. It has danceable "street" rhythms.
2. It speaks to the soul of young urban listeners.
3. It deals with important issues for my generation.

As you can see, Billie's plan is the better one. The reasons that are given can be supported with facts, rather than emotions.

Check your list again. Did you

- choose a specific type of music as your favorite?
- give three good reasons for your choice?

Warm-up Exercise—Strengthening by Combining Details

Take another look at Billie's list. Can any of the details listed be combined because they are similar? Actually, the second and third points share a similarity. When music "speaks to the soul of young urban listeners," it surely can be said that it "deals with issues for my (Billie's) generation." Therefore, these two details can be combined in this way: "It speaks to the soul of young urban listeners because it deals with important issues for my generation." This complex style of thinking is rewarded on the NJ PARCC, especially because writing is the placement of thoughts on paper. Complex thought should therefore inspire complex writing.

Warm-up Exercise—Supporting Details

Okay, now write three supporting details for each of your main points. Be sure to give clear, specific reasons. Remember that this essay is going to require that you state a strong argument from an opposing point of view to your own. You must then give evidence that shows that this argument either does not apply in this instance or that it is not as strong as those supporting your position. This style of arguing resembles that which is used during debating, as well as the authoring of papers that are comprehensive and carefully planned. As you progress throughout the remainder of your academic career, the argumentative essay will be viewed more favorably than the persuasive one because it addresses both sides of the issue.

Hip hop music is the best music for my generation to listen to.

Writing an Argumentative Essay • 13

I like this music because:

1. _It is perfect type to dance on_
   a. _Beats are easier to follow_
   b. _Dancing is freestyle_
   c. _The style is unique to dance_
2. _It refers to lives of teens_
   a. _It understands relationships_
   b. _It understands stress_
   c. _It understands love & sadness_
3. _It matches the lives of this genera_
   a. _It describes a person_
   b. _It describes breakups_
   c. _It describes nature_

As you have just seen, each of your main points needs to be supported with more details. Let's look at one of the ways that Billie's pre-writing list can be expanded.

Hip hop music is the best music for my generation to listen to.

I like this music because:

A. It has danceable "street" rhythms.

1. The beats are easy to follow.
2. The dancing is freestyle and energetic.
3. The dance style is unique (one-of-a-kind).

B. It speaks to the soul of young urban listeners.

1. It understands problems with parents and other generations.
2. It deals with issues including mistrust, anger, poverty, and rebellion.
3. It gives us energy when we're tired or depressed.

C. Opposing Point of View and Counter

1. The music often contains too much anger and little, if any, harmony.

   a. The present generation needs an outlet for its frustrations and energies, and hip hop provides that outlet.
   b. The protest music of the 60s contained anger and a large amount of "metal" sound, and many positive social changes were instituted by the young people who were listening to this music.

Billie's plan should be more successful than Ronnie's plan. You see, Billie's thesis (main point) is: "Hip hop music is the best music for my generation to listen to." The three reasons are clear and distinct. They're not just restatements of reasons already given. Finally, the supporting details help to explain each position.

Billie is heading for success because good planning leads to success. Ronnie, however, needs to do more work to focus on reasons, rather than emotions. Even though Ronnie feels connected with hip hop music, the reader won't feel the same connection unless Ronnie states clearly the way Billie has done both a mindful thesis and thoughtful points.

Ronnie's Plan—Can It Be Better?

Ronnie actually can make a better plan. It's good to love hip hop music. Ronnie just needs to do a few simple things to write effectively.

A. Think of the first statement: "I like my music (hip hop) because it's awesome!" Next, ask the question "Why?"

We know that Ronnie enjoys listening to hip hop. Now Ronnie needs to identify what's "awesome" about hip hop.

1. Does the beat make it "awesome"?
2. Is it easy to dance to?
3. Is it different than the other music that's being played and recorded?

B. Think of the second statement: "It (hip hop) really gives me a rush." Again, ask the question "Why?"

- Maybe Ronnie likes the fact that the music deals with problems like those he faces at school or at home.
- Maybe it's not like the music that adults listen to.
- Hip hop may even let Ronnie get away from some problems and "get lost" in the words and the beat.

C. Think of the third statement: "It's (hip hop's) great to listen to!" Ronnie can identify the reasons why hip hop is "great to listen to."

- Maybe Ronnie has a problem (trouble with a friend who can't be trusted, for example) that is also in a song by a favorite singer or group.
- Maybe Ronnie understands the anger in the music because of his own lack of money or a safe place to live.
- Maybe both Ronnie and the musicians don't see much hope for the future.

Whatever the case may be, Ronnie's essay can be a good one if it includes some hard facts that give reasons for the feelings that have been written down.

Prewriting Your Way to Success

Let's take a look at the first five steps of the **Ten-Step Strategic Plan for Success**. We'll practice these together. They are the prewriting steps. They'll help to make your writing clear and complete. Like Billie, you'll create a plan that's thoughtful, carefully put together, and headed toward success. With practice, you'll get better at coming up with the most important information for your essay. You'll be starting your writing with a solid plan.*

Before the Test Begins—Focus and Prepare to Write

This step may be taken for granted, but it's critical in your effort to succeed. Unless you're giving it all of your attention, your chances for success will begin to lessen. To be successful, you need to do the following:

- Give your full attention to writing an effective argumentative essay.
- Choose a compositional risk to use in your opening paragraph both to catch and then hold your reader's attention.
- Relax, take a deep breath or two, and get ready to do your best.

Remember, you need to be ready right from the start for this challenging test. There is not a lot of time for warming up.

Please note:

- When you take the test, remember to leave yourself enough time to write and edit your work.
- Write the response that you are being asked to write. If the directions say to write an essay, you should write an essay. On the other hand, you should write a letter if you are being asked to do so. Also, don't write a poem when you are being asked to write an essay or a letter.

- Remember, a good essay or letter is specific. Your writing must also be specific.
- At the conclusion of your essay, be sure to include at least one insight. Write down something that you have learned or observed as you have written your essay. Also, make sure that your insight is stated clearly. Otherwise, your reader may not understand it and you won't receive the credit you are trying to receive.

TEN-STEP STRATEGIC PLAN FOR SUCCESS

Let's look at the sample prompt. We'll go through each of the first five Prewriting Steps together. After each Step, a **Suggested Answer** is given. Compare each answer with the one that you've given.

Step 1—Read the Prompt and Directions

This step is very important because it'll help you to start off well. Be sure to find out exactly what your topic is. This will help you to write directly for the prompt and address the questions that you've been given. Even if your essay is technically perfect, you'll receive a lower score if you didn't follow the prompt and all the necessary directions. Also, be sure to state your position clearly and concisely. Otherwise, you won't earn the high score you are looking to earn.

Writing Prompt

As a seventh grade student, you probably lead an active life. You go to school every day, do your homework after school, and then spend time doing things like playing sports, taking music lessons, surfing the Internet, or playing video games.

Because you don't always have a lot of time each day to do the things you like to do, you and other seventh graders often skip breakfast, lunch, and even dinner. Instead, you may often eat an unhealthy snack. This type of eating can lead to many health problems, including obesity, high blood pressure, and diabetes. Moreover, these poor eating habits could actually hurt your ability to focus clearly in class. Your school, therefore, wants to eliminate all unhealthy meals and serve only healthy food and snacks in the cafeteria and in all vending machines.

Directions: Write an argumentative essay about your school's new policy to eliminate unhealthy foods and drinks from cafeteria meals and vending machines. Do you think this is a good policy? Do you think these changes will help you and your classmates eat healthier? Do you believe that a policy like this one can actually change the eating habits of you and your friends? When you state your opinion, be specific. Make sure that you give enough supporting evidence for your argument. You may wish to include valid facts and examples, as well as brief anecdotes (very short personal stories) to prove your point.

Remember that your essay is argumentative. That means that you have two main points to develop. Those are your two strongest points. You must also state a strong counter argument that someone who opposes your position might have. Once you do so, you must then counter their argument by either disproving it or by explaining why their position does not apply to this particular instance. As always, be sure to include your thesis (main point) in your opening paragraph.

Strategic Practice

Answer the following questions concerning the **Writing Prompt** and the **Directions** for the sample essay. After you answer these three questions, check your answers against those provided.

1. The practice of seventh-grade students skipping meals may lead to ___D___

    A. obesity
    B. high blood pressure
    C. diabetes
    D. all of the above

2. The new policy mentioned in the **Directions** would ___A___

    A. eliminate unhealthy foods and drinks from your school's cafeteria meals and vending machines.
    B. eliminate unhealthy meals and drinks from your school's vending machines.
    C. eliminate certain unhealthy foods and drinks from your school's vending machines.
    D. begin a study to determine whether unhealthy foods and drinks should be eliminated from your school's cafeteria meals and vending machines.

3. You, the argumentative essay writer, must __E__

   A. include a compositional risk in the opening paragraph and insight in the conclusion.
   B. state your opinion specifically.
   C. use facts to support your argument and disprove the counter argument you present.
   D. include a compositional risk in the opening paragraph and insight in the conclusion.
   E. all of the above ✓

Answer Explanations

1. The practice of seventh-grade students skipping meals may lead to: **D** (all of the above). Look at the first two sentences of the second paragraph. These clearly state that the poor eating habits of many seventh graders "*can lead to many health problems, including obesity, high blood pressure, and diabetes.*"

2. The new policy mentioned in the **Directions** would: **A** (eliminate unhealthy foods and drinks from the school's cafeteria meals and vending machines). This answer is found in the first sentence of the **Directions** section: "*Write an essay about your school's new policy to eliminate unhealthy foods and drinks from cafeteria meals and vending machines.*" This is the statement that you will use to create your main idea (or thesis). This is the basis of your entire essay. Answer B doesn't mention "your school's cafeteria meals," and answer C is incorrect because of the word "certain." (By the way, answer D ["*Begin a study to determine …*"] is never mentioned in the **Directions** and is therefore incorrect.)

3. You, the essay writer, must: **E** (all of the above). You must A include a compositional risk in the opening paragraph and insight in the conclusion, B state your opinion specifically, C use facts to support your argument and disprove the counter argument you present, and D include a compositional risk in the opening paragraph and insight in the conclusion. These strategies have been discussed throughout this section of this book. Also, be sure that you leave yourself enough time to proofread your work. Otherwise, your haste may prevent you from catching your mistakes and changing them before your time runs out for this section of the test.

How Am I Doing? Should I Move Ahead or Practice?

How did you do with these questions? Were they easy for you to answer, or were they difficult? **If you did well** on this section, then **skip** to **Step 2—Working Title**. **If you struggled** with this section, however, then you may be having trouble remembering the main points being covered. **Try practicing** by skimming over the material quickly and jotting down the key words that you find. Either practice this technique on a separate sheet of paper or simply highlight the key words in the **Writing Prompt** and **Directions**.

Now that you've finished, compare your list with the following one.

- ☑ seventh-grade students
- ☑ active lives
- ☑ skip meals . . . for unhealthy snack
- ☑ health problems
- ☑ new policy
- ☑ eliminate unhealthy foods

Once this practice exercise is completed, return to the **Writing Prompt** and the **Directions**. Re-read them carefully. This strategy should help you to improve your comprehension.

Now move on to **Step 2—Working Title**.

Step 2—Working Title

Steps 2 and 3 are "organizing" steps that will help you create a "map" for your writing. First begin by thinking of a **Working Title**. Next, list your thesis (main idea). You may wish to use a graphic organizer (flow chart, idea web, or writing wheel), a formal outline, or a series of notes for each paragraph. For this exercise, a graphic organizer will be used with boxes containing bullet points.

Good Time for a Title?

An author will often change the title of an essay before settling on the final one. It's good practice, however, to begin writing with a working title in place. This working title gives direction to your essay. It can be a guide to tell you whether your thoughts are staying on topic or wandering from your original direction.

When deciding on a working title, always keep in mind the position that you're taking. Your title must directly reflect your stance. Otherwise, the first impression you make on the evaluators of your test will not be positive. At the start, your title and your thesis (main point) will look a lot like each other.

Strategic Practice

Here's Your Task: Create your own effective writing plan. Take a clear, specific position for this task: "Write an essay about the new policy that would eliminate unhealthy foods and drinks from your school's cafeteria meals and vending machines." Your main idea will be your position on this statement: Do you support or oppose the position? For this exercise, we will take the position that "unhealthy foods and drinks" should be eliminated from your school's cafeteria meals and vending machines." However, let's not forget that we have been assigned to write an argumentative essay. Therefore, our fourth paragraph must contain a statement of a counter argument that is followed by our disproving of the argument.

Let's examine the following sample titles and decide which ones we may or may not use for this essay.

1. **Kids Should Eat Healthy Foods**
   This title makes good sense with its message. Even so, it does not directly address the main question.

2. **Parents Need to Feed Their Kids Better Meals**
   This title is a supporting detail and is therefore not strong enough to stand alone as a main point.

3. **We Need Healthier Food and Drink Choices in My School**
   This title does address the main question, and it is a good one.

4. **Kids at My School Eat Too Much Junk**
   This title is a supporting detail that is a bit too general: we don't know how much junk food and drinks are actually too much.

5. **My School Should Stop Selling Junk Food and Drinks**
   This title does address the main question and may be a possibility.

6. **A Junk Food Ban at My School**
   This title would be a good one if it also included drink choices.

7. **Junk Food Is My Fave!**
   Not only does this title state the opposing point of view, but the word "Fav" is slang and therefore should not be used.

At this point, a graphic organizer would look this way.

> **Working Title**
> We Need Healthier Food and Drink Choices in My School

Step 3—Thesis Statement (Main Idea)

Now that you have your **Working Title**, you need to write a clear **Thesis Statement (Main Idea)**. Remember, your thesis is just a restatement of your **Working Title** in sentence form.

Strategic Practice

The **Working Title** is "We Need Healthier Food and Drink Choices in My School." Place a checkmark in the blank before the **Thesis Statement (Main Idea)** that you feel is the best one for this essay.

- [ ] Unhealthy foods should be banned from schools.
- [ ] Unhealthy drinks should be banned from my school.
- [x] Unhealthy foods and drinks should be eliminated in my school.
- [ ] We should be allowed to eat anything we want in school.

Answer Explanations

1. The statement "Unhealthy foods should be banned from schools" does not include either unhealthy drinks or the term "my school," which are mentioned in the **Working Title**.

2. The statement "Unhealthy drinks should be banned from my school" does not include unhealthy foods, which are mentioned in the **Working Title**.

3. The statement "Unhealthy foods and drinks should be eliminated in my school" is the best one because it includes all the important information from the **Working Title**.

4. The statement "We should be allowed to eat anything we want in school" is the opposite of the information presented in the **Working Title**. This statement, however, is a good one for the counter argument that will be included in the fourth paragraph, along with your disproving of the counter argument.

Now, fill in the graphic organizer with the **Working Title** and **Answer 3** from the exercise you have just completed.

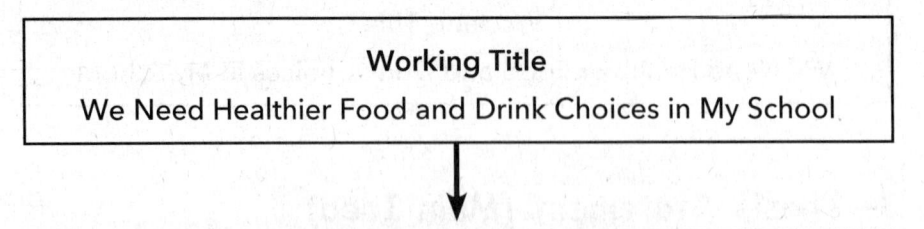

Working Title

We Need Healthier Food and Drink Choices in My School

↓

Thesis Statement (Main Idea)

Unhealthy foods and drinks should be eliminated in my school.

Step 4—Make a Common Sense Check

Before continuing with the next step, consider these questions:

- Does my **Thesis Statement (Main Idea)** make sense?
- Am I stating my thesis clearly?
- Am I saying what I want to say?
- Does my idea make sense?

A common sense check is a good strategy to use when practicing for the NJ PARCC Test. This strategy will also help you when you are actually taking the test.

Step 5—Main Points and Supporting Details

Before writing the essay, let's continue getting organized. This step helps you to make a clear "map" to follow as you compose your thoughts. You should be able to stay on topic easier. Also, you should reduce your chances of forgetting a main point in your essay.

Main Points—Identification

Let's identify our three main points. Your first and second arguments should be your two strongest ones. Your first argument gives the test reviewer a strong first impression of your essay. In addition, your second point should further strengthen your position. Do not include a weaker point for any reason.

Moreover, your next point listed will be the counter argument from the opposing side of the issue. It is a good strategy to build a solid foundation with your two strongest arguments before you share the counter argument. That gives your position more credibility.

Strategic Practice

Here's Your Task: Let's check these possible main points to see which ones are acceptable. Then, let's see which one is the best. Remember, the main point of each paragraph needs to connect with the main idea (or thesis) of your essay.

1. **Kids today are eating too much.**
   This statement may or may not be true. What is important is this statement does not strongly support the thesis ("Unhealthy meals and drinks should be eliminated in my school").

2. **Parents need to feed their kids better meals.**
   This statement is not strong enough to be the first main point of this essay. Rather, it is possibly a supporting detail.

3. ✓ **We concentrate better when we're healthy.**
   Students who concentrate on their lessons usually do well in school. This point is a good one to use in your essay.

4. **Kids at my school eat too much junk food.**
   Even though both *school* and *junk food* are mentioned, you may wish to use it as a supporting detail instead of a main point.

5. ✓ **Our bodies are still growing so we need healthy food.**
   This is a reason based on medical fact. Good nutrition is important not just for seventh graders, but also for everyone. This is another good point to make in your essay.

6. **Consuming only healthy foods and drinks helps our families to take good care of us.**
   Parents are responsible for their children's health and welfare. Your school can help parents by serving healthy foods and drinks. This is a good point for your essay.

Notice that points number 3 and 5 are your strongest ones. Point 6 can actually help to support 5.

After completing this exercise, we can agree that we have found two solid main points. Since you only will have a total of 45 minutes to complete the essay writing section of the test, it is wise to use only two points to develop your essay. You also have to state the opposing point of view and then disprove it. You may not have time to finish your essay if you try to write too much, and that will hurt your score a lot.

24 • New Jersey Grade 7 ELA/Literacy Test

Let's look at our plan so far. We have four paragraphs. **First,** you'll use a compositional risk to catch your reader's attention. **Next,** you'll write the final (**Change "one" to "paragraph"** (Paragraph 5). You see, it will have your summary and any little bit of extra thought you can add ("**insight**").

Fill in the Blanks

Directions: Take a look at the Thesis (Main Idea) and Paragraphs 2–4. First, after you review the information for paragraph 1, see if you can begin the first paragraph with a compositional risk. Practice by focusing on the idea of "risk taking" and the fact that it's not always a wise thing to do. Next, see if you can fill in the blanks with the Supporting Details for the Main Points in Paragraphs 2, 3, and 4.

Compositional Risk Dealing with "Risk Taking"

Many of us arent eating healthy food and drink. This doesn't help concentrate. Our bodies are still growing. Thats the reason why we need healthy foods & drinks

Paragraph 1—Thesis (Main Idea)
Unhealthy foods and drinks should be eliminated in my school.

- We concentrate better when we're healthy.
- Our bodies are still growing. That's the reason why we need healthy foods and drinks.

Paragraph 2—First Main Point
We concentrate better when we're healthy.
(*Hints:* How will being able to concentrate better help you in school? What are the benefits of better concentration?)

Supporting Detail 1: _If we eat healthy food it will help us concentrate better._

Supporting Detail 2: _The benefits of better concentration are they help get your grad up_

Writing an Argumentative Essay • 25

Supporting Detail 3: _It helps family take good care of us_

Paragraph 3—Second Main Point
Our bodies are still growing. That's the reason why we need healthy foods and drinks. Having only healthy foods and drinks in our school helps our families to take good care of us. (Hints: What is the problem with fatty foods and sweet drinks? What are the benefits of avoiding them?)

Supporting Detail 1: _Our bodies are still growing so we need healthy food._

Supporting Detail 2: _Sugary, fatty drinks should be avoided_

Supporting Detail 3: _Healthy food can fight off disease_

Paragraph 4—Opposing Point of View
Students should be allowed to make their own choices. How else are they ever going to become responsible? Counter Argument: State two reasons why this position is a weak one. (Hints: Think about the negative impact on concentration for those students who may be choosing their food unwisely. Consider the primary responsibility of all students. Also, think about the negative results that poor food choices may have on a young body that is still growing and developing.)

Supporting Detail 1: _But they should be taught to make proper dission_

Supporting Detail 2: _Bad eating habits have negative impact on their childhood and adulthood too._

Supporting Detail 3: _The poor eating habbit will make a child obsed or unhealthy_

Check Out the Sample Answers

Now that you have filled in the blanks, take a look at the sample plan contained in the graphic organizer. Are your ideas similar to those in the organizer? If your plan is a better one, congratulations! If you struggled with this exercise, then carefully look over the sample plan and see if there is anything that could be added to your information.

Working Title
We Need Healthier Food and Drink Choices in My School

↓

Compositional Risk
Risks may seem to be exciting to take when riding on a new super rollercoaster or trying to ski down a hill that has always intimidated you. However, they are not good to take when you are dealing with your health.

↓

Main Idea (Thesis Statement)
Eliminating unhealthy meals and snacks in my school is a good idea.

↓

Main Point 1—We concentrate better when we're healthy.
Supporting Details

- We can pay attention better.
- We can ask better questions and get better test scores.
- We can learn more.

↓

Writing an Argumentative Essay • 27

Main Point 2—Our growing bodies need healthy food.
Supporting Details

- We should avoid salty, fatty, sugary foods and caffeinated, sugary drinks.
- Healthy foods and drinks can help us students to fight off diseases, colds, and flu and be healthy.
- With full schedules and working parents, eating healthy at home can be challenging. The school can help us to manage this difficult situation.

Opposing Argument
Students need to make their own choices so they may learn how to do so when they become adults.

Counterpoint—
Supporting Details

- While students should be encouraged to make their own choices, they should be taught how to make proper choices and become better learners—their primary purpose for going to school.
- Poor eating habits for youngsters have extremely negative impacts upon their health in adulthood including obesity, diabetes, and heart-related problems.

Summary Conclusion
Restate the Thesis (Main Idea).
Restate the Two Main Points.
Add the Final Conclusion and Insight.

Step 6—Summary Conclusion

Now that you have completed the exercise dealing with **Main Points and Supporting Details,** you need to **begin with your Compositional Risk and** restate your **Thesis Statement (Main Idea)** and each of your **Main Points** clearly in your **Summary Conclusion,** along with your **Insight.**

Strategic Practice

So far, you have practiced with the first four paragraphs of your essay. These may be the hardest to write. Once you get to the fifth paragraph, you'll restate your thesis (main idea). Next, you'll summarize (highlight) the main point you have made in each paragraph. You'll then draw a final conclusion from the points you have made, being sure to add your insight.

It's Time to Close

Now, write a sample closing paragraph. Use either the supporting details that you made in the previous exercise or use the information in the sample graphic organizer.

With healthier food we concentrate better. Our bodies need halthy food so they can be good in physical shape. It helps family take care of us. It help us get good grades. Moreover good nutional choices benefits us for rest of our lives.

Compare your **Summary Conclusion** with the following one. As you do, ask yourself: Did I remember to

- begin with my **Thesis Statement (Main Idea)**?
- restate each of my **Main Points**?
- make a thoughtful closing statement?

Sample Summary Conclusion

Healthier foods and drinks in my school could give us students a better chance to be healthy each day. We can concentrate better when we are healthy Our growing bodies need healthy food so our bodies can be in good physical shape, thereby helping our families to ensure that we shall be making better nutritional choices. Moreover, by making these good nutritional choices we are developing good habits that will benefit us for the rest of our lives.

HELPFUL HINT

When you're writing your essay, there's a chance you won't know your final conclusion until you reach the end of the essay. **Don't panic!** Often, your final conclusion will seem to magically appear as you're finishing your essay. You simply need to write a summary of your main points first then ask yourself, "Why is the information I'm presenting important? Who should care?" The answer to those questions will give you your insight for your conclusion.

Step 7—Use Transitions

Transitional phrases are a critical element to help you to succeed on the ELA/Literacy Test for grade 7. They indicate many things including **time** ("Immediately" or "Then"), **sequence** ("First of all" or "At this point"), **comparison** ("However" or "Nonetheless"), or **summary** ("Therefore" or "As a result").

Strategic Practice

Let's practice using transitional phrases. For each sentence, choose the correct transitional word or phrase to fill in the blank.

1. If we consume healthier foods and drinks in school, ____ we have a better chance to concentrate better.

    ○ A. next
    ○ B. when
    ● C. then
    ○ D. therefore

2. Our growing bodies need healthy food. _____, we should eat a healthy diet both at home and at school.

    - ● A. Therefore
    - ○ B. In contrast
    - ○ C. Also
    - ○ D. First of all

3. We should avoid salty snacks. _____, we should avoid sugary snacks and drinks.

    - ○ A. Therefore
    - ○ B. In contrast
    - ● C. Also
    - ○ D. Finally

Answer Explanations

1. A. The word *next* doesn't work well here since consuming *healthier food and drinks in school* should result in *a better chance* for the students *to concentrate better*. The word *next* would work better if this sentence were describing steps in a sequence: *First of all*, *Second*, and *Next*.

    B. The word *when* doesn't work. It creates a sentence fragment.

    C. The word *then* is the correct choice. The phrase *If . . . then* uses correct grammar and connects the two main parts of the sentence.

    D. Even though the word *therefore* introduces a conclusion, it is nonetheless not the proper choice. Should the word *If* be omitted at the beginning of the sentence, then the use of the word *therefore* would be acceptable to begin the second sentence.

2. A. The word *Therefore* is used correctly because it shows that eating *a healthy diet both at home and at school* is an appropriate choice because *Our growing bodies need healthy food*. The second statement directly supports the first.

    B. The phrase *In contrast* is incorrect in this sentence since the second statement is the result of the first. There is no *contrast*.

    C. The word *Also* is not the best choice here since the two sentences are connected. *Also* is better used for additional information that is not necessarily related directly to the first sentence.

    D. *First of all* is not a good choice unless it is part of a larger paragraph. It needs to introduce this point as the first of one or more additional points.

3. A. *Therefore* is not a good choice since the second statement (*avoid sugary snacks and drinks*) is an additional statement to support the first one (*avoid salty snacks*).

   B. *In contrast* is not a good choice. The two sentences are closely related and not opposites.

   C. *Also* is the correct choice since it shows that the second sentence is being added to the first. Use *Also* in a similar way to your use of a plus sign (+) in math class.

   D. *Finally* is not a good choice since there is only one sentence coming before the second and final sentence. The word *Finally* should be used only in a series of three or more sentences or ideas.

Step 8—Begin with a Compositional Risk

All successful argumentative essays raise the reader's interest or get their attention through the use of grabbers. These are often used by public speakers to capture the audience's attention quickly. You can do the same for the evaluators of your essay.

Think of a compositional risk as a first impression. When you meet people who seems to be interesting, there is a greater chance that you will want to know more about them. They have captured your interest, and your attention is now focused on them. The same is true for your essays. When you effectively use a compositional risk to capture your reader's attention, and piqued his/her interest, you tempt them to read more of your essay.

An effective compositional risk should make the reader want to learn more about the subject you're covering in your essay. The grabber should always relate directly to the topic of the essay, even when it is shocking. Otherwise, the effect is similar to your hearing a door slam while you're watching a tense moment in a movie, a drama, or a sporting event on TV. The noise shocks you, but it has no relation to what you're watching. You may quickly look around to find out where the noise is coming from, but then you turn your attention back to your TV set. An effective grabber, therefore, should not be similar to the sound of a slamming door. Rather, it should be similar to a pleasant invitation, a welcoming handshake, or a meaningful shock.

When you write your essay, try one of the following devices.

Sample Compositional Risks

Rhetorical Question
A **rhetorical question** is one that you do not expect to be answered. It is asked to get your readers to wonder about an issue. You, the writer, will supply the appropriate answer.

Here are some examples.

- Have you ever considered . . . ?
- What pops into your mind when you hear the word . . . ?
- When you are invited to a friend's birthday party, do you ever think about . . . ?

Interesting Fact or Observation
An **interesting fact or observation** leads the reader to become interested in your essay. When you relate this information, you expect your reader to smile, to nod in agreement, or to feel that (s)he has just learned something important.

Here are some examples.

- Margarine has one less molecule than plastic.
- The first Harley-Davidson motorcycle used a tomato can for a carburetor (old-fashioned fuel regulator on a car's engine).
- Your body has ten times more bacteria cells than human cells.
- There are over 100 million websites on the Internet.

Startling Statement
Use a **startling statement** to shock or get an emotional reaction from your reader. Use statements that are thought to be common knowledge because you can't look them up during the test.

- Excessive cell phone use may expose you to harmful radiation.
- Secondhand smoke kills many innocent victims each year.
- Drug abuse is found not only in poor communities, but also in rich ones.

Simile or Metaphor
A simile or metaphor allows you, the writer, to introduce figurative language into your compositional risk. A simile is a comparison using "like" or "as." "The plane glides like a sled on a slippery, snow-covered hill" and "My new shoes squeak like an old door hinge that needs to be oiled" are examples of similes. A metaphor, on the other hand, is a figurative comparison that does not use like" or "as." For example, "The waves of the ocean sang me to sleep with a rhythmic lullaby" and "My mind was a cloud drifting aimlessly through the sky as I dreamed about my upcoming vacation plans" are examples of metaphors. Actually, the first metaphor

"The waves of the ocean sang…" is also an example of personification since "The waves" are given life-like qualities.

Warning
Be careful not to use a simile that is overused. These trite, stale phrases lack their original impact. "I ran like the wind" or "My cousin is as strong as an ox" are examples of similes that are known as clichés since they are overused.

Magic Threes
Magic threes are defined in two ways. Some think of them as three of the same parts of speech used to capture the reader's attention. For example, take the following sentence: "As I entered the dining room, I noticed an object that was metallic, oddly-shaped, and completely unfamiliar to me." This sentence uses the adjectives "metallic," "oddly-shaped," and "unfamiliar" to create a picture for the reader.

The other approach for magic threes is a bit longer. Each of the three phrases must include a subject and a verb. For example, "I opened my eyes, I turned toward my alarm clock, and I noticed that summer must have officially begun. You see, it was 8:30 A.M. and I was still in bed." The magic threes here are "I opened," "I turned," and "I noticed."

Why do we use the magic threes? Actually, our brains remember things best in groups of three, four, and five. Notice that your phone number has a three digit area code, a three digit exchange, and a four digit personal number (Ex. 555-001-5555). Your postal zip code is five digits followed by four digits (Ex. 99999-0001).

Hyperbole
Exaggeration for effect is an example of hyperbole. You, the writer, give one or more qualities that are beyond logic and reason. For example, a marathon runner after a grueling race might state that she thought the last mile of the race took an eternity to complete. The music lover who states at a concert that he could spend the rest of his life partying to the music is using hyperbole for effect.

Hyphenated Modifier
The hyphenated modifier adds a little bit of edge or attitude while presenting an idea in a series of words that are more descriptive or appropriate than a single word or phrase may be. Rather than saying that someone's hair is beautiful, you might wish to describe the person's hair as having that "I-just-can't-get-enough-compliments kind of hair."

> 💡 **HELPFUL HINT**
>
> Often, it is easier to write your "Grabber" after you have compiled all your information. In this way, you will have a better chance that your "Grabber" will fit your essay.

Remember, compositional risks are a great way to grab a reader's attention. These are used in narrative, argumentative, and sometimes even in informational writing. When you are writing informational pieces, however, be sure to restate any question that you are answering.

If you wish to practice more with using compositional risks, then ask your English teacher for some help and search the Internet for a variety of sources. Be sure to fit the compositional risk to the writing, and be sure that the compositional risk makes sense. Otherwise, you may simply confuse your reader with an anecdote that is clever but does not relate to the main idea of your essay.

Strategic Practice

Sometimes the hardest part of writing an essay is writing the opening line. With a good opening line, your essay will get off to a great start. The idea is to grab the reader's attention by making her/him interested in hearing the main points of your argument. For example, for an essay about replacing grades at your school with a "Pass/Fail" system, you might write: "Learning a skill or different information should be important because it is helpful, not because it leads to a grade in school."

Also, be sure that you think about your main idea (thesis). Your opening to your essay should build a bridge of words that leads to the direct statement of your theme. Try, for example, to think of a newscaster preparing to "send" the audience out to a remote location (outside of the studio) for a story about a grandmother who has used a bucket and a long piece of rope to rescue five kittens trapped in a well that is crumbling. The newscaster won't say, "Our next story is about a grandmother who has saved some kittens" because that does not grab the viewer's attention. It also doesn't focus on the important details: a grandmother, five kittens, danger, and a rescue. Therefore, the newscaster will be better served to say, "Two of the things we love most in life are grandmothers and kittens. Well, who would have thought that by using a little bit of ingenuity and some common household items, a grandmother from Springfield would face danger to rescue five cute kittens she now calls her own? Let's go to our reporter in the field Sidney Sanger for the latest update on this story." The main idea of this news lead (called a "throw" in the media) focuses on a grandmother's ingenuity and bravery that helps her to rescue the kittens.

Let's practice by writing some opening first lines for the topics listed.

Topic 1: Students should not be allowed to use electronic devices in school.

Imagine when a teacher yells five times on the class just to get students attention

Topic 2: There should not be Saturday detention in your school.

Imagine when your parents really want to go out somewhere and they need you there but you got detention on saturday

Topic 3: Your school should extend the day one hour so you and your classmates can complete homework assignments.

When Kids go home they have so many activites to do so if school provides 1 hour just for homework students can finally finish their work.

Possible Opening Lines

Topic 1: Students should not be allowed to use electronic devices in school.

- Imagine a class where the teacher has to compete with the lures of social media to get the attention of the students.
- When parents send their children to school each day, should they have to worry that the children are "surfing the Web" and possibly visiting some undesirable sites when they should be concentrating on the lessons being taught?

Topic 2: There should not be Saturday detention in your school.

- Students need to be punished when they disobey in school, but the punishment needs to be immediate to have any consequence. Detention on Saturday is as ineffective as a mother telling her disobedient child, "Wait until your father gets home."
- Family time is important, especially in today's world when families just don't have enough time to spend together. Saturday detention will take even more of that precious time away from families.

Topic 3: Your school should extend the day one hour so you and your classmates can complete homework assignments.

- At the end of a school day, students have been working hard for seven hours or more. What they really need is a break to relax, maybe have a snack, and clear their minds so they can do their homework with a fresh approach.
- Extending the school day another hour to allow students time to complete their homework may sound like a good idea, but what happens to the after-school sports programs that begin immediately after school? Scheduling becomes difficult, especially for outdoor sports in the fall and winter.

Step 9—Writing

This is the step to use to create your argumentative essay. The assignment during the test allows you 45 minutes to plan, write, and edit your essay. When you actually take the test, allow yourself enough time to write your essay. As you begin practicing, try to take no more than ten minutes of planning before you begin writing. With practice, your goal should be to reduce your pre-writing time to five minutes or so.

Strategy

Here are some strategies to use as you practice your essay writing for the test.

- Once you've completed your pre-writing and before you begin your essay, look at the clock to see how much of the original 45 minutes remain.
- After you complete your first two paragraphs, glance at the clock to see how much time you now have left.
  - If you have plenty of time, don't rush but don't slow down either. Instead, be sure to maintain your steady pace.
  - If you lag behind a bit, then you'll need to increase your pace.
  - It is important that you finish your essay since your score will be lowered for a partial essay.

- After you finish writing your essay, look at your title again.
  - If it fits your essay, then keep it.
  - If the title doesn't fit, then change it.
- When you write your essay, be sure to use words that you know are used correctly and spelled correctly.

HELPFUL HINT

If you're not sure of either the meaning or the proper spelling of a word, then use a different word that you are sure of. Correct spelling and good word choice do make a difference in your score.

Step 10—Proofread and Edit

This is the final step in writing your essay. Once you've finished writing, take a deep breath. This will only take a few seconds, but it should relax you enough to get you ready to proofread and edit your essay. Carefully read over your essay. You should only need to add a finishing touch or two.

It is important for you to plan carefully **before** you begin to write your final draft. In this way, you can avoid any major rewrites that will take up too much time. To make sure that your essay receives the best score, you must proofread and edit your final draft. Remember, the content and the development of your essay are important. Also, don't forget that spelling, punctuation, and grammar count, too.

Writing Checklist for the NJ PARCC

As you read over your essay, be sure that you use the NJ PARCC Writer's Checklist. This is available at http://www.state.nj.us/education/sca/parcc/. This site is sponsored by the New Jersey Department of Education. Just go to the website and type "NJ PARCC Writer's Checklist" in the "Search" box.

Here is a brief version of the NJ PARCC Writer's Checklist. It covers all the major points in the Writer's Checklist you might see on test day. Use either checklist to evaluate the four major areas of your writing.

- ✔ Have I started with an overview paragraph that contains my main point (thesis)?
- ✔ Does my formal argumentative essay make sense?
- ✔ Is my position clear?
- ✔ Have I given details, explanations, and examples to support each of my three main points?
- ✔ Am I bringing my essay to a logical conclusion by restating my main points?
- ✔ Are my sentences clear and varied?
- ✔ Are my words specific, powerful, academically complex, and appropriate to my topic?
- ✔ Have I used my words correctly?
- ✔ Is my capitalization, spelling, and punctuation correct?

Strategic Practice

Let's practice with the following essay draft that a student like you might write. As you edit the essay, look for spelling mistakes, grammar mistakes, and logic errors. Mark up all the mistakes you find.

Remember, this is your thesis and two main points.

Unhealthy foods and drinks should be eliminated in my school.

- We concentrate better when we're healthy.
- Our bodies are still growing. That's the reason why we need healthy foods and drinks.

This is the opposing argument and your counter.

- *Students should be allowed to make their own choices. How else are they ever going to become responsible?*

When you have completed editing the essay, check your answers with those from the sample. You might find some helpful editing suggestions.

Sample Essay

We Need ~~Better~~ Healthier Food and Drink Choices ~~in~~ at My School

If our school gave grades for the meals and drinks that many of us are eating and drinking in school, would we get a lot of failing grades? ~~Many~~ It seems that many of us students aren't eating healthy lunches and snacks. These poor choices are harmful ones. Our general health and concentration is being negatively affected. And our families can't always provide us with the right nutritional choices. ~~So,~~ Therefore, we should eliminate the serving of unhealthy meals and snacks in our school.

By making better nutritional choices, we can increase our chances of focusing more directly on our lessons. Sugar and caffeine, which are common ingredients in many snack foods and drinks, have an adverse ~~bad~~ affect on our ability to maintain our concentration. We can pay attention in class and ask more thoughtful questions when we are not being distracted by the "rush" and the "slump" we get from these snacks. When we learn more, we can have a better chance to get higher scores on our quizzes, tests, and projects.

Eliminating unhealthy meals and snacks in school will help our bodies to develop more properly. We should avoid foods and snacks that are not only high in sugar and caffeine, but also ~~in~~ fats and salt. We need to stay strong to fight off and prevent various diseases like the common cold and the ~~flu~~. We should try to stay healthy in our young years to avoid increasing our chances of becoming a victim of various diseases including high blood pressure, diabetes, bone diseases, and heart problems as we get older. And by making healthy food choices, we can also help our parents or guardians. All of us have very busy schedules each day that don't match with those of our parents or guardians. That is why we need help to make the correct nutritional choices, and our school can actually help us by making sure that our food and snacks are healthy ones.

There are those who believe that ~~we~~ us students should be allowed to make ~~our~~ their own choices. How else are we ever going to become responsible? While becoming responsible is a necessary skill for us to learn, we are to young to be aloud [allowed] to make decisions that are gonna [going to] effect us in the future. If we are aloud [allowed] to make silly choices, who is gonna [going to] make sure that we do well in school, stay healthy, and grow us to be healthy and productive members of our society? Freedom to decide is only good [prevented] when we can show that we are responsible enough to make these important, critical decisions for ourselves.

By not eating the right foods and snacks in school, we are potentially causing ourselves a great deal of harm. We are hurting ourselves in the classroom by affecting our ability not only to concentrate, but also to do our best work. We are hurting our bodies by weakening our defences against everyday problems like colds and flu and more severe problems including diabetes and heart disease. We are hurting our parents's or guardians's chances of helping us to be healthy since we are all following busy and hectic schedules that do not always allow us time to make the best food choices. We often choose the most convenient choices instead. I therefore believe that eliminating unhealthy meals and snacks in school is an idea that should be adopted today. Shouldn't we all try to receive [strive] a passing grade for our food choices as we grow up to be reasonable, intelligent, and healthy adults?

Check pages 229–230 for a sample of this essay again with corrections. Keep these corrections in mind as you write your next essay.

INDEPENDENT WRITING PRACTICE

Now that you have followed the entire writing process from beginning to end, it's time to practice your argumentative writing skills by yourself. Use the space provided to pre-write. Organize your ideas in a flow chart, ideas web, outline with bullet points, or any reasonable way that works best for you.

Writing an Argumentative Essay • 41

Topic 1

"Parents for Change," a local community group of concerned parents, is challenging the standard grading scale used in your school. They believe that under the present system, high grades are too easy to achieve. That is the reason they are calling for a stricter scale that would change the traditional ten-point scale (100 to 90 is an A, 89 to 80 is a B, etc.) to a seven-point scale (100 to 93 is an A, 92 to 85 is a B, etc.). Write a letter to this group and explain your opinion to them.

Pre-writing Section

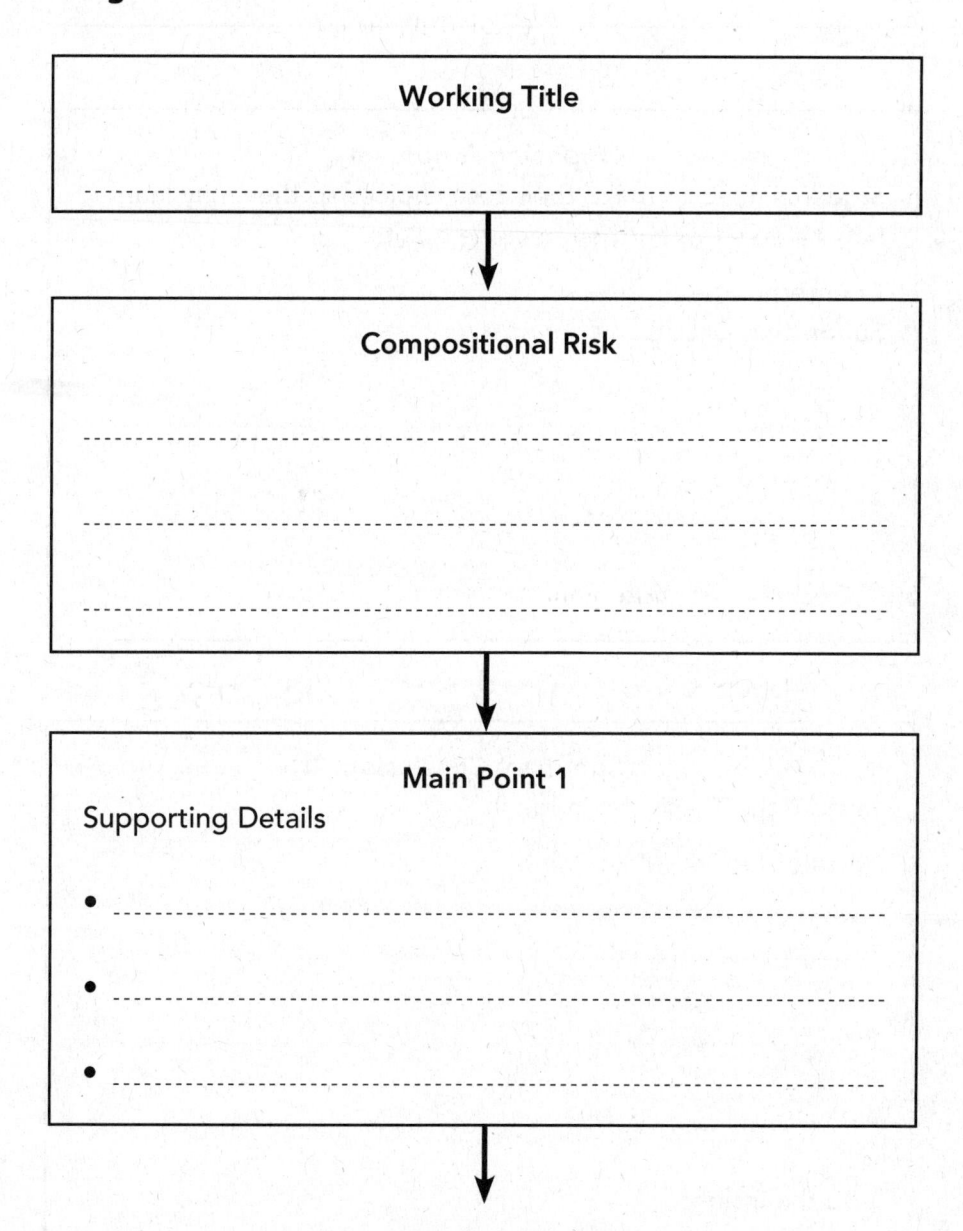

Working Title

↓

Compositional Risk

↓

Main Point 1

Supporting Details

- ------
- ------
- ------

↓

Main Point 2

Supporting Details

- ....
- ....
- ....

Opposing Argument

Students need to make their own choices so they may learn how to do so when they become adults.

Counterpoint—
Supporting Details

- ....
- ....
- ....

Summary Conclusion

Restate the Thesis (Main Idea).

Restate the Two Main Points.

- ....
- ....
- ....

Add the Insight.

Argumentative Writing/Letter

Be sure to check the Suggested Main Points listed on page 231 against your argumentative writing.

Writing a Speculative Essay

CHAPTER 2

WHAT IS A SPECULATIVE ESSAY?

A speculative essay requires you to write a story or scenario (a brief scene) from a few details given in the test directions. When writing a speculative essay, a good imagination comes in handy. First, you will need a good idea to begin writing your story. Your story should focus around a conflict with a resolution. Then, you will need to give enough details so your reader understands your story. Finally, bring your story to a logical conclusion and always make sure to use correct grammar and spelling.

What will I have to write about?

You will be given a brief description of a situation. Then, you will be asked to think about what you feel might happen as the situation develops. In other words, you'll be asked to write a story from the details you're given. For example, if you're given a situation in which a youngster has wandered too far from home, you might be asked to tell the story of the things that happen next. Possibly, you may decide to write about the youngster's challenge to find his/her way home.

What should I include in my story?

You should write your story so your reader knows exactly what is happening. Make sure that your story makes sense. Write your story to answer the question you're being asked. In other words, don't write about an adventure in an amusement park if your question deals with a lost child trying to return home. Catch your reader's attention in the opening paragraph by using a solid compositional risk. Make sure that your risk sets the tone you wish to set. For example, avoid using a startling statement for a story with a comforting mood. Moreover, be sure to use a higher level (academic) vocabulary that uses words such as "microscopic" instead of "tiny."

Should I pre-write (make notes to plan my writing) before I actually begin?

You should always pre-write before you begin writing. By doing so, you will organize your thoughts, create your plan for writing, and actually warm up your brain to prepare yourself for a good writing session. Moreover, the majority of current research has found that your chances for writing successfully increase when you carefully pre-write before you begin composing.

CREATING A STORY PLAN

My Writing Plan

Writing a story for the speculative writing portion of the NJ PARCC grade 7 ELA/Literacy test is different than writing an argumentative essay. In the first chapter of this book, you were concerned with taking a position and developing a thoughtful argument that was supported by two main points. You also made sure that you stated the opposing point of view, gave your strongest supporting argument, and then countered that argument with contrary proof that supported your position. That strategy won't work for this section.

To write an effective story, you need a new plan. For your argumentative essay, you practiced using mostly logic and reason to create an effective argument. For your speculative essay, you're going to use your imagination to "speculate" or describe what might happen in a certain situation. You will not be arguing your point. Instead, you will be addressing the main question, "What do you think is happening?"

Time to Practice

Imagine that you have a Chihuahua puppy. Your Chihuahua puppy is a very excitable dog that always seems to have a lot of energy. Today, you hear your dog barking more loudly than usual. Think about what might be causing your dog to be so excited.

Once you decide upon the cause of your Chihuahua's barking, then create a story and fill in the details of that story. Remember, your story should be based on events that most people would understand. Otherwise, you may not made a connection with the picture prompt.

Please remember that our practice throughout this book is meant to be completed at a slower pace than you will have when you take the actual test itself. By practicing in the book, you should be able to gain the skills needed to work at a much faster pace.

Writing a Speculative Essay • 47

TEN-STEP STRATEGIC PLAN FOR SUCCESS

Follow these ten steps to help you write a speculative essay successfully.

Step 1—Create the Realistic Main Conflict

The first thing we need to do is to think about possible situations (story lines or plots) for this story. These will each be created from a main conflict (problem). For this exercise, we will use the following scenario: Your best friend hears the sounds of a puppy barking in the kitchen excitedly. For the conflict, let's imagine that the puppy smells smoke that is coming from the oven because the breakfast muffins are burning.

Second, think about the reason why the puppy might be discovering the beginning of a major problem. Consider not only the loss of one of the muffins for breakfast, but more importantly the safety hazard that might occur. These actions would be rising actions, which are events that authors use to strengthen a reader's interest in the plot. In the space given below, write down both what you think the main conflict is and the reason why the muffins burning could be a problem.

Conflict and Reason

A possible response may be that the muffins that are baking in the oven have started to smoke and will soon catch fire. The smoke has just started and hasn't yet reached the detector. Even so, this situation is dangerous because your friend's mom is in the backyard and doesn't see that the muffins are starting to burn. Your friend has just awakened and is getting out of bed upstairs. The puppy has noticed the smoke, and it begins to bark while running back and forth in front of the stove. Meanwhile, if the muffins catch fire, then the entire kitchen might also catch fire. That would be terrible.

Consider now what the main conflict is. Is it…

- Your friend not realizing that the puppy's barking is really a warning of a possible fire in the house?
- The muffins smoking and being close to catching fire?

The main problem is the possible fire in the house. Even so, this situation has become a problem because your friend does not realize that the muffins are starting to burn. Your friend being awakened when (s)he hears the puppy barking and scurrying around is a good starting point for the story.

Step 2—Create the Plot (Plan of Action)

The next step to is to create a plot line. You may use the plot line as a plan of action in your story. You will focus on "setting the stage," by identifying the problem (conflict), creating the action (rising action), and then solving the problem (resolution or falling action). Use the questions below to start building your plan of action.

1. What is the reason for the puppy barking and running around so much?

   ----

2. Does your friend investigate immediately the reason why the puppy is excited, or does (s)he wait a few moments? Why? (Remember, this is the beginning of the rising action).

   ----

3. When the muffins catch fire, what happens next? (This is the main event leading to the climax).

   ----

4. How does your friend deal with the fire? Was anything badly damaged? (This is the resolution, also known as the falling action.)

Step 3—Create the Setting

Think about the setting of your story. When you write your story for the test, be sure to include details. This makes your story seem realistic. Be sure to paint a thorough word picture to give your reader a clear view of your scenes. Also, be sure to include a compositional risk in your opening to grab your reader's attention.

As an exercise, write down one detail to describe your friend's room. If you practice this technique, you'll train your mind to begin to think of these details automatically. On the actual test, you won't have much time to improve your story. You will need to jot down details quickly. The amount of detail that you will be able to include and the length of your story will depend on the amount of time it takes you to write an effective story. Remember, this is a timed test. Once the time runs out, you cannot return to the test to finish an item. Practice writing down some details.

Detail

Next, do the same for your friend's kitchen.

Detail

Here is a possible detail for your room.

- Detail— There is an old clock radio that wakes your friend up in the morning.

Here is a possible detail for your friend's kitchen.

- Detail—The window shade was blocking the sun from shining directly on the door leading into the kitchen.

Step 4—Give Each Main Character a Personality

Now it's time to jot down a brief outline of the facts of the story so far. Fill in the information next to each section.

Two (or More) Personality Traits and a Name for Each Main Character

Friend

Trait 1 _____

When does your friend show this trait?

_____

_____

_____

Trait 2 _____

When does your friend show this trait?

_____

_____

_____

Name _____

Puppy

Trait 1 ....

When does the dog show this trait?

....

....

....

Trait 2 ....

When does the dog show this trait?

....

....

....

Name ....

Here are some possible responses:

Friend
- Name—JJ Wilburn
- Gender—Female
- Trait 1— Reliable
- When does your friend show this trait? (S)he always helps out in an emergency. (S)he fed the dog belonging to Mr. Barnes, a neighbor, every day until he returned from the hospital last summer.
- Trait 2—Quick to take action
- When does your friend show this trait? When another student was being bullied at school, your friend stepped in and told the others to stop. (S)he didn't hesitate at all.

Dog
- Name—Frisky
- Gender—Male
- Trait 1—Full of Energy
- When does the dog show this trait? Like most puppies, this one seems to have an unlimited supply of energy. One day, the puppy ran around the house almost non-stop for ten minutes. One minute later, the puppy was gobbling down its food. Ten minutes later, the puppy was sleeping to rest up for the next dash around the house.
- Trait 2— Loyal
- When does the dog show this trait? The puppy appreciates the love he receives in the Wilburn house. JJ is always taking him for walks and play sessions outside. Mrs. Wilburn lets the dog sit in her lap after JJ goes to sleep. While Mrs. Wilburn watches her favorite program, Frisky falls asleep too.

Step 5—Develop the Story (Plot Line)

The next step is to create a plot line. You may use the plot line as a plan for the action in your story. You will focus on "setting the stage," identifying the problem (conflict), creating the action (rising action), and then solving the problem (resolution).

Action

Think about the action taking place. After waking up and getting out of bed, your friend hears the new puppy barking and scurrying around the kitchen. Consider these questions as you prepare to write your story.

1. What does your friend think is the reason for the puppy barking and running around so much?

   ----

2. Does your friend investigate immediately the reason why the puppy is excited, or does (s)he wait a few moments? Why?

Writing a Speculative Essay • 53

3. When the muffins catch fire, what happens next?

   _____

   _____

4. How does your friend deal with the fire? Was anything badly damaged?

   _____

   _____

5. What is the lesson that your friend and her mom learn from this experience?

   _____

   _____

Here are some possible responses to the questions that were just asked.

1. What does your friend think is the reason for the puppy barking and running around so much?

   Your friend might think that the puppy is just excited about one of his toys or maybe a bird that has flown by.

2. Does your friend investigate immediately the reason why the puppy is excited, or does (s)he wait a few moments? Why?

   Your friend might yawn, stretch a little, and then walk downstairs to try to find out the reason why the puppy is barking so much.

3. When the muffins were smoking and almost ready to catch fire, what happens next?

   Your friend might start to fill up a bucket with water to throw on the flames. However, (s)he might remember the previous conversation with Uncle Ralph, the firefighter, about throwing water on a fire. You friend may also realize that there may be an exposed electrical wire, and water could also be dangerous in that situation. Therefore, before the fire gets too large to manage, your friend opens a box of salt and throws it on the fire to douse it.

Step 6—Write the Solution for the Problem (Resolve the Conflict)

This is the point where your story begins to wrap up. The events have developed, and the solution lies just ahead.

Here are some questions for you to consider for this step.

1. How does your friend deal with the fire? Was anything badly damaged?

   Luckily, your friend thought clearly and was able to put out the fire.

2. What is the lesson that your friend and her/his mom learn from this experience?

The lesson might be, "When you are cooking or baking, don't ever leave the stove unattended."

> Please note that the second question is requiring you to be introspective. The NJ PARCC evaluators are looking for writing that demonstrates how a writer has thought about the situation at hand.

Step 7—Give Your Story a Working Title

When you write a story, you must always give it a title. This title should relate to the events of your story. It should, in fact, reflect the main conflict in some way. Also, it should make the reader want to read your story because the title sounds exciting.

Which of these titles do you think fits your story the best?

1. My New Puppy
2. My Friend JJ's Noisy Puppy
3. My Friend Hates to Wake Up

The first title "My New Puppy" would be better for a story about a friend getting a new puppy. The second title is a better one because it relates somewhat to the action of the story. The third one isn't good because it sounds like the story deals with your friend's dislike for waking up.

Even though the second title is not a great one, it's the best one of the bunch. Let's use it for now until you actually write the story. Once you're done, the title may be easier to write.

Using the information that you have gathered from our guided pre-write, please write a draft of your speculative story. Be sure to get all your ideas down on paper before you even begin to think about editing. Make sure that you do the following as you write:

Start with a realistic situation.

- Consider writing about things you know.
- Keep your ideas realistic, or at least clear and precise.

Grab your audience's attention in the same way that a good author or public speaker captures the audience's attention: use a compositional risk to *grab* that audience's attention.

Introduce your main conflict. Tell about:

- The problem that seems to be happening.
- The reason that the situation being described is a problem.

Pay attention to the plot of your story.

- Write your story so it relates directly to your plot.
- Be sure that your story makes sense so the adults who will be scoring your test can understand it.

Give each of your characters a personality. Let your reader get close to your characters by:

- Describing the way they look.
- Showing their traits.

Create the setting by:

- "Painting a word picture" that describes the characters and places in the scene.
- Making sure that your scene "fits" your story and is not "out of place" or confusing.

Develop the plot by:

- Writing your story so the events follow a regular pattern.
- Making sure that the events relate directly to your main conflict.

Decide what the resolution will be.

- Heroic action.
- Unlikely happening.

Give your story a working title. You may change it after the story is written. For now, however, it will give your story a point you can use to focus it.

Consider whether or not a lesson was learned by the main character(s).

- If so, does the lesson make sense from the story you have written?
- If not, does the story come to a definite conclusion?

Step 8—Write Your First Draft

Speculative Story First Draft

Title: _____

Writing a Speculative Essay • 57

Here's a possible essay draft.

My Friend JJ's Noisy Puppy

As the sun came up, JJ heard her alarm clock go off. She was asleep when some noise woke her up. The noise was from downstairs, and it was loud. She figured her mom would take care of business, but she didn't. How much louder could the noise become?

JJ always helped people. She stopped some bullies at school one time. She took care of a neighbor's dog.

As she walks out of her room, she was able to tell that the noise was being made buy Frisky. Frisky sounded excited, but JJ figured that her puppy was acting the way it always did. This puppy would run around for almost ten minutes at a time. The barking was probably just Frisky's way of being psyched.

When JJ got downstairs, however, she noticed that something was berning. JJ called to her mom to ask if nothing was wrong, but her mom didn't answer. JJ called again, but she still didn't get an answer.

As JJ opened the door to the kitchen, the sun that would usually be in JJ's eyes was blocked since her mom had pulled down the shade. At once, JJ noticed that Frisky was barking and running around in circles. Before she tried to calm down her puppy, JJ noticed smoke. JJ had to act quick.

She started to fill up a bucket with water, but JJ remembered a conversation last week with her Uncle Ralph. JJ asked him if you throw water on a fire. He told her to do so if the fire isn't a grease or electrical fire. For those, he said to open a box of salt and throw the salt on the fire.

JJ was able to take as box of salt in case she needed to use it to put out the fire, make sure the fire hadn't started, open the door, and take out the muffins. JJ's mom raced into the kitchen.

JJ's mom asked her what had happened. JJ told her that Frisky woke her up, and she came down to turn off the oven. JJ thought that Frisky was now a hero.

Her mom thought JJ was a hero too because JJ may have saved their lives. JJ did ask her mom to promise not to go outside again if the oven was on. JJ's mom agreed.

Step 9—Add Dialogue

Now that you have written your draft, consider adding dialogue to make your story sound more realistic. This dialogue will also help your reader to hear directly the thoughts of those who are speaking.

Notice that when you write dialogue, you change the paragraph every time you change the speaker. Also, make sure that the dialogue fits the character who is speaking. A child on the playground will not sound like a college professor. At the same time, a parent should not be using language common to second graders.

JJ was worried. (S)he didn't know what to do. (S)he had never had to put out a fire before.

Suddenly, JJ remembered a conversation (s)he had had with her/his Uncle Ralph, a fireman, at dinner last week.

JJ asked, "Should you throw water on a fire?"

Uncle Ralph replied, "Not if the fire is a grease fire--you know, like the ones in a kitchen."

Now that you have found some places in your story where you can include dialogue, proofread your work for mistakes the same way you did in the first chapter of this book when you wrote your essay. Also, look for places where you can add more detail.

> Remember: When you write dialogue, you change the paragraph every time you change the speaker.

Step 10—Edit and Submit Your Essay

10. (A) Check Your Grammar and Spelling

Always check for grammar and spelling mistakes. By correcting these, you can give yourself a good chance of getting a higher score. An essay with good ideas but a lot of spelling and grammar mistakes will not receive a good score.

The first mistake is contained in the fourth sentence of the first paragraph. Instead of saying "She figured her mom would take care of business," the writer should say "She figured her mom would solve the problem." Slang phrases should always be avoided in formal writing, especially on a test.

The next mistake is contained in the first sentence of the third paragraph: "As she walks out of her room, she was able to tell that the noise was being made buy Frisky." You should not shift tenses in a paragraph. If you are writing in the past tense, then continue to write in the past tense. The verb "walks" should be "walked" since the entire paragraph is being written in the past tense. Also the word "buy" is incorrect. It should be "by."

Did you notice the third mistake? It is also contained in the third paragraph. It actually appears in the final sentence of the paragraph: "The barking was probably just Frisky's way of being psyched." The word "psyched" is slang. A better word to use would be the word "excited."

The next three mistakes are in the fourth paragraph. The first mistake in the paragraph is in the first sentence: "When JJ got downstairs, however, she noticed that something was berning." The word "berning" should be spelled "burning."

For the next mistake in the paragraph, look at the second sentence: "JJ called to her mom to ask if nothing was wrong ..." Instead of the word "nothing," the word "anything" should be used. There would not be a problem if "nothing" was wrong. JJ is concerned, however, since she is unsure if "anything was wrong."

The third and final mistake in the paragraph is contained in the last sentence: "JJ had to act quick." The word "quick" needs to be changed to "quickly" since the word being modified (to act) is a verb form. Only the adverb "quickly" and not the adjective "quick" can modify a verb form.

10. (B) Check Your Content

Make sure that you also edit to improve the content of your essay. Let's return to the first paragraph of the sample essay draft. Concentrate on editing for content this time. Try to rewrite this paragraph to contain more specific detail. Think about the following questions:

1. What did JJ see when she opened her eyes?
2. What slang expression should the writer change?
3. In the last sentence, the author said, "How much louder could the noise become?" Is the noise the problem, or is there more to the situation?

Consider the first question: "What did JJ see when she opened her eyes?" Instead of saying, "JJ heard her alarm clock go off," it's more effective to say, "JJ looked at the alarm clock as she lay in bed." There's a combination of action and detail in the revised sentence.

Next, look at the second question: "What slang expression should the writer change?" The sentence "She figured her mom would take care of business, but she didn't" is weakened by the slang phrase "take care of business." This overused, stale phrase is an example of a cliché. Always avoid using clichés in your writing.

Finally, think about the quote mentioned in the third question: "How much louder could the noise become?" The loudness of the noise is not the issue in the story. Instead, the issue is Frisky's barking and scurrying, which fortunately wakes up JJ.

10. (C) Submit Your Final Draft
Now it's time to submit your final draft. Give this writing your best effort. Make sure that you concentrate on the elements that we have discussed.

- Set the scene. Let your reader get close to the characters by:
  - Describing the way they look.
  - Showing their traits.
  - "Painting a word picture" that describes the characters and places in the scene.

- Introduce your conflict. Tell about:
  - The problem that seems to be happening.
  - The reason that the situation being described is a problem.

- Decide the way in which the problem will be solved.
  - Heroic action.
  - Unlikely happening.

- Consider whether or not a lesson was learned by the main character(s).
  - If so, does the lesson make sense from the story you have written?
  - If not, does the story come to a definite conclusion?

- Think of a title that truly relates to your story. Be as specific as possible.

Speculative Story Final Draft

Title: _____

Writing a Speculative Essay • 63

Be sure to check the sample response on pages 232–234 against your essay.

Don't Forget to Follow the Guidelines

Remember, when you write a story, always be sure to follow these guidelines.

1. Create the Realistic Main Conflict.
2. Create the Plot (Plan of Action).
3. Create the Setting.
4. Give Each Main Character a Personality.
5. Develop the Story (Plot Line).
6. Write the Solution for the Problem (Resolve the Conflict).
7. Give Your Story a Working Title.
8. Write your first draft and include a compositional risk (and some insight, if appropriate).
9. Add Dialogue.
10. Edit and Submit Your Final Draft.

   (A) Check Your Grammar and Spelling.
   (B) Check Your Content.
   (C) Hand in Your Final Draft.

INDEPENDENT WRITING PRACTICE

Now that you have followed the entire writing process from beginning to end, it's time to practice your speculative writing skills by yourself. Use the space provided to write a speculative essay on the topic below.

When you finish, check the **Suggested Main Points** listed on pages 234–235. Your points may be just as good, if not better than the ones given.

Writing Topic
You are walking along the street when you notice there is a large box wrapped in birthday wrapping. The tag on the box has a name written on it, but it's hard to read since it is a little smeared.

Think about the box that you have found. Now create a story and fill in the details of that story. Remember, your story should be based on events that most people would understand.

Do **not** simply describe what you see in your mind. Instead, make up a story about what is going on. You may wish to include some details that have happened even before the picture was taken.

Speculative Essay

Title: _____

Writing a Speculative Essay • 67

Reading: Literature and Informational Text

CHAPTER 3

TEST CHANGES

This section of the test has been changed significantly. No longer are you going to be asked to comment on a fictional passage, poem, or piece of informational writing separately.

The New Jersey Grade 7 ELA/Literacy test now contains three main sections dealing with fiction and non-fiction.

- Literary Analysis
- Research
- Writing

We shall address the first two sections (Literary Analysis and Research) before we address the Writing section.

Let's look at the first two sections one at a time.

First of all, let's examine the section known as "Literary Analysis." You will be given either excerpts from long works or brief works in their entirety. After you have read these works, you will be directed to write analytical essays.

Writing Analytical Essays

There is a good chance that you will be given the task of focusing on a certain theme that is covered in the writings. Most likely, the theme will be covered differently in each passage. Therefore, you likely will be asked to compare the way each author developed the theme. You will be required to find similarities, as well as differences. One of the ways this may be done is by having you compare the way a theme is used in a classical piece of literature and in a more modern piece of literature. Moreover, the structure of the piece is important and needs to be addressed. A poem, for example, is written in stanzas while a piece of informational text is written in language that does not necessarily rely on literary devices such as metaphor, simile, alliteration, and onomatopoeia. In addition, the author's purpose for the piece is important. While an informational piece may be written to instruct or to share knowledge, a literary piece may be written to teach a lesson or to resolve a conflict.

Multiple-Choice Questions

The multiple-choice questions that you will be seeing on the PARCC differ greatly from the ones that you have seen in the past. The questions will be paired together, and the answer on the first must be related to the second. For example, you may be asked to select the correct definition of *hubris* (excessive pride) from a list of five or six options. Your next task will be to examine five or more possible supports for your choice. The supports will be based on evidence (examples) from the text. More than one choice may be correct, and you will need to choose all of the correct answers. If you answer the first question correctly but have one or more incorrect answers on the second part, you will receive one-half credit since you answered the first part correctly. However, if you miss the first part of the question and guess correctly on the second part, you will receive no credit for any of your answers to that question.

Multiple-Meaning Words

If a word has more than one meaning when it is used in the passage, then you will be required to choose the correct meanings (two or more) from the list of multiple options of five or more meanings. Let's look at a very simple example. Let's imagine that the weather in a passage may be described as "cool" while a character in the same passage may be referred to by his friends as being "cool." Five or more possible meanings for the word cool may be included as optional answers. The correct answers would refer to a temperature between hot and cold, as well as a desirable quality of one's personality. However, a definition of "cool" as the process to bring down the temperature in food would be incorrect. There likely would be an antonym (opposite) such as raising the temperature of food, as well as a definition such as the sound that a dove makes—which is actually "coo." These two definitions are also incorrect.

> **Remember:** This test will be given on a computer. You will be asked to click and drag the correct answers to a certain place like a central Venn diagram or a set of boxes into which you will place your answers. You may even be asked to take events from the story and put them in a correct order. There will likely be more events than boxes since some of the events may either not have occurred during the story or they may be from a different part of the story than the one that the question is addressing. The key is to be sure not to rush through your answers. Take a reasonable amount of time while you ensure that you have examined all the possible responses and have chosen the correct ones.

Research, Research, Research

For this exam, you are most likely going to be reading informational (non-fiction) passages. You will be asked questions about what you think the author is trying to communicate to his/her audience and also about the structure of the piece (the way it is arranged). This will include considerations such as chronological order, comparison and contrast, and order of importance. For example, a piece featuring a certain vacation experience may focus on the order in which the events of the vacation occurred. This would be an example of chronological order. A piece using comparison and contrast would possibly showcase the differences of the writer's expectations for the vacation and compare and contrast those with the actual events. Furthermore, a piece written using order of importance would feature the events of the vacation from the most important or memorable to the least important or memorable—without considering the order in which these events occurred.

The NJ PARCC pairs a piece of fiction with a piece of non-fiction. There may even be an additional video to watch. Furthermore, some questions will ask you to compare the information from each passage (and video), as well as the manner in which it is presented. You will be required to find both similarities and differences between not only what is covered in the pieces, but also what you think each author may have intended in his/her piece. You'll complete two major tasks in this section of the test. First, you'll answer questions based on the passage. They'll deal with literary concepts like plot, character, and setting. Second, you'll write both brief and lengthy responses to questions also based on the passages. For these, you'll directly address the questions being raised. Your writing must demonstrate a high ability level.

Using the right strategies can help you to be very successful. We'll begin with the literary questions and move directly to the writing section.

Use the Preview Technique (PT) to Be Successful

Because these tests are timed, you might think that the best strategy is to read the passage(s) and then answer the questions. Actually, that way is NOT the best way to take this test. Instead, use the Preview Technique (or PT) before you read each passage.

The Key Steps

Step 1–Preview the Questions
Read the questions given for the passage before you read the passage.

Step 2–Preview the Material
Skim through the essay and look for key words and phrases.

Step 3—Read the Entire Passage
Get all the information you'll need to answer the questions.

Step 4—Address the Prompt Directly
Be sure that you restate the question and make specific text references.

MAJOR TASK 1: ANSWER QUESTIONS BASED ON LITERATURE—LITERARY ANALYSIS

For the Reading—Narrative section of this exam, you will answer questions based mostly on excerpts from long fiction works, short stories, and poetry. Some questions will be based on the text, and others will be inferred (hinted at).

First, let's do a warm-up exercise to become familiar with some important skills you will need not only for this test, but also to help you as you become an effective reader.

SKILLS PRACTICE—WARM-UP EXERCISES

Practice 1—Essential Reading Skills: Questioning, Clarifying, and Predicting

Questioning is the effective use of questions to gather information. **Clarifying** is the way to find out further information about a topic. **Predicting** is making educated guesses based on both the information that you have already found out and information that you already know.

Strategy
As you are doing your reading, use these strategies.

- For effective **Questioning**, make sure that your questions are designed to bring you the information that you seek. Be specific.
- Use specific questions when you need help **Clarifying** information.
- When you are **Predicting**, make sure that your predictions are based on logic and common sense.

Practice
The passage that we'll read is a 7th grade student's journal entry entitled *My First Day of School*. The following questions deal with **Questioning**, **Clarifying**, and **Predicting**.

Read the passage then answer the questions by using the PT below.

> **PREVIEW TECHNIQUE**
>
> 1. Preview the questions.
> 2. Preview the material.
> 3. Read the entire passage.

My First Day of School
by Pat Cole

When I set my alarm last night, I realized that tomorrow I would be following a different routine for the next few months. Since school had let out last June, I suddenly had a lot more freedom. I could sleep a little later, eat lunch whenever I wanted to, watch my favorite daytime television
(5) programs, and just hang out with my friends. Tomorrow morning, it was time to go back to school.

The next morning, my mom woke me up even before my alarm rang. She told me that I had to make sure that I was awake. I couldn't go back to sleep. If I did, I would be late for the first day of school. She said, "That's
(10) not the way you want to start out your school year, is it?" I just grumbled "No" and slid out of my bed. I found my way to the bathroom and jumped in the shower. During the summer, I never had to take my shower before breakfast. I always made some cereal, poured a glass of juice, and settled in with my favorite television program on one of the music channels. Today,
(15) however, I had to finish my shower, dry my hair, and have a little breakfast. Oh, I couldn't do these things in slow motion. My mom kept reminded me to "Hurry up!" so I wouldn't be late. She also reminded me to wear the new outfit we had bought last week. "You should always make a good first impression, especially on the first day of school," she said. It would
(20) feel funny dressing up for breakfast after an entire summer of eating while wearing my pajamas.

My mom made me hot cereal, toast, and juice for breakfast. She also cut up some melon for me. I was still a little tired and didn't feel like eating much. My mom told me that I would be hungry before lunch if I didn't eat a good breakfast, but I just wasn't hungry. Besides, lunch was only a few hours away, wasn't it?

After I had finished my breakfast, I walked out the door. I noticed that my skateboard was hanging from the hook near the door. I wonder what would happen if I took my skateboard and rode it one last time down my driveway. The bus isn't due for another minute. Besides, aren't the buses always late on the first day? Oh, it's just my luck. Here's comes the bus—right on schedule.

Well, I least I'm getting to be with my friends on the ride to school. We talk about all the things we always talk about, but it's different today. Before we know it, the bus pulls up to the school. We all get off and head to our homerooms.

Classes aren't too bad. Miss Washington is still greeting every one of her students at her front door. Vice-Principal Palmer is disciplining a rowdy student for getting in trouble near the lockers. I only have to carry my math and public speaking textbooks this year because most of our classes let us keep an extra book at home.

Things actually didn't go too badly all throughout my day, but I did have one little problem. Around ten o'clock in the morning, I was hungry. Lunch wasn't on my schedule until noon. I had to sit in three different classes and listen to my stomach reminding me that I should have eaten my breakfast. What's worse is we had a discussion in English class of the ways fast food restaurants try to influence us so they can sell us their burgers, fries, tacos, and chicken. I could almost hear the food calling me by my name.

After I had lunch, the rest of the day seemed to fly by. I enjoyed my social studies class because Mr. Barns is a great guy. He doesn't hassle his students, and he never makes fun of anyone in his class. Gym was great because I got to blow off a little steam. Miss Springer let us choose an activity today, so my friends and I played dodgeball.

When the day was over, I got on the bus and headed home. I didn't think it was fair that we were assigned a one-page journal entry in English class, but I guess I can finish by just writing about my day.

Boy, I hope the weekend gets here quickly. I'm going to sleep late on Saturday.

Reading: Literature and Informational Text • 75

Answer the questions based on this passage using our PT. Fill in or check each correct answer.

1. Select Pat's attitude after setting the alarm for the morning of the first day of school.

    - [x] A. Happy because the summer was boring.
    - [ ] B. Angry because Pat loathed going to school.
    - [ ] C. Afraid because the school was in a different town.
    - [ ] D. Upset because there would be less freedom in school.

2. Which of the following answers best predict what was likely going to happen when Pat used the excuse "lunch was only a few hours away, wasn't it?" to disregard mom's advice to eat a good breakfast?

    - [x] A. Pat's mom would be right.
    - [ ] B. Pat would be right.
    - [ ] C. Pat's brother would be right.
    - [ ] D. Pat wanted to watch TV.
    - [ ] E. "A" and "C"
    - [ ] F. Pat's family didn't own a TV.

3. If Pat had taken his skateboard and ridden it "one last time down (his) driveway" before the bus came, which of the following answers would indicate reasons why Pat's mom might be upset?

    - [ ] A. Pat had never ridden a skateboard before.
    - [ ] B. Pat's new clothes might be ruined.
    - [x] C. Pat might get hurt and miss the first day of school.
    - [ ] D. Pat might have to stay away from the class bully on the bus.
    - [x] E. Pat might miss the bus.
    - [ ] F. None of the above
    - [ ] G. All of the above

4. During the morning of the second day of school, what is Pat likely to do?

    - [ ] A. Sleep late.
    - [x] B. Eat the breakfast Pat's mother has made.
    - [ ] C. Send a message on social media to his girlfriend.
    - [ ] D. Remember to put the completed diary assignment in the school bag.
    - [ ] E. Walk the dog.
    - [ ] F. Go to the local store and get the morning newspaper.

5. In the phrase "the ways fast food restaurants try to influence us" (lines 45–46), what does the word *influence* mean?

   ☐ A. Tell a story
   ☐ B. Broadcast an idea
   ☐ C. Create a market
   ☐ D. Prepare food
   ☐ E. Advertise
   ☒ F. Have an effect

Be sure to check your answers with those on page 235.

Practice 2—Essential Reading Skills: Fact vs. Opinion

A **Fact** is information that can be measured and proven. An **Opinion** shows the way someone feels about a Fact.

Strategy

As you are doing your reading, use these strategies.

A **fact** is something that is easy to measure and prove.

- Look for measurements for proof (for example, *gallons*, *days*, and *inches*).
- Look for quotes and citations from books and newspapers.

An **opinion** is an interpretation.

- Look for key words or phrases, such as *Sometimes* or *As I see it*.

A Letter to the Mayor

14 Pleasant Avenue
Springtown, NJ 09151

March 25, 2007

Dear Mayor Patel,

    I believe that we should have a place in town where all the kids can get together. The park near the river used to have a building where we could play games or just sit with our friends and talk. There was even some blacktop where we used to roller skate or ride our skateboards. Now, the
(5) building is closed because there's no one to take care of it. Mr. Ross used to volunteer his time on the weekends to make sure the building was kept up for us kids, but he retired and moved to Florida.

    A meeting place for us kids is a great idea for our town. Right now, we have no place to go where we can be with our friends. When we go to the

(10) movies, the security guards are mean to us. They're always chasing us away. Sometimes, they even holler at us for laughing too loudly. How can we help it if something's funny? Don't you laugh out loud sometimes, too?

Every time we ask for a meeting place for us teens, we're told that large groups of teens cause trouble. Why do people say this to us? We don't look (15) for trouble. Now, I know that some kids can cause problems, but that's why there are adults to watch us. If you put a large group of adults together, don't you think that some of them would get in trouble too? If you don't believe me, just look at the police records for the past month. Are teens the only ones causing trouble?

(20) Last month when we came to a town council meeting to ask for a teen center, you became upset with us. You told us that there were too many kids hanging out in the Maple Grove Shopping Center parking lot behind the movie theater. You told us that you were concerned that nine teenagers had been arrested for fighting during the last month. That may be so, but those (25) kids don't represent all of us in town who really want a place to go at night. If you gave us a teen center, there wouldn't be any more trouble in town because we'd be off the streets. We'd all want to be with our friends.

Please reconsider my request for a teen center in town. It's a place we really need.

(30) Without it, we'll probably just keep having trouble in town.

Sincerely,

Victoria Martinez

1. Which of the following statements are facts?

   ☐ A. Mr. Ross continues to volunteer his time so the building where the kids would skate and skateboard is "kept up for us kids."

   ☑ B. Victoria Martinez wrote the letter to Mayor Patel and requested a new teen center.

   ☐ C. Victoria Martinez tells Mayor Patel that she has also written a letter to her friends to ask for their support.

   ☐ D. Mayor Patel is hearing for the first time this request from Victoria Martinez and her friends for a new teen center.

   ☐ E. Mayor Patel believes that there is already a problem with "too many kids hanging out in the Maple Grove Shopping Center parking lot behind the movie theater."

   ☐ F. Mayor Patel once agreed to build a new teen center, but the request was not able to be realized because of a budget deficit.

2. Which of these statements are opinion statements?

   - ☐ A. "I believe that we should have a place in town where all the kids can get together."
   - ☐ B. "The park near the river used to have a building where we could play games or just sit with our friends and talk."
   - ☐ C. "There was even some blacktop where we used to roller skate or ride our skateboards."
   - ☐ D. "A meeting place for us kids is a great idea for our town.
   - ☐ E. "When we go to the movies, the security guards are mean to us."
   - ☐ F. "We don't look for trouble."

Be sure to check your answers with those on page 236.

Practice 3—Essential Reading Skills: Following Directions

To do something well, we should make sure that we follow directions carefully. These are our guides for success.

Strategy

As you are doing your reading, use these strategies.

Directions are given in order. We must follow the order to get the desired result.

- Look for key words and phrases—for example, *First*, *Next*, and *After completing Step 1*.
- Look for warning phrases—for example, *Before continuing* and *Be sure to*.
- Only use the directions that are given to write your essay. Do not wander from the topic. Follow the directions that you have been given.

The passage that we'll read contains the guidelines to a Guided-Reading Book Report for 7th grade. The focus is on following directions.

Read the passage thoroughly then answer the questions. **Be sure to:**

PREVIEW TECHNIQUE

1. Preview the questions.
2. Preview the material.
3. Read the entire passage.

Guided-Reading Book Report Guidelines

Reading a good novel can be exciting. Finding out about the different characters and learning how the author blends each action and scene together are only some of the thrills you can have while reading. This experience can be a good one. If you read your book with a friend, then you can discuss the book together. That means that it's OK to pick out a book to read with a friend, read the book together, and then discuss it too.

Once you select your book, you will need to follow these steps.

1. Find a friend who also wants to read the same book.
2. Have your parent/guardian sign your book permission slip.
3. Return your slip to Mr. Rhoades by February 26.
4. Write down the following information in your personal guided reading log:

    a. Your name.
    b. Your reading partner's name.
    c. The title and author of the book that you and your partner are reading.

5. Divide your book into three sections. Enter the page numbers into your reading log.
6. Write down the dates that you plan to discuss each section of your book. Be sure to schedule a meeting at least once a week so you and your partner can complete the assignment no later than March 18.

You will be expected to finish reading the book and complete all the discussions with your partner. If you wish to read more quickly than the rest of the class, you may do so without worrying about discussing sections that you were not yet assigned to read. Sometimes when you are really interested in a book, you want to read ahead. This unit has been designed to encourage you to do that.

Once a week, you and your partner will form a guided reading small discussion group. You will meet for no more than 20 minutes with another pair of students who are reading a different book. One of you will serve as a group facilitator who will keep the discussion "on track." You will also select a recorder who will take notes that will be signed by all group members and submitted to Mr. Rhoades. Your group must answer the following questions each time you meet:

- What are the major events that have happened in this section of the novel?
- Who are the major characters, and what are their roles?
- What conflicts are occurring?
- What is the biggest change you have observed from the beginning to the end of the section?
- Who is your favorite character in this section and why?
- What advice would you give to the main characters at this stage of the book?
- What grade (A, B, etc.) would you give this section of the book and why?

When you finish your student meetings, you will then share your responses with Mr. Rhoades. You must complete all three sessions by the March 18 deadline stated to receive two "A+" grades. Completing two sessions will earn you two "C" grades. Completing one session will earn you two "D" grades. A failure to complete any sessions will result in two "0" grades.

If you have any questions during this unit, please ask Mr. Rhoades at once. Also, please share with Mr. Rhoades any difficulties and successes that you may have.

1. Which of the following statements may be considered to be factual concerning the book report?

    - ☐ A. "Reading a good novel can be exciting."
    - ☐ B. "Finding out about the different characters and learning how the author blends each action and scene together are only some of the thrills you can have while reading."
    - ☐ C. "If you read your book with a friend, then you may discuss the book together."
    - ☐ D. "Have your parent/guardian sign your book permission slip."
    - ☐ E. "Sometimes when you are really interested in a book, you want to read ahead."
    - ☐ F. "Once a week, you and your partner will form a guided-reading, small-discussion group."

2. **Part A:** Which of the following book genres are being assigned for the Guided-Reading Book Report?

    ☐ A. Free-Choice
    ☐ B. Free-Choice Fiction
    ☐ C. Free-Choice Non-fiction
    ☐ D. Free-Choice Biography
    ☐ E. Free-Choice Autobiography
    ☐ F. None of the above

    Part B: Which qualities are not generic to the type of genre being assigned?

    ☐ A. The genre only deals with the past.
    ☐ B. The genre only deals with the present.
    ☐ C. The genre only deals with the future.
    ☐ D. The story contains a fictional main plot, conflict, and a resolution.
    ☐ E. The story is based on a real person's life story.
    ☐ F. The story is written by the person whose life is featured.

3. Which of the following information does NOT need to be included "in your personal guided-reading log"?

    ☐ A. Your reading partner's name.
    ☐ B. Your parent/guardian's signature.
    ☐ C. The title and author of the book that you and your partner are reading.
    ☐ D. Your homeroom teacher's name.
    ☐ E. The amount of books you have read so far during the marking period.

4. Which of these statements is true concerning this assignment?

    ☐ A. You may not read a book that anyone else in class is already reading.
    ☐ B. A permission slip is suggested but not necessary.
    ☐ C. The deadline for the project is February 26.
    ☐ D. You must keep a reading log.
    ☐ E. You may not read ahead of the rest of the class.
    ☐ F. For each session, you must discuss with your group the conflicts in the book.

Be sure to check your answers with those on pages 236–237.

Target Skills 1-3: Plot, Characters, and Setting

- **Plot** is the basic story line: the major events. The plot can be either simple or complex.
- **Characters** are the "players" in the work. The most important ones are main characters. Those who aren't as important are minor characters.
- **Setting** is the location in which the action takes place. When the action shifts to another place, the setting changes.

Strategy

- The minor events in the **plot** affect the major ones.
- **Characters** often have opposite points of view and different situations. These can help you to understand the reasons (motives) for the **characters'** actions.
- The **setting** helps the author get the main message (**theme**) across. For example, if the setting's peaceful, the author may want the actions to be peaceful.

The first passage we'll look at is from L. Frank Baum's classic novel, *The Wonderful Wizard of Oz*. Even if you know the story well, you should still use the **PT** to help you to make the best decisions on your test. **Be sure to:**

PREVIEW TECHNIQUE

1. Preview the questions.
2. Preview the material.
3. Read the entire passage.

The Wonderful Wizard of Oz

by L. Frank Baum

Chapter 1. The Cyclone

Dorothy lived in the midst of the great Kansas prairies, with Uncle Henry, who was a farmer, and Aunt Em, who was the farmer's wife. Their house was small, for the lumber to build it had to be carried by wagon many miles. There were four walls, a floor and a roof, which made one room; and this
(5) room contained a rusty looking cookstove, a cupboard for the dishes, a table, three or four chairs, and the beds. Uncle Henry and Aunt Em had a big bed

in one corner, and Dorothy a little bed in another corner. There was no garret (attic)
at all, and no cellar—except a small hole dug in the ground, called a cyclone
cellar, where the family could go in case one of those great whirlwinds arose,
(10) mighty enough to crush any building in its path. It was reached by a trap
door in the middle of the floor, from which a ladder led down into the small,
dark hole.

When Dorothy stood in the doorway and looked around, she could see
nothing but the great gray prairie on every side. Not a tree nor a house broke
(15) the broad sweep of flat country that reached to the edge of the sky in all
directions. The sun had baked the plowed land into a gray mass, with little
cracks running through it. Even the grass was not green, for the sun had
burned the tops of the long blades until they were the same gray color to be
seen everywhere. Once the house had been painted, but the sun blistered the
(20) paint and the rains washed it away, and now the house was as dull and gray
as everything else. When Aunt Em came there to live she was a young, pretty
wife. The sun and wind had changed her, too. They had taken the sparkle
from her eyes and left them a sober gray; they had taken the red from her
cheeks and lips, and they were gray also. She was thin and gaunt, and never
(25) smiled now. When Dorothy, who was an orphan, first came to her, Aunt Em
had been so startled by the child's laughter that she would scream and press
her hand upon her heart whenever Dorothy's merry voice reached her ears;
and she still looked at the little girl with wonder that she could find anything
to laugh at.

(30) Uncle Henry never laughed. He worked hard from morning till night and
did not know what joy was. He was gray also, from his long beard to his
rough boots, and he looked stern and solemn, and rarely spoke. It was Toto
that made Dorothy laugh, and saved her from growing as gray as her other
surroundings. Toto was not gray; he was a little black dog, with long silky
(35) hair and small black eyes that twinkled merrily on either side of his funny,
wee nose. Toto played all day long, and Dorothy played with him, and loved
him dearly.

Today, however, they were not playing. Uncle Henry sat upon the
doorstep and looked anxiously at the sky, which was even grayer than usual.
(40) Dorothy stood in the door with Toto in her arms, and looked at the sky too.
Aunt Em was washing the dishes.

From the far north they heard a low wail of the wind, and Henry and
Dorothy could see where the long grass bowed in waves before the coming

84 • New Jersey Grade 7 ELA/Literacy Test

(45) storm. There now came a sharp whistling in the air from the south, and as they turned their eyes that way they saw ripples in the grass coming from that direction also.

Suddenly Uncle Henry stood up. "There's a cyclone coming, Em," he called to his wife. "I'll go look after the stock." Then he ran toward the sheds where the cows and horses were kept.

(50) Aunt Em dropped her work and came to the door. One glance told her of the danger close at hand. "Quick, Dorothy!" she screamed. "Run for the cellar!"

1. Which of these actions does NOT take place in this passage?

    ☐ A. Dorothy lived with her Uncle Henry and Aunt Em.
    ☒ B. Uncle Henry always laughed.
    ☐ C. Uncle Henry and Dorothy heard "a low wail of the wind" that came from the south.
    ☐ D. Aunt Em warned Dorothy to go in the cellar to protect herself from the cyclone that was coming.
    ☐ E. The tornado ripped through the house, destroying everything.

2. Which of these statements best describes Dorothy and Toto?

    ○ A. Dorothy adopted Toto from a shelter, and he never left her side.
    ○ B. Uncle Henry and Aunt Em gave Toto to Dorothy, and now Dorothy and Toto are always together.
    ● C. Toto always made Dorothy laugh.
    ● D. Dorothy loved Toto dearly.
    ○ E. Dorothy loved Toto even more than she loved Uncle Henry and Aunt Em.

3. Select the events in the correct sequence from the order given below. Drag each one into the corresponding boxes.

    A. Dorothy saw "nothing but the great gray prairie on every side" of her.
    B. Aunt Em warned Dorothy to "Run for the cellar!"
    C. Uncle Henry sat on the doorstep and looked anxiously at the sky.
    D. Uncle Henry "ran toward the sheds where the cows and horses were kept."
    E. Uncle Henry said to his wife, "There's a cyclone coming, Em."

    1. A   3. E   5. B
    2. C   4. D

4. **Part A:** The phrase "and he looked stern," is used in paragraph 3 to describe Uncle Henry. Which of the following answers fit the story's definition of *stern*?

- ☐ A. Austere
- ☐ B. Out of control
- ☐ C. Filled with laughter
- ☐ D. Sincere
- ☒ E. Seldom amused

Part B: Which of the following details best relate to the answer to Part A?

- ☐ A. "There now came a sharp whistling in the air from the south…"
- ☒ B. "Uncle Henry never laughed."
- ☐ C. "Aunt Em had been so startled by the child's laughter…"
- ☐ D. "It was Toto that made Dorothy laugh…"
- ☐ E. "'Quick, Dorothy!' she screamed. 'Run for the cellar!'"
- ☒ F. "(He) did not know what joy was."

5. **Part A:** Read the following sentence from the passage.

   "There was no garret at all, and no cellar—except a small hole dug in the ground, called a cyclone cellar…"

   The word *cyclone* refers to?

- ○ A. A weather map
- ○ B. A heat wave
- ○ C. A desert breeze
- ● D. A storm with swirling winds

Part B: Select the quotes from the passage that best relate to the answer to Part A.

- ☐ A. "…the sky, which was greyer than usual."
- ☐ B. "…she could see nothing but the great gray prairie on every side."
- ☐ C. "…a small hole dug in the ground…"
- ☐ D. "The sun had baked the plowed land into a gray mass…"
- ☒ E. "…the sun blistered the paint and the rains washed it away…"

6. Part A: Which of the following statements best describes the setting of the story?

   ○ A. An orphanage
   ○ B. The mountains and prairies in Kansas
   ○ C. The eastern coast of the United States
   ● D. A farm on the prairies in Kansas

   Part B: Which details from the passage best supports the answer for Part A?

   ☐ A. "When Dorothy, who was an orphan …"
   ☐ B. "…the broad sweep of flat country that reached to the edge of the sky in all directions."
   ☑ C. "…she could see nothing but the great gray prairie on every side."
   ☑ D. "Dorothy lived in the midst of the great Kansas prairies…"
   ☑ E. "…the lumber to build it had to be carried by wagon many miles."

Be sure to check your answers with those on pages 237–239.

MAJOR TASK 2: ANSWER QUESTIONS BASED ON PAIRED PASSAGES—RESEARCH

Before we begin to analyze a passage that has a similar topic covered in *The Wonderful Wizard of Oz*, let's take a moment to discuss the ways informational text is organized. This information is critical for you to be successful on the NJ PARCC since you will be asked questions about the structural patterns of selected informational texts.

Informational Text—Patterns

Chronological
The first structural pattern is a common one known as chronological. This pattern arranges facts according to the time at which they have occurred. For example, a social studies text covering the events of the Revolutionary War will often arrange battles as they occurred.

You are likely to find a timeline or chart that lists the most important events in the order in which they took place. For example, The Battle of Lexington and Concord is considered by many to be the first major battle of the Revolutionary War. Since it occurred in April 1775, it is listed before the Battle of Bunker Hill, which was fought in June 1775. A mention of the Battle of Saratoga would need to follow the Battle of Trenton since Trenton was fought in December 1776 while Saratoga was fought in

October 1777. Other battles would need to be placed in the text according to the time order in which they took place.

When dealing with chronological order, common transitional phrases include *first of all*, *secondly*, *next*, *then*, *later*, and *finally*, along with any qualifying dates and times of the year.

Problem/Solution

Another method is known as problem/solution. Think of the beginning of a chapter in your math book in which you learn about key concepts. Often, your text will introduce a problem that includes the concept being taught. A step-by-step explanation will be shown that leads to the solution of the problem. When you are studying the associative property, for example, the problem will require you to use grouping. The problem asking you to solve 4(2x) requires that you regroup and then simplify. Therefore 4(2x) is regrouped to be (4 × 2)x.

When the multiplication is done, then you can see that (4 × 2)x = 8x. For an argumentative essay, the problem being addressed is explored and a solution is presented, along with a counter to the opposing side's strongest argument.

For problem/solution pieces, chronological order is important for each step. Common transitional phrases besides those already noted include numbered steps (*Step 1*, *Step 2...*), *therefore*, *as a result*, *nonetheless*, *also*, *furthermore*, *moreover*, and *in conclusion*.

Cause and Effect

In a cause and effect essay, a writer is often attempting to prove that certain causes have led directly to a resultant effect. Simply put, the stated result has occurred because of conditions *a*, *b*, *c*, and *d*. Text written about word events will explain causes that led up to a major event taking place. This event is the effect of the causes. For example, a paper for an environmental science assignment may focus on the causes of pollution in a community. Some of these may be a result of poor waste disposal methods, a lack of a comprehensive recycling program, excessive highway noise, and the excessive use of woodlands for commercial building projects. The effect is a harsh negative impact on the local environment. This will probably result in imbalances and maybe toxicity in the land, water, and air. There may also be a negative impact on the plant and animal life, as well as on the people living in the area. A key to writing a successful cause-and-effect piece is being sure to use textual evidence to support your point of view. References to the text should actually be direct quotes rather than indirect ones. The reason is simple. A reader is unlikely to miss material that is highlighted in quotations, but a text reference can easily be missed if a reader doesn't realize that the information being given is being taken directly from the text. For cause-and-effect pieces, common transitional phrases besides those already noted include, *since*, *because of the fact*, *for that reason*, *provided that*, *thus*, and *for this reason*.

Compare and Contrast

To create a compare and contrast essay, you must focus upon similarities and differences among two or more topics. Imagine that your English teacher has assigned you to write an essay comparing the writing styles of Ray Bradbury and John Steinbeck. You can compare the two by illustrating the passion each had for the topics that they addressed. Bradbury and Steinbeck both showed the ways that people can sometimes be a bit harsh. Both Bradbury and Steinbeck wrote of characters who were the victims of an unthinkable and at times harsh society. However, Bradbury's prose has a definite poetry in its descriptiveness although that sometimes became excessive. On the other hand, Steinbeck used a more economical and less flowery style to describe his characters and scenes.

For comparison and contrast pieces, common transitional phrases besides those already noted include *despite*, *nevertheless*, *nonetheless*, *on the one hand*, *on the other hand*, *similarly*, *in contrast*, and *in similar fashion*.

Description

When writing an essay using description, your major task is to paint a clear word picture.

You must give the details in such a way that those who have little experience in the area can still understand your point clearly. Let's say that your teacher has assigned you a descriptive essay. You decide to describe the general rules of baseball. You decide that including the major areas of the game: pitching, hitting, fielding, throwing, base running, and strategy is too daunting a task. Therefore, you concentrate on hitting. You must consider the selection of a bat, the grip of the bat, the stance, the swing, and strategy. To do so effectively, you decide to take each area and explain it in detail so even someone who is not familiar with baseball can understand your points. Effective description will allow you to do this.

For description pieces, common transitional phrases besides those already noted include *in front of*, *behind*, *next to*, *across*, *over*, and *on top of*.

Paired Passages

Now that you have practiced with a single passage, let's now move to the second one called a paired passage. *The Wonderful Wizard of Oz* is a novel that features the weather phenomena known as cyclones, or tornadoes. In the NJ PARCC, you will be asked questions that are similar to the ones that you have just completed. However, another passage will be introduced. This passage will be similar to the previous one since it will contain material that somehow relates to the first passage. In this case, tornadoes are a plot device in the first work while they are the main topic in the second. Please read this second passage and then answer the questions that follow.

Tornadoes—The Facts

What exactly are tornadoes?

They are defined as violently spinning columns of air that both extend between and make contact with a cloud and the earth's surface. The winds of the most powerful tornadoes have been known to reach speeds of 200 miles an hour. Surprisingly, the winds of some tornadoes have even been
(5) measured at more than 250 miles an hour.

It is interesting to note that the speeds which a tornado's winds achieve are not measured during the weather event. Rather, they are determined once the tornado has moved on. The determining factor for figuring these speeds is the amount of damage that has been produced. Furthermore, a
(10) scale is used to determine the strength of each tornado. This scale is known as the Enhanced Fujita Scale. It uses a number progression from one to five to categorize the tornado's power. A rating of zero is assigned to the weakest tornadoes while a rating of five is assigned to those with the most intense power. According to the National Oceanic and Atmospheric Administration
(15) (NOAA), tornadoes cause about 70 deaths and 1,500 injuries each year.

Tornadoes are often mistakenly referred to as cyclones, as L. Frank Baum did in *The Wonderful Wizard of Oz*. It should be noted that Baum made this meteorological error by calling the tornado in the story a cyclone. Actually, a cyclone is a hurricane and not a tornado.

Is there a pattern that tornadoes follow?

(20) Tornadoes are quite unpredictable. It seems that they can touch down in an area one at a time. However, they can also travel in clusters. When they do so, their potential to wreak havoc and cause devastation to homes, farms,

buildings, and any edifice and area in their paths increases greatly. Generally, the pattern that tornadoes follow is variable and somewhat unpredictable. (25) They are capable of leveling an area as small as less than 100 yards wide and as large as more than a mile or two wide. In fact, some tornadoes can travel on the ground for more than 50 miles.

Can a person see through tornadoes?

At first, tornadoes may be almost transparent. However, as they travel, they gather up a collection of dust and debris. As these begin to accumulate (30) inside the tunnels of the tornadoes, the transparency lessens considerably. It is interesting to note that tornadoes tend to move from the southwest to the northeast, but they have been seen moving in any direction.

Where are tornadoes most common?

Unfortunately for Americans, the United States reports the highest incidence of tornadoes. Even though fewer than 25 or so tornadoes may (35) be reported by the media during the year, over 1,000 tornadoes devastate some part of the country during a typical year. It seems that there are certain geographical factors that make this possible. For instance, Canada to the north sends down its air from the North Pole. The Gulf of Mexico supplies warm, moist air. The Southwest region is also a factor by supplying (40) very dry air. Whenever these three fronts combine, the potential for both thunderstorms and tornadoes rises dramatically.

Is there a section of the U.S. where tornadoes are the most common?

In the United States, the state of Texas has the highest incidence of tornadoes with an average of almost 140 tornadoes each year. The next highest state on average is Oklahoma with 57 every year. Kansas and Florida (45) are tied for third place with an average of 55 a year.

The United States has the highest incidence of tornadoes worldwide, with more than 1,000 occurring every year. This is due to the unique geography that brings together polar air from Canada, tropical air from the Gulf of Mexico, and dry air from the Southwest to clash in the middle of the country, (50) producing thunderstorms and the tornadoes they spawn.

What should people do if they hear that a tornado warning has been issued? First of all, note that a tornado watch is issued when severe stormy weather is predicted within the upcoming hours. At this time, it is wise to

(55) take shelter. Listen to the local radio and TV reports to stay current with the weather situation. Find a safe, solid shelter and go there if you have time. Do not open your windows to alleviate the pressure from the tornado because you may be injured by flying glass while you are opening the windows. Besides, there is no advantage gained by opening the windows.

If a tornado is coming in your direction, what should you do?

(60) If you see a tornado approaching, run in the opposite direction of its path. Your main concern is your own safety and that of your family. The best course of action is to leave the area of the storm before it becomes visible. Forget about your possessions. Those can be replaced. You and your family cannot.

In *The Wonderful Wizard of Oz*, L. Frank Baum wrote that a "cyclone" swept up Dorothy and Toto. Doesn't "cyclone" refer to a hurricane and not a tornado?

(55) When L. Frank Baum wrote his novel, he actually misused the term "cyclone." It does indeed refer to a hurricane, but the twister that Dorothy experienced was a tornado. A hurricane generally has strong, blowing winds, but those winds are not necessarily swirling. Therefore, Baum's "cyclone" was actually a tornado. For the following questions, we shall use the term "tornado" and "cyclone" interchangeably to reflect Baum's intent.

1. Which of the following two facts mentioned in the second passage are not supported in *The Wonderful Wizard of Oz*?

   ☐ A. Tornadoes have the potential to be dangerous.
   ☒ B. The winds of the most powerful tornadoes have been known to reach speeds of 200 miles an hour.
   ☐ C. Tornadoes are not common in Kansas.
   ☐ D. The United States has the highest incidence of tornadoes.
   ☒ E. Some tornadoes have been known to travel along the ground for 50 miles.

2. When comparing *The Wonderful Wizard of Oz* with "Tornadoes—The Facts," select the two answers that are in both pieces of writing.

   ☐ A. *The Wonderful Wizard of Oz* is written to inform and "Tornadoes—The Facts" is written to entertain.

   ☐ B. *The Wonderful Wizard of Oz* gives advice for anyone who sees a cyclone approaching and "Tornadoes—The Facts" does not.

   ☒ C. *The Wonderful Wizard of Oz* refers to the weather phenomenon as a cyclone while "Tornadoes—The Facts" refers to the weather phenomenon as a tornado.

   ☒ D. *The Wonderful Wizard of Oz* portrays a set of fictional characters who are dealing with a cyclone and "Tornadoes—The Facts" contains advice but no characters.

   ☐ E. *The Wonderful Wizard of Oz* is non-fictional, and "Tornadoes—The Facts" is fictional.

3. What information from "Tornadoes—The Facts" is important to include in a summary? Choose from the list below and arrange them in the correct order to create a summary.

   A. Tornadoes make contact with a cloud and the surface of the earth over which they are traveling.

   B. *The Wonderful Wizard of Oz* is set in Kansas and features a cyclone, which is another name for a blizzard.

   C. Some people have been known to follow tornadoes while recording these "twisters" on cameras.

   D. More tornadoes occur in the United States than they do in any other part of the world.

   E. People should turn off their radios and TV sets during a tornado to conserve electricity.

   F. Even though tornadoes generally move from the southwest to the northeast, they have been known to travel in every direction.

4. Which of the following two facts does "Tornadoes—The Facts" present to support the idea that tornadoes can be very dangerous?

- ☐ A. Every tornado is almost completely transparent as it travels across the ground.
- ☐ B. The winds of a tornado are seldom more than 125 miles per hour.
- ☐ C. The pattern of a tornado is at times unpredictable and variable.
- ☐ D. The Enhanced Fujita Scale, used to measure the strength of tornadoes, assigns a rating of five to the most powerful tornadoes.
- ☐ E. Opening your windows during a tornado will help to equalize the pressure in your house and thereby help to keep it safe.
- ☐ F. When a tornado watch is announced, it is wise to take shelter.

5. What is the pattern in which this text is arranged?
- ○ A. Cause and effect
- ○ B. Compare and contrast
- ○ C. Description
- ○ D. Problem/Solution

Be sure to check your answers with those on pages 239–241.

MAJOR TASK 3: WRITING CLEAR, THOROUGH ESSAYS BASED ON READING PASSAGES

You'll be writing essays dealing with questions relating to the themes, structures, characters, people, and/or concepts, and purposes of paired fictional and non-fictional pieces. The short answers are scored 4 (high) to 0 (low). To earn a score of 4, you must answer the question thoroughly, support your main point(s) with details from the passage, add insight (thinking beyond obvious points), and use correct grammar, spelling, and vocabulary. A 2 is average. A 0 means the response either didn't answer the question or address the topic.

The first prompt requires a literary analysis of Baum's *The Wonderful Wizard of Oz*. You are asked to write about the author's use of description in the passage. You must remember to do the following things to be successful:

- Prewrite—Think about the prompt and sketch out a plan of action for your essay. Your plan should include direct textual evidence ("quotes") from the work. When you quote directly, there is no chance that a reviewer will miss your reference. The same is not always true for an indirect quote. This step should take five minutes or less to complete.
- Restate the question.

- As you begin to write, be sure to refer to your plan. Deviate from it only if it is absolutely necessary since you are being given no more than 30 minutes to complete the full task.
- When you are halfway finished with your essay, check to see that you have enough time to complete your task. If you are running behind schedule, then you may need to combine the important points so they get covered in your essay. Also, make sure that you are staying on topic. Do not "bird walk" (go off on a tangent). Stick to the prompt.
- When you finish writing, you should have at least five more minutes to edit your work. Be sure to check your spelling, sentence structure, and grammar. Make sure that you have used commas to separate compound sentences, used words correctly, changed to a simpler word if you are not sure of the meaning, substituted "happens when," "occurs when," or "takes place when," for "is when," and avoided mistakes at the beginning and the end of your piece. Those are the worst places to make a mistake since those are the places where you can make a good or bad first and last impression.

HELPFUL HINTS FOR ESSAYS

Step 1—Preview the Questions
Read the questions given for the passage before you read the passage.

Step 2—Preview the Material
Skim through the essay and look for key words and phrases.

Step 3—Read the Entire Passage
Get all the information you'll need to answer the questions.

Step 4—Address the Prompt Directly
Be sure that you restate the question and make specific text references.

Essay for Plot, Character, and Setting

The setting of *The Wonderful Wizard of Oz* is a farm in Kansas. Explain how the author uses the setting (literary analysis) to show how difficult it must be to live there. Use the details in "Tornadoes—The Facts" to support your position.

PREWRITING SECTION
Use the empty space provided to make a writing plan for your essay before you begin writing.

ESSAY

Be sure to check your essay against the sample responses and suggestions on pages 241–245.

Target Skills 4, 5, and 6: Theme, Cause and Effect, and Point of View

The **theme** is the main message that the author wants you to get while you're reading the work.

Every event has at least one **cause** that results in an **effect**.

Point of view deals either with the way a character sees things or the way a story is told. It's the "voice" that tells the story. A **first person narrator** tells the story in the "I" or "We" voice. A **second person narrator** tells the story in the "You" voice. A **third person narrator** tells the story using "she," "he," "it," or "they."

Strategy

When you're looking for the **theme**, ask yourself the following questions:

- What did I learn from this novel, story, or poem?
- What has the author had the main characters do to show the theme?
- Has the author made this point easy to see, or did (s)he hide it?

Look to connect the cause with the effect that results. Phrases like "As a result" and "Therefore" help to make the connection.

A **first person narrator** is a character who tells the story in the "I" or "We" voice. This allows you, the reader to be told the story by a character. A **second person narrator** speaks directly to "You" and often teaches a lesson. A **third person narrator** tells the story from someone who isn't usually part of the story.

Target Skills 7 and 8: Details and Sequence of Events

- Reading passages always have **details**, the facts that explain the information you're reading.
- The **sequence of events** is the order in which things happen.

Strategy

When looking for **details**, concentrate on the facts and not on opinions.

When looking for the **sequence of events**:

- Look for transition words and phrases like "first," "next," and "the final step."
- Look for numbers or bullet points to guide you.
- Look for the abbreviations "AM" and "PM" for time sequences.

Practice

The poem that you will read is one that you may have seen before. It is *The Road Not Taken* by Robert Frost.

Read the poem thoroughly then answer the questions. **Be sure to:**

> **PREVIEW TECHNIQUE**
>
> 1. Preview the questions.
> 2. Preview the material.
> 3. Read the entire passage.

The Road Not Taken
by Robert Frost

Two roads diverged in a yellow wood,
And sorry I could not travel both
And be one traveler, long I stood
And looked down one as far as I could
(5) To where it bent in the undergrowth

Then took the other, as just as fair,
And having perhaps the better claim,
Because it was grassy and wanted wear;
Though as for that the passing there
(10) Had worn them really about the same,

And both that morning equally lay
In leaves no step had trodden black.
Oh, I kept the first for another day!
Yet knowing how way leads on to way,
(15) I doubted if I should ever come back.

I shall be telling this with a sigh
Somewhere ages and ages hence:
Two roads diverged in a wood, and I—
I took the one less traveled by,
(20) And that has made all the difference.

1. From which point of view is the story of the poem being told?

    A. First person
    B. Second person
    C. Third person
    D. Both "A" and "C"

2. **Part A:** What is the main idea in the first stanza (paragraph in poetry)?

    A. The traveler was lost.
    B. The traveler was hungry.
    C. The traveler was happy that he could travel both roads.
    D. The traveler was sad that he couldn't travel both roads.

    Part B: What line(s) in the poem provide the details to support the position in Part A?

    A. "Two roads diverged in a yellow wood" (Line 1)
    B. "And sorry I could not travel both" (Line 2)
    C. "To where it bent in the undergrowth" (Line 5)
    D. "Because it was grassy and wanted wear; (Line 8)

3. The traveler hoped someday to take the road that "bent in the undergrowth," but what did he believe that the effect of his hopes would be?

    A. The traveler doubted he would take the other road some day.
    B. The traveler was sure he would take the other road some day.
    C. The traveler was paralyzed with fear.
    D. The traveler was encouraged by his friend to take the other road.
    E. The traveler was addled.

4. **Part A:** Which of the following four details does not appear in the poem?

- ☒ A. Two roads ran parallel in the woods. 1
- ☐ B. The narrator took the more traveled road.
- ☐ C. The narrator couldn't decide which road to travel and thus took neither.
- ☐ D. The narrator took the road that had not been traveled as much as the other road. 19
- ☐ E. The narrator walked down each road before he made a decision about which one to travel.
- ☐ F. Each road was used about the same amount.
- ☐ G. The narrator believes that the course he chose to take has made a significant difference in his own life. 20
- ☐ H. The narrator isn't sure if he'll ever return to the road he had not taken. 15
- ☐ I. The narrator consulted with a good friend before deciding which road to take.

Part B: Drag the details that *do* occur in the poem and drop them in the boxes below. Make sure to place them in the order in which they are mentioned.

- Ⓐ Two roads ran parallel in the woods. 1
- B. The narrator took the more traveled road.
- C. The narrator couldn't decide which road to travel and thus took neither.
- Ⓓ The narrator took the road that had not been traveled as much as the other road. 19
- E. The narrator walked down each road before he made a decision about which one to travel.
- F. Each road was used about the same amount.
- Ⓖ The narrator believes that the course he chose to take has made a significant difference in his own life. 20
- Ⓗ The narrator isn't sure if he'll ever return to the road he had not taken. 15
- I. The narrator consulted with a good friend before deciding which road to take.

☐
☐
☐
☐
☐

5. Which of these statements describes the main theme of the poem?

   ○ A. The choice of the road taken happens in a dream.
   ○ B. The choice of the road taken is no challenge.
   ● C. The choice of the road taken changes the traveler's life.
   ○ D. The choice of the road taken frustrated the traveler.

6. What is the rhyme scheme of the second stanza of the poem?

   ○ A. aabbc
   ○ B. abcbc
   ○ C. abbba
   ● D. abaab

Be sure to check your answers with those on pages 245–246.

Target Skill 9: Fact vs. Opinion

A **fact** is information that can be measured and proven. An **opinion** shows the way someone feels about a **fact**.

Strategy

As you are doing your reading, use these strategies.

A **fact** is something that is easy to measure and prove.

- Look for measurements for proof (for example, *gallons*, *days*, and *inches*).
- Look for quotes and citations from books and newspapers.

An **opinion** is an interpretation.

- Look for key words or phrases, such as *Sometimes* or *As I see it*.

Paired Passage

How Do We Handle a Challenge?
by Philip Postrun

Our lives are often filled with many challenges. There are problems that we need to solve, difficult questions that we need to answer, and obstacles that we have to overcome. We can either face those challenges or give in to them. Both options, however, can lead us in different directions in our lives.

(5) Take, for example, an important assignment that we have been given. This assignment will count for one-third of our grade. Our options are fairly basic: we can work with a plan, divide up our time, and proceed to complete the task both well and on time. Our other option is to proceed without a plan. We may decide that there are friends that we would like to see, movies that we (10) would like to watch, and games we would like to play. Eventually, however, the time will come to pass when our assignment will be due.

If we haven't worked hard so far, then we have placed ourselves in an unenviable position. We may wish to complete our work now, but we likely have run out of enough time to do the assignment effectively. We are (15) definitely in a bind.

Imagine that a friend comes by and offers to help us to complete the assignment. He says that he can have someone get him a completed assignment. It will cost us some money, and we can't ask any questions. He also promises that he will deny helping to get the assignment if there is (20) any trouble in the future. Do we give in, knowing that there's a chance that we could get caught cheating? If we are caught, then we shall be in serious trouble both at school and at home. If we don't cheat, however, then one-third of our grade may be an "F." That will also get us in trouble.

What should we do? Should we take the easy way out, or should we be (25) honest and accept the consequences of our negligence, even though there will also be consequences for our honest actions? The answer is not a simple one, but it is one that we must each decide ourselves.

104 • New Jersey Grade 7 ELA/Literacy Test

1. Which statement contains the theme of this essay?

    - ⊘ A. "Our lives are often filled with many challenges."
    - ○ B. "There are problems that we need to solve, difficult questions that we need to answer, and obstacles that we have to overcome."
    - ○ C. "We can either face those challenges or give in to them."
    - ○ D. "Facing these challenges is never easy, but we must ultimately face these challenges ourselves."

2. Which of these four statements are opinion statements, rather than factual statements? Select each opinion.

    - ☑ A. "Our lives are often filled with many challenges."
    - ☑ B. "Both options, however, can lead us in different directions in our lives."
    - ☐ C. "This assignment will count for one-third of our grade."
    - ☐ D. "…the time will come to pass when our assignment will be due."
    - ☑ E. "If we haven't worked hard so far, then we have placed ourselves in an unenviable position."
    - ☐ F. "He says that he can have someone get him a completed assignment."
    - ☑ G. "The answer is not a simple one…"

3. Part A: How is this essay organized?

    - ⊘ A. Cause and effect
    - ○ B. Compare and contrast
    - ○ C. Description
    - ⊘ D. Problem/Solution

    Part B: Select the two words from the passage that are common for the correct organizational pattern of the piece.

    - ☐ A. "often"
    - ☑ B. "challenges"
    - ☐ C. "imagine"
    - ☐ D. "assignment"
    - ☐ E. "consequences"

4. Select the phrase from "How Do We Handle a Challenge?" that reflects the main idea in "The Road Not Taken."

    ☐ A. "Take, for example, an important assignment that we have been given."
    ☐ B. "If we haven't worked hard so far, then we have placed ourselves in an unenviable position."
    ☐ C. "Do we give in, knowing that there's a chance that we could get caught cheating?"
    ☒ D. "What should we do?"

5. In the sentence, "If we haven't worked hard so far, then we have placed ourselves in an unenviable position," what does the word *unenviable* mean?

    ● A. difficult
    ○ B. inane
    ○ C. complicated
    ○ D. advantageous

Be sure to check your answers with those on pages 246–247.

Paired Passage

Essay for Theme, Cause and Effect, Point of View, Details, Sequence, and Fact vs. Opinion

Both Robert Frost and Philip Postrun deal with the concept of facing a challenge. Compare the way each addresses the main idea, being sure to include the impact of the text structure, the similarities and differences in the causes and effects of the challenges, the author's point of view, and the author's intended response from the reader.

PREWRITING SECTION

Use the empty space provided to make a writing plan for your essay before you begin writing.

ESSAY

Be sure to check your essay against the sample response and suggestions on pages 247–248.

Target Skills 8 and 9: Conflict/Resolution and Making Predictions

Conflict
The **conflict** refers to a problem. The main conflict is the main problem being faced by one or more of the protagonists (heroes) in the work.

Resolution
The **resolution** is the solution to the conflict. When the conflict is resolved, the resolution isn't always one that the protagonist(s) may have wanted.

Making Predictions
Making predictions helps you to use the information that you've read and to predict the action that's likely to take place.

Strategy
- The **conflict** should appear early in the work. One or more main characters are going to be challenged. This challenge will be the **main conflict**. In novels, there are often **minor conflicts** that make the **major conflict** appear even worse.
- The **resolution** happens when the problem is solved. Be sure to look for hints (**foreshadowing**) the author may give you to help you to guess the resolution. As you read the following passage, *The Queen Bee*, consider how the marble horses and the absence of men **foreshadow** the fate that will come to pass upon the two older brothers.
- Whether you **make predictions** about events likely to occur in the story or after the story ends, base them only on the story's information.

Practice

The fable that you will read is *The Queen Bee* by the Brothers Grimm. It deals with the struggles faced by three brothers. Answer the questions based on this passage. Be sure to:

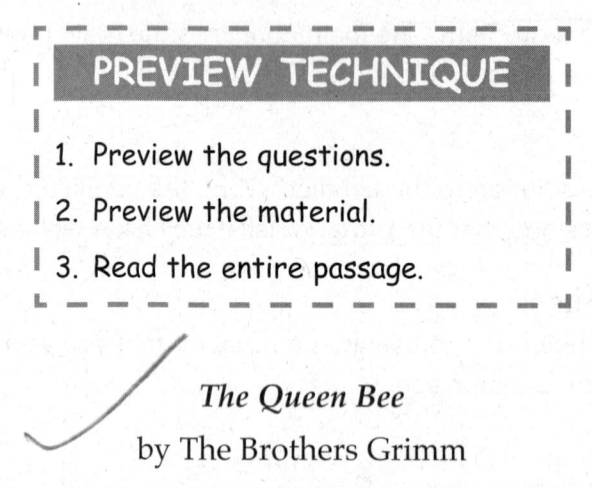

PREVIEW TECHNIQUE

1. Preview the questions.
2. Preview the material.
3. Read the entire passage.

The Queen Bee
by The Brothers Grimm

Two kings' sons once upon a time went into the world to seek their fortunes; but they soon fell into a wasteful foolish way of living, so that they could not return home again. Then their brother, who was a little insignificant dwarf, went out to seek for his brothers: but when he had found them they (5) only laughed at him, to think that he, who was so young and simple, should try to travel through the world, when they, who were so much wiser, had been unable to get on. However, they all set out on their journey together, and came at last to an ant hill. The two elder brothers would have pulled it down, in order to see how the poor ants in their fright would run about (10) and carry off their eggs. But the little dwarf said, "Let the poor things enjoy themselves; I will not suffer you to trouble them."

So on they went, and came to a lake where many ducks were swimming about. The two brothers wanted to catch two, and roast them. But the dwarf said, "Let the poor things enjoy themselves; you shall not kill them." Next (15) they came to a bees nest in a hollow tree, and there was so much honey that it ran down the trunk; and the two brothers wanted to light a fire under the tree and kill the bees so they could get their honey. But the dwarf held them back and said, 'Let the pretty insects enjoy themselves; I cannot let you burn them."

(20) At length the three brothers came to a castle: and as they passed by the stables they saw fine horses standing there, but all were of marble, and no man was to be seen.

Then they went through all the rooms, until they came to a door on which were three locks: but in the middle of the door was a wicket, so that they could look into the next room. There they saw a little grey old man sitting at a table; and they called to him once or twice, but he did not hear: however, they called a third time, and then he rose and came out to them.

He said nothing, but took hold of them and led them to a beautiful table covered with all sorts of good things; and when they had eaten and drunk, he showed each of them to a bed-chamber.

The next morning he came to the eldest and took him to a marble table, where there were three tablets, containing an account of the means by which the castle might be disenchanted. The first tablet said: "In the wood, under the moss, lie the thousand pearls belonging to the king's daughter; they must all be found: and if one be missing by set of sun, he who seeks them will be turned into marble."

The eldest brother set out, and sought for the pearls the whole day: but the evening came, and he had not found the first hundred: so he was turned into stone as the tablet had foretold.

The next day the second brother undertook the task; but he succeeded no better than the first; for he could only find the second hundred of the pearls; and therefore he too was turned into stone.

At last came the little dwarf's turn; and he looked in the moss; but it was so hard to find the pearls, and the job was so tiresome!—so he sat down upon a stone and cried. And as he sat there, the king of the ants (whose life he had saved) came to help him, with five thousand ants; and it was not long before they had found all the pearls and laid them in a heap.

The second tablet said: "The key of the princess's bed-chamber must be fished up out of the lake." And as the dwarf came to the brink of it, he saw the two ducks whose lives he had saved swimming about; and they dived down and soon brought in the key from the bottom.

The third task was the hardest. It was to choose the youngest and the best of the king's three daughters. Now they were all beautiful, and all exactly alike: but he was told that the eldest had eaten a piece of sugar, the next some sweet syrup, and the youngest a spoonful of honey; so he was to guess which it was that had eaten the honey.

Then came the queen of the bees, who had been saved by the little dwarf from the fire, and she tried the lips of all three; but at last she sat upon the lips of the one that had eaten the honey: and so the dwarf knew which was (60) the youngest. Thus the spell was broken, and all who had been turned into stones awoke, and took their proper forms. And the dwarf married the youngest and the best of the princesses, and was king after her father's death; but his two brothers married the other two sisters.

1. Which of the brothers seems to shy away from conflict?
   - A. The youngest (the dwarf)
   - B. Second oldest
   - ● C. Oldest
   - D. All of the above

2. Part A: When the king's youngest son is referred to as "a little insignificant dwarf," the word *insignificant* means:
   - ● A. unimportant.
   - B. important
   - C. wealthy
   - D. precocious

   Part B: Select the two phrases/sentences that refer to the opposite of the king's younger son's insignificance.
   - A. "…they soon fell into a wasteful foolish way of living."
   - B. "when he had found them they only laughed at him."
   - ☒ C. "Let the pretty insects enjoy themselves; I cannot let you burn them."
   - D. "they saw fine horses standing there, but all were of marble."
   - E. "he could only find the second hundred of the pearls."
   - ☒ F. "the dwarf married the youngest and the best of the princesses."

3. What conflict does the old man gives the oldest brother to resolve?
   - ● A. Find the first hundred pearls or be turned into marble.
   - B. Find all the missing pearls or be turned into marble.
   - C. Find the dwarf or be turned into stone.
   - D. Find the princess or be turned into stone.

4. When "The next day the second brother undertook the task," he:

    - ○ A. ran away.
    - ○ B. locked the old man in a prison and escaped with his brothers.
    - ○ C. accepted the challenge and succeeded.
    - ⊘ D. accepted the challenge and failed, also getting turned into marble.
    - ○ E. killed the duck that was helping him to search for the honey.

5. Because the little brother (dwarf) had shown kindness to the ants, ducks, and bees, you can predict that:

    - ○ A. They would attack him because he's a dwarf.
    - ○ B. They would pay him money.
    - ○ C. They would run away because they're afraid of dwarfs.
    - ⊘ D. They would help him later in the story.

"Friends, Romans, countrymen, lend me your ears"
William Shakespeare

Taken from *Julius Caesar* and spoken by Marc Antony (Act 3, Scene 2)

Friends, Romans, countrymen, lend me your ears;
I come to bury Caesar, not to praise him.
The evil that men do lives after them;
The good is oft interred with their bones;
So let it be with Caesar. The noble Brutus
(5) Hath told you Caesar was ambitious:
If it were so, it was a grievous fault,
And grievously hath Caesar answer'd it.
Here, under leave of Brutus and the rest–
For Brutus is an honourable man;
(10) So are they all, all honourable men–
Come I to speak in Caesar's funeral.
He was my friend, faithful and just to me:
But Brutus says he was ambitious;
And Brutus is an honourable man.
(15) He hath brought many captives home to Rome
Whose ransoms did the general coffers fill:

　　　　　Did this in Caesar seem ambitious?
　　　　　When that the poor have cried, Caesar hath wept:
(20)　　　Ambition should be made of sterner stuff:
　　　　　Yet Brutus says he was ambitious;
　　　　　And Brutus is an honourable man.
　　　　　You all did see that on the Lupercal
　　　　　I thrice presented him a kingly crown,
(25)　　　Which he did thrice refuse: was this ambition?
　　　　　Yet Brutus says he was ambitious;
　　　　　And, sure, he is an honourable man.
　　　　　I speak not to disprove what Brutus spoke,
　　　　　But here I am to speak what I do know.
(30)　　　You all did love him once, not without cause:
　　　　　What cause withholds you then, to mourn for him?
　　　　　O judgment! thou art fled to brutish beasts,
　　　　　And men have lost their reason. Bear with me;
　　　　　My heart is in the coffin there with Caesar,
(35)　　　And I must pause till it come back to me.

1. **Part A:** The word "ambitious" means:
   - A. nervous.
   - B. uncaring.
   - C. somewhat dishonest.
   - D. severe.

   Part B: Marc Antony's purpose in this speech is to demonstrate that:
   - A. there was a conflict between Caesar and Brutus caused by Brutus's ambition.
   - B. there was a conflict between Caesar and Brutus caused by Antony's ambition.
   - C. there was a conflict between Caesar and Brutus caused by Caesar's ambition.
   - D. the implied conflict is between Caesar and Antony.

2. **Part A:** When looking only at the opening two lines of Marc Antony's speech, "Friends, Romans, countrymen, lend me your ears; I come to bury Caesar, not to praise him," one could infer that:

   ○ A. Marc Antony wished to portray Caesar as a hero.
   ○ B. Marc Antony was not liked by the citizens of Rome.
   ○ C. Marc Antony disliked Caesar.
   ○ D. Marc Antony was related to Caesar

   Part B: When Marc Antony says, "When that the poor have cried, Caesar hath wept: Ambition should be made of sterner stuff: Yet Brutus says he was ambitious; And Brutus is an honourable man," Marc Antony is actually saying:

   ○ A. Caesar was overly emotional, and stress had caused his death.
   ○ B. Brutus was honorable, and Caesar was not.
   ○ C. Caesar was a poor man when he died.
   ○ D. Caesar was honorable, and Brutus was not.

3. **Part A:** What does the word *sterner* mean when Marc Antony says, "Ambition should be made of sterner stuff"?

   ○ A. more serious
   ○ B. more intelligent
   ○ C. more imaginative
   ○ D. more creative

   Part B: At this point in the speech, it can be concluded that the statement "Ambition should be made of sterner stuff" the quote from Part A, means

   ○ A. Marc Antony is falsely accusing Brutus of stealing gold from Caesar's treasury.
   ○ B. Marc Antony says that Brutus's accusation that Caesar was "ambitious" is false.
   ○ C. Marc Antony is glad that Caesar has been killed so he (Antony) can ascend to the throne.
   ○ D. Marc Antony is angry that he has not received any praise for killing Caesar.

Be sure to check your answers with those on pages 249–251.

Essay for Conflict/Resolution and Making Predictions

Both the "dwarf" in "The Queen Bee" and Marc Antony in his speech from Shakespeare's *Julius Caesar* were faced with a conflict that was not easy to resolve. Compare and contrast the challenge that each of these two individuals faced. Explain how the paths that led each one to the resolution of his problem were developed by the authors. You are encouraged to acknowledge the use of the literary devices used by the authors.

PREWRITING SECTION
Use the empty space provided to make a writing plan for your essay before you begin writing.

Reading: Literature and Informational Text • 117

ESSAY

Be sure to check your essay against the sample responses and suggestions on pages 251–253.

Target Skills 10 and 11: Mood and Tone

Mood
Mood is the general feeling "in the air" in a work. The mood could be gloomy, realistic, hopeful, or even romantic.

Tone
Tone is the attitude or way the speaker presents himself/herself. The tone could be serious, angry, happy, sad, or formal.

Strategy
- When reading, pretend that the narrator and main character(s) are speaking directly to you. As you listen to their words, consider how the situation feels to you. Is it hopeful? Are things dark and depressing? To find the mood, just listen to the way the story's being told. It may help you to understand mood if you place yourself directly into a situation that has occurred in your favorite story, novel, movie, TV show, or even song. Next, examine the feelings that you are experiencing. If there is hope for a brighter future, then the mood would likely be positive and uplifting. On the other hand, a feeling of hopelessness would set a quite somber mood.
- You can find the tone in a similar way. What emotions are the narrator and main character(s) feeling? Are they discussing serious issues, yelling during a fight, smiling, or speaking formally? What types of words are they using? Are these words supportive ("I'll help you right away," for example) or are these words displaying displeasure ("You'll never be able to steal from me again, you horrible thief!")? These emotions reflect the tone of the text.

> It is important for you to be able to analyze the mood and tone of a piece. Many of the concepts being tested, including author's intent, motivation, irony, and foreshadowing can be impacted by both mood and tone.

Practice

In *The Children's Hour* a poem by Henry Wadsworth Longfellow he shares his thoughts about an evening spent while playing with his children, to whom he was very devoted.

Read the poem thoroughly then answer the questions. **Be sure to:**

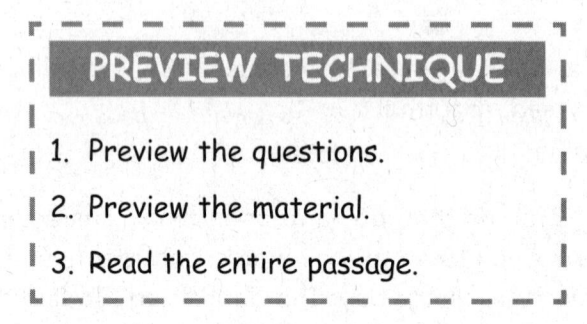

> **PREVIEW TECHNIQUE**
>
> 1. Preview the questions.
> 2. Preview the material.
> 3. Read the entire passage.

The Children's Hour

by Henry Wadsworth Longfellow

(1) Between the dark and the daylight,
When the night is beginning to lower,
Comes a pause in the day's occupations,
That is known as the Children's Hour.

I hear in the chamber above me
(6) The patter of little feet,
The sound of a door that is opened,
And voices soft and sweet.

From my study I see in the lamplight,
(10) Descending the broad hall stair,
Grave Alice, and laughing Allegra,
And Edith with golden hair.

A whisper, and then a silence:
Yet I know by their merry eyes
(15) They are plotting and planning together
To take me by surprise.

A sudden rush from the stairway,
A sudden raid from the hall!
By three doors left unguarded
(20) They enter my castle wall!

They climb up into my turret
O'er the arms and back of my chair;
If I try to escape, they surround me;
They seem to be everywhere.

(25) They almost devour me with kisses,
Their arms about me entwine,
Till I think of the Bishop of Bingen
In his Mouse-Tower on the Rhine!

Do you think, o blue-eyed banditti,
(30) Because you have scaled the wall,
Such an old mustache as I am
Is not a match for you all!

I have you fast in my fortress,
And will not let you depart,
(35) But put you down into the dungeon
In the round-tower of my heart.

And there will I keep you forever,
Yes, forever and a day,
Till the walls shall crumble to ruin,
(40) And moulder in dust away!

122 • New Jersey Grade 7 ELA/Literacy Test

1. What is the rhyme scheme used by Longfellow in his poem?

   - A. aaab
   - B. aabb
   - C. aaba
   - D. abcb

2. Which two of the following is/are NOT possible tone(s) of the poem's first four lines "Between the dark and the daylight, when the night is beginning to lower, comes a pause in the day's occupations, that is known as the Children's Hour"?

   - A. formal
   - B. clear
   - C. realistic
   - D. gloomy
   - E. insincere

3. What word describes the tone of lines 13–16 "A whisper, and then a silence: Yet I know by their merry eyes—they are plotting and planning together—to take me by surprise."

   - A. nasty
   - B. playful
   - C. angry
   - D. sad

4. Part A: In line 21, Longfellow uses the word *turret*. Select the two choices that are correct definitions.

   - A. a small tower
   - B. bookcase
   - C. a tank missile
   - D. stairway
   - E. lap
   - F. a gunner's enclosure

Part B: Which four words from lines 21–24 connect with the term *turret* from Part A?

- ☒ A. climb
- ☐ B. arms
- ☐ C. back
- ☒ D. escape
- ☒ E. surround
- ☒ F. everywhere

5. Choose the tone of lines 29–32 "Do you think, o blue-eyed banditti, because you have scaled the wall, Such an old mustache as I am is not a match for you all!"

- ○ A. angry
- ○ B. pompous
- ⊘ C. sad
- ○ D. challenging

6. What is the mood of the narrator in lines 33–40 "I have you fast in my fortress, and will not let you depart, . . . till the walls shall crumble to ruin, and moulder in dust away!"?

- ⊘ A. worried
- ○ B. sad
- ○ C. vengeful
- ○ D. playful

Be sure to check your answers with those on pages 253–254.

"We Shall Fight on the Beaches"
by Winston Churchill

Excerpts from a speech presented to the House of Commons on June 4, 1940

We are told that Herr Hitler has a plan for invading the British Isles. This has often been thought of before. When Napoleon lay at Boulogne for a year with his flat-bottomed boats and his Grand Army, he was told by someone. "There are bitter weeds in England." There are certainly a great many more
(5) of them since the British Expeditionary Force returned.

We have found it necessary to take measures of increasing stringency, not only against enemy aliens and suspicious characters of other nationalities, but also against British subjects who may become a danger or a nuisance should the war be transported to the United Kingdom. I know there are a great many
(10) people affected by the orders which we have made who are the passionate enemies of Nazi Germany. I am very sorry for them, but we cannot, at the present time and under the present stress, draw all the distinctions which we should like to do. If parachute landings were attempted and fierce fighting attendant upon them followed, these unfortunate people would be far better
(15) out of the way, for their own sakes as well as for ours. There is, however, another class, for which I feel not the slightest sympathy. Parliament has given us the powers to put down Fifth Column activities with a strong hand, and we shall use those powers subject to the supervision and correction of the House, without the slightest hesitation until we are satisfied, and more than
(20) satisfied, that this malignancy in our midst has been effectively stamped out.

Turning once again, and this time more generally, to the question of invasion, I would observe that there has never been a period in all these long centuries of which we boast when an absolute guarantee against invasion, still less against serious raids, could have been given to our people. In the
(25) days of Napoleon the same wind which would have carried his transports across the Channel might have driven away the blockading fleet. There was always the chance, and it is that chance which has excited and befooled the imaginations of many Continental tyrants. Many are the tales that are told. We are assured that novel methods will be adopted, and when we see the
(30) originality of malice, the ingenuity of aggression, which our enemy displays, we may certainly prepare ourselves for every kind of novel stratagem and

every kind of brutal and treacherous maneuver. I think that no idea is so outlandish that it should not be considered and viewed with a searching, but at the same time, I hope, with a steady eye. We must never forget the solid assurances of sea power and those which belong to air power if it can be locally exercised.

I have, myself, full confidence that if all do their duty, if nothing is neglected, and if the best arrangements are made, as they are being made, we shall prove ourselves once again able to defend our Island home, to ride out the storm of war, and to outlive the menace of tyranny, if necessary for years, if necessary alone. At any rate, that is what we are going to try to do. That is the resolve of His Majesty's Government-every man of them. That is the will of Parliament and the nation. The British Empire and the French Republic, linked together in their cause and in their need, will defend to the death their 40 native soil, aiding each other like good comrades to the utmost of their strength. Even though large tracts of Europe and many old and famous States have fallen or may fall into the grip of the Gestapo and all the odious apparatus of Nazi rule, we shall not flag or fail. We shall go on to the end, we shall fight in France, we shall fight on the seas and oceans, we shall fight with growing confidence and growing strength in the air, we shall defend our Island, whatever the cost may be, we shall fight on the beaches, we shall fight on the landing grounds, we shall fight in the fields and in the streets, we shall fight in the hills; we shall never surrender, and even if, which I do not for a moment believe, this Island or a large part of it were subjugated and starving, then our Empire beyond the seas, armed and guarded by the British Fleet, would carry on the struggle, until, in God's good time, the New World, with all its power and might, steps forth to the rescue and the liberation of the old.

1. **Part A:** Winston Churchill states that when Napoleon had prepared to invade England, he was told by someone that "There are bitter weeds in England." Select the two answers that correctly define the phrase "bitter weeds":

   ☐ A. England could not defend itself.
   ☐ B. England was in the midst of a drought.
   ☐ C. England was a country known for its farms.
   ☐ D. England would not be an easy target for any invaders.
   ☐ E. England was prepared to defend itself, but it would prefer a peaceful solution.
   ☐ F. England was prepared to defend itself aggressively as it had done in the past.

   Part B: When Winston Churchill uses the phrase "There are bitter weeds in England" from Part A, his tone is

   ○ A. timid.
   ○ B. inconsistent.
   ○ C. determined.
   ○ D. light-hearted.

2. Winston Churchill states that "We have found it necessary to take measures of increasing stringency." What does the word *stringency* mean?

   ○ A. rigor
   ○ B. exhaustion
   ○ C. mildness
   ○ D. creativity

3. **Part A:** Winston Churchill uses the term "Fifth Column activities." Choose the two answers that refer to the term.

   ☐ A. patriotism
   ☐ B. loyalty
   ☐ C. espionage
   ☐ D. oratory
   ☐ E. faith-based
   ☐ F. sabotage

Part B: Winston Churchill asserts, "We shall use those powers... until we are satisfied... that this malignancy in our midst has been effectively stamped out." To whom or to what group is he referring?
- A. Napoleon's army
- B. The British Expeditionary Force
- C. British subjects
- D. Fifth columnists

4. **Part A:** Which two of the following words best describe the mood at the beginning of this excerpt?
   - A. reassuring
   - B. insensitive
   - C. vengeful
   - D. aggressive
   - E. hopeful

   Part B: What two words best describe the mood at the conclusion of the excerpt that might be different from the example in Part A?
   - A. timid
   - B. inconsistent
   - C. determined
   - D. light-hearted
   - E. antagonistic
   - F. uplifting

5. When Winston Churchill keeps saying the phrase "We shall fight...," what literary term does he use?
   - A. simile
   - B. metaphor
   - C. personification
   - D. repetition for effect

Be sure to check your answers with those on pages 254–255.

Essay for Mood and Tone

Winston Churchill's excerpted speech deals with an invasion, as does Henry Wadsworth Longfellow's poem. Each has a particular purpose in mind. State each author's purpose and tell how each writer used the idea of a battle. Consider the intent of both authors, as well as the literary devices each uses to craft his piece.

Briefly explain what the tone of the poem is in the first four stanzas (paragraphs in poetry). Is Longfellow angry, serious, or sad? Is he formal, suspicious, or witty (clever)? Is the tone different than the choices mentioned?

PREWRITING SECTION
Use the empty space provided to make a writing plan for your essay before you begin writing.

ESSAY

Be sure to check your essay against the sample responses and suggestions on pages 255–258.

Target Skills 14–18: Poetic Devices—Metaphor, Simile, Personification, Rhyme Scheme, and Alliteration

Metaphor

A metaphor shows how two objects or ideas are similar, even though they're usually not similar. For example, "The cloud is a soft pillow."

An extended metaphor "connects" two objects or ideas. Moreover, it's used throughout the work instead of in just one section.

Simile

A simile also shows how two objects or ideas are similar, even though they're usually not similar. However, a simile uses "like" or "as" to make the comparison. A metaphor doesn't. For example, "The cloud is as soft as a pillow" or "She runs like a jaguar in the jungle."

Personification

Personification gives human or living qualities to non-human or non-living things. For example, "The river sang a peaceful song of hope to the weary travelers."

Rhyme Scheme

Rhyme scheme is the pattern of words that sound alike in two or more lines of a stanza (poetry paragraph). Look at the last word in the line to find the rhyme. In the following example, notice that lines one and three rhyme.

Example:
I went to the park
To play baseball.
When it became dark
I went home.

Alliteration

Alliteration repeats the beginning sounds (usually consonants) of words that are close by. It can be used along with rhyme (see the first example). Also, alliteration can sometimes be used instead of rhyme (see the second example).

First example:
All the animals are alive.
The forest has been saved by you five.

Second example:
Many more military men will receive medals this morning.
Most of the militia will be mentioned.

Strategy
Metaphors and similes add vivid description to literature.

- They provide vivid descriptions. For example, "The cloud is (as soft as) a pillow."
- They use the traits of the object or idea in the comparison. For example, "She was as stubborn as a forged bar of steel" suggests that the girl's will power is very strong.
- Metaphors and similes help you to see clearly the writer's images.

Personification adds life to descriptions. For example, "The ocean scolded the fishermen by slapping their boats with its powerful waves and roaring disapproval."

Practice

As you read Joyce Kilmer's poem, *Trees*, notice Kilmer's use of metaphor, simile, and personification. Also, look for an extended metaphor.

Read the poem thoroughly then answer the questions. **Be sure to:**

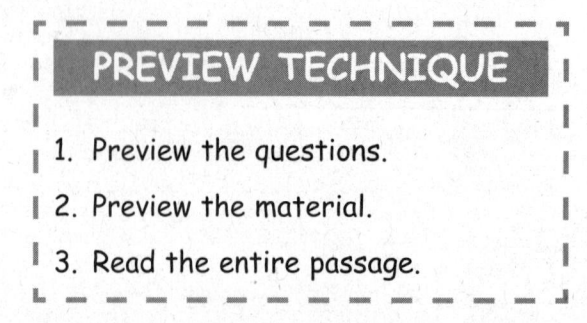

> **PREVIEW TECHNIQUE**
>
> 1. Preview the questions.
> 2. Preview the material.
> 3. Read the entire passage.

Trees

By Joyce Kilmer

I think that I shall never see
A poem lovely as a tree.

A tree whose hungry mouth is prest (pressed)
Against the earth's sweet flowing breast;

(5) A tree that looks at God all day,
And lifts her leafy arms to pray;

A tree that may in Summer wear
A nest of robins in her hair;

Upon whose bosom snow has lain;
(10) Who intimately lives with rain.

Poems are made by fools like me,
But only God can make a tree.

1. The simile used in line 2 of the poem compares the poem to what object?
   - ● A. a tree
   - ○ B. grass
   - ○ C. a mouth
   - ○ D. robins

2. In line 3 of the poem, select one of the following answers that describes what the tree's "hungry mouth" is doing.
   - ☐ A. speak
   - ☑ B. cry
   - ☑ C. get nourishment
   - ☑ D. yawn
   - ☐ E. shelter the birds
   - ☐ F. play with the rain

3. Part A: In line 6 of the poem, "And lifts her leafy arms to pray," select the three literary devices being used.

- ☐ A. simile
- ☐ B. metaphor
- ☒ C. personification
- ☐ D. alliteration
- ☐ E. rhyme scheme

Part B: Which two words relate to the image from Part A?

- ☐ A. practical
- ☒ B. romanticizing
- ☒ C. neutral
- ☐ D. preliminary
- ☐ E. insidious
- ☐ F. imaginary

4. Lines 7 and 8 of the poem state, "A tree that may in Summer wear / A nest of robins in her hair." Choose the answer that explains the way the author is portraying the tree.

- ○ A. A hungry predator
- ○ B. A living form of shelter
- ⊘ C. A fashion model
- ○ D. The poet

5. Select from the following statements the two that would accurately portray Joyce Kilmer's feelings about trees as expressed in the poem.

- ☐ A. Trees exhaust all the nutrients from the earth.
- ☐ B. Trees are nice until they have to be cut down.
- ☒ C. Trees are a beautiful part of nature.
- ☐ D. Trees are a beautiful part of nature, but they can be dangerous for birds.
- ☐ E. Trees like the snow, but they don't enjoy the rain because it washes away the soil.
- ☐ F. Trees think that Joyce Kilmer is foolish.
- ☐ G. Trees can figuratively pray.

Be sure to check your answers with those on pages 258–259.

Forest Trees of Wisconsin: How to Know Them

(Published by the Department of Natural Resources—
Madison, Wisconsin—Division of Forestry)

—Excerpted http://dnr.wi.gov/files/PDF/pubs/fr/FR0053.pdf

Introduction

Trees, like all living things, grow and mature and die while the forest, which is a community of trees, may live indefinitely because the trees reproduce before they die.

Vegetative Reproduction

(5) Many trees reproduce vegetatively under certain conditions, for example, most of the broad leaf trees will sprout if cut when small, while some like basswood will sprout regardless of age. Others like the quaking aspen and black locust will send up shoots from the roots at considerable distance from the parent tree.

The only American conifer (cone-bearing tree) which sprouts is the
(10) redwood, but we have one conifer in Wisconsin which often reproduces vegetatively, but by a method other than sprouting. Lower limbs of black spruce often touch the ground and, where moss grows over the limb back of the tips, roots develop, and finally the tip of the branch becomes a new tree.

Man uses the ability of some trees to reproduce vegetatively. Cuttings from
(15) small branches of willow or eastern cottonwood bearing several buds can be set in the ground to grow, because they will develop roots. Other methods like budding and grafting are used to propagate horticultural varieties. We cannot grow Baldwin apple trees from seed, but must graft a twig from a Baldwin tree onto a seedling apple tree.

Reproduction by Seed

(20) However, most of our forest trees grow from seed and the way the seeds are produced is the basis for classifying plants. For example, white pine seeds grow in pairs on the inner surface of the cone scales, while the hickory seed is enclosed in a nut. This really is the difference between the conifers or evergreens, and the broadleaf trees. In this bulletin the word "fruit" is used

in the botanical sense, meaning the seeds and seed bearing part, therefore, the acorn and its cup together constitute a fruit.

The Formation of Seed

Some seed is produced from "perfect" flowers, like the cherries where both stamens and pistils are found in the same tree. This is best illustrated with the corn plant, where the tassel or staminate flower produces the pollen which must fertilize the grains in the ear. You have all seen ears of corn where some of the kernels did not develop because they were not fertilized by pollen.

With some species like the ashes and the poplars, some trees have only staminate flowers and others only pistillate flowers, so that the female trees will not bear seed unless there are staminate trees in the vicinity. The Lombardy poplar which is a horticultural variety of the European poplar never bears seed because the variety was developed as a mutation and there are no Lombardy poplars bearing staminate flowers. Therefore, it is always reproduced vegetatively; that is, by cutting or sprouts.

Distribution of Seed

Since some trees mature their seed in spring while others ripen later, seeds developed several methods of scattering or planting themselves. Seeds from the aspens are very light and so perishable that they must come in contact with moist mineral soil within a few hours. As they are covered with cottony down they are carried by the wind. These two characteristics have enabled the aspen to reforest many of the burned over areas. Pin cherry also comes in on areas after forest fires because birds eat the cherries and may drop the seed far from the parent tree.

Seeds of pine, maple and basswood have wings so that they are carried farther by wind, while the heavy nuts and acorns are often buried by squirrels and then forgotten. Seeds of trees which grow along the stream banks are carried by the water.

Jack pine is especially interesting because it protects its seeds from fire. While most of the cones will open the first autumn, a few will remain closed, sometimes for many years. Then following a forest fire, these cones will open from the heat and drop seeds on the denuded land. In this way jack pine predominates on lands which originally carried mostly Norway or white pine. If jack pine grows in your vicinity look for some of these unopened cones and place one on a hot stove and watch the scales open.

How Trees Grow

(60) The growth of new wood in any year forms a complete layer over the entire tree. That is why we can determine the age of a tree from the number of rings on the stump. Height growth occurs only in the new wood of any one year. If a nail is driven into the trunk of a ten foot tree at five feet from the ground, it will still be five feet from the ground when the tree is a hundred feet tall.

(65) The form of trees depends on the growing space. A close spacing between trees, shades the tree stems by restricting sunlight and causes side branches to die and fall off, leaving tall straight clean stems which are valuable for timber. Shade trees which have room to spread out have a large crown with spreading limbs and a short stem. Notice the trees at the edge of a forest,
(70) they have branches on the side towards the open while the other side is free of branches.

Variations in Trees

Since form and size or color and character of bark vary with size and growing conditions, too much importance should not be placed on them in identifying trees. The leaves from the lower branches of a tree may have a
(75) very different outline than those from the tip of the tree, while leaves on the sprouts from a tree which was cut may be excessively large and of unusual shape. Notice the difference between the twigs and needles of balsam trees when one has had full sunlight and the other grew in the shade.

An effort has been made to point out several distinguishing characteristics
(80) in describing each tree. After you have identified the trees, they can be recognized as you recognize your friends on the street even though you cannot describe them so that a stranger will recognize them.

1. **Part A:** Select the two statements that are true from the "Introduction."

    ☐ A. Trees and forests are both communities.
    ☐ B. Neither trees nor forests are communities.
    ☐ C. Trees are communities, and forests are not.
    ☐ D. Forests are communities, and trees are not.
    ☐ E. Trees and forests have the same lifespan.
    ☐ F. Trees and forests have different lifespans.

    Part B: Which one of the following statements best supports the answer to Part A and explains the way in which the "Introduction" is structured?

    ○ A. Chronological
    ○ B. Problem/Solution
    ○ C. Cause and Effect
    ○ D. Compare and Contrast

2. Select the two statements that are true about vegetative reproduction.

    ☐ A. Seeds or nuts from the trees are used in vegetative reproduction.
    ☐ B. Cuttings are used in vegetative reproduction.
    ☐ C. All conifers reproduce vegetatively by sprouting.
    ☐ D. Regardless of age, most conifers reproduce vegetatively by sprouting.
    ☐ E. Baldwin apple trees can grow from seeds and not from grafting.
    ☐ F. Most trees in the forest grow from seeds, not vegetative reproduction.

3. Choose the two statements that are true about forest trees that grow from seed.

    ☐ A. The acorn is considered to be a botanical fruit.
    ☐ B. The corn plant reproduces vegetatively, not by seed.
    ☐ C. For trees like the ashes and the poplars, "the female trees will not bear seed" unless there are pistillate trees "in the vicinity."
    ☐ D. The Lombardy poplar bears no staminate flowers since it was developed as a mutation.
    ☐ E. The Lombardy poplar can reproduce both vegetatively and through the formation of seed.

4. In the sentence "In this way jack pine predominates on lands which originally carried mostly Norway or white pine," what does the word *predominates* mean?

   - A. Grows
   - B. Simplifies
   - C. Explores
   - D. Prevails

5. Select the following statement(s) that you think is/are true.

   - ☐ A. Since seeds from the aspen "are very light and so perishable" and their "cottony down covers" make them easy to be "carried by the wind," they are able to reforest any area that is not "burned over."
   - ☐ B. After birds eat pin cherries, they "may drop the seed far from the parent tree" and thereby help to reforest areas "after forest fires."
   - ☐ C. "Seeds of pine, maple and basswood have wings so that they are carried farther by wind," thereby helping in the reproduction process.
   - ☐ D. Since the jack pine "protects its seeds from fire," it is a good reforestation tree "following a forest fire."
   - ☐ E. The "growing space" for trees has a direct effect on the "form of trees" growing in the space.
   - ☐ F. When looking at "the trees at the edge of a forest," notice that the side that is "towards the open" part of the forest "is free of branches."

Be sure to check your answers with those on pages 259–260.

Essay for Poetic Devices—Metaphor, Simile, Personification, Rhyme Scheme, and Alliteration

Both Joyce Kilmer and The Wisconsin Division of Forestry had a different purpose in mind when writing about trees. Compare and contrast the pieces and focus on the genre they used, the way they created their imagery, and the method of explaining their topic. Also consider how the style and structure influenced their writing.

PREWRITING SECTION
Use the empty space provided to make a writing plan for your essay before you begin writing.

ESSAY

Be sure to check your essay against the sample responses and suggestions on pages 260–262.

Reading: Informational (Everyday) Text

CHAPTER 4

WHAT IS EVERYDAY READING

In English class, you read many poems, stories, novels, grammar exercises, and more. In other classes and outside of school, you may be reading newspapers, magazines, e-mails, IM's (Instant Messages), **text messages**, and other printed material. This is **informational (everyday) reading**.

> Text messages are casual forms of writing that do not necessarily follow the rules of grammar and spelling. Therefore, text message form should not be used when you write any of your responses on the exam.

Reading every day will help you to be a better reader. It is important to keep practicing and keep up your skills.

Strategy
To answer questions in this category, you must read the passages carefully. Before you do so, continue to use the **PT (Preview Technique) Strategy**.

PREVIEW TECHNIQUE

1. Preview the questions you actually need to answer.
2. Preview the material.
3. Read the entire passage to find key lines or phrases that relate to the questions.

143

MAJOR TASK: ANSWER QUESTIONS BASED ON INFORMATIONAL TEXT

This section of the test will give you reading selections found in textbooks, magazines, reference books, or other sources. Even though you may find a topic or person that you don't know a lot about, read the entire passage carefully since the questions are based on the passage.

Target Skills 1 and 2: Details and Sequence of Events

- Reading passages always have **details**, the facts that explain the information you're reading.
- The **sequence of events** is the order in which things happen.

Strategy

When looking for **details**, concentrate on the facts and **not** on opinions.

When looking for the **sequence of events**:

- Look for transition words and phrases, such as, "first," "next," and "the final step."
- Look for numbers or bullet points to guide you.
- Look for the abbreviations "AM" and "PM" for time sequences.

PRACTICE FOR TARGET SKILLS

This passage is entitled *Things Had Really Changed!* It deals with a young boy who doesn't start out being happy on the first day of school. Use only facts from the passage to answer the questions that follow.

Things Had Really Changed!

When Jonathan had walked into his 7th grade homeroom on the last day of class in school, he wasn't as happy as he thought he would be. Yes, he loved the freedom in the summer. He wouldn't have to follow a schedule every day. On the first day of school in September, Jonathan had quickly written a note in his planner as he sat down at his desk. The note said, "Only 179 more days to go until summer comes back!" He never expected that he might actually enjoy school this year.

Jonathan's previous years in school had not been that bad, but they also weren't great. He got into trouble sometimes, but he had never been suspended. He always knew when to stop his fooling around with his friends.

He didn't think that he would like any of his classes this year, but he was actually wrong. He found that he liked Miss Rumson's English class the best. She had encouraged him to write when he was in central detention with her last year. She had looked at some of his writing and even laughed at his story about falling off his bike while showing off to his friends.

Things would get even better in Miss Rumson's class. After he had handed in his first assignment, she told him that he has a lot of writing talent. A lot of teachers had said that to Jonathan before, but this was different somehow. Miss Rumson seemed to take a personal interest in Jonathan's writing.

For the first month of school, Miss Rumson tried to get Jonathan to join the school newspaper. He resisted at first, but Miss Rumson was persistent. Finally, he agreed and was assigned to cover the school's wrestling matches. Jonathan had never gone to a school event before because his friends would think he wasn't "cool." That's the reason why he didn't tell his friends that he was going.

When he was at the first match, he noticed that the head cheerleader, Katie, smiled at him. He smiled back, but he didn't think anything about it. When his story came out about the school team's first win of the year,

Jonathan knew that his friends would make fun of him. Actually, that didn't happen because the captain of the team was also the brother of one of his good friends.

School really began to change for Jonathan. He started to take his books home every night. Sometimes he went out with his friends instead of studying, but there were times when he actually did study. After one of those times when he studied, he received the second highest grade on Miss Rumson's test. Who had received the top grade? Katie earned a perfect score, of course.

His friends teased Jonathan a little more for his high score on the test, but he didn't get as upset about it as he had thought he would. In fact, something good happened. Katie asked him if he would study with her for the next test. Jonathan was shocked, but he was also very pleased.

Jonathan believed that no one had ever thought that he was a good student. He remembered that his fourth grade teacher had told him he could be a very good student if he would just work a little harder. He hadn't listened because most of his friends didn't study. Jonathan hadn't wanted to lose his friends.

Things were different now. Jonathan was on the school newspaper. The older brother of one of his friends was on the team so Jonathan wouldn't be teased for covering the wrestlers for the school newspaper. More importantly, the head cheerleader, Katie, wanted to study with him.

Two weeks later, Jonathan had become a little uneasy. When he had arrived home after school, his mom mentioned that Miss Rumson had called. Even though he didn't remember doing anything wrong in school, he was ready to apologize. He figured that he must have done something wrong. Why else would the teacher be calling?

Well, things couldn't have been better for Jonathan. He learned that he had received the highest grade in the class on the last test. His grade was actually one point higher than Katie's. He also learned that Miss Rumson liked his reporting skills so much that she had contacted the local newspaper. The editor said that he would be willing to take Jonathan's reports about the school wrestling team and place them in the paper.

Jonathan had not been very happy when the school year had started. Now, he looked at things completely differently. The next day, Jonathan wrote in his planner that 7th grade wasn't so bad.

1. Starting with Jonathan's first day in 7th grade, which event is out of sequence?

    A. First, "Jonathan had quickly written a note in his planner as he sat down at his desk."
    B. Second, Jonathan "was assigned to cover the school's wrestling matches."
    C. Third, Jonathan "had received the highest grade in the class on the last test."
    D. All events are listed in sequence.

2. During all his years in school, how many times had Jonathan been suspended?

    A. none
    B. one
    C. two
    D. five

3. Why didn't Jonathan tell his friends that he was covering the wrestling team?

    A. His best friend had been thrown off the team.
    B. He thought his friends wouldn't think he was "cool."
    C. He thought Katie wouldn't think he was "cool."
    D. He thought his teachers wouldn't think he was "cool."

4. For what group did Jonathan cover the wrestling team?

    A. The principal's newsletter.
    B. The parent-teacher group's newsletter.
    C. The class newspaper.
    D. The school newspaper.

Be sure to check your answers against those on pages 262–263.

Essay for Details and Sequence of Events

Explain how "School really began to change for Jonathan." Next, relate how you have dealt successfully with a change that you have faced.

> **PREWRITING SECTION**
> Use the empty space provided to make a writing plan for your essay before you begin writing.

ESSAY

Be sure to check your essay against the suggestions made on page 263.

Target Skill 3: Central Idea or Theme

The **central idea** or **theme** in a passage tells you what the main topic is. A passage about a famous mountain climber, for example, may feature the courage of the climber as the **central idea** or **theme**.

Strategy

As you are reading a chapter in your textbook, an article on the Internet, or a story about a famous person, try these strategies to help you to find the **central idea** or **theme**.

- Look at the title since it may often contain the **central idea** or **theme**.
- Look at the first sentence in the first paragraph. It may either contain the theme or be leading you directly to it.
- Look for a summary or a closing comment at the end of the passage, as well.

Practice

You will read an article entitled "Vacation." It is about the places in New Jersey where you can go to take a vacation.

Read the passage thoroughly and then answer the questions. **Be sure to:**

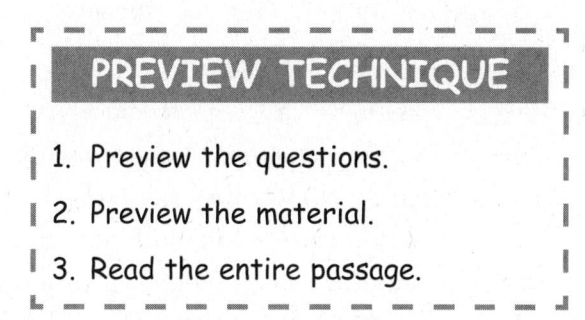

> **PREVIEW TECHNIQUE**
> 1. Preview the questions.
> 2. Preview the material.
> 3. Read the entire passage.

Vacation

Many of us travel long distances to take our vacations. Even though it's nice to travel, did you know that you could take a vacation without leaving our state of New Jersey? Whether we like the mountains, the ocean, shopping or sightseeing, there are many interesting attractions to see throughout the state. New Jersey is your in-state vacation spot.

If the mountains interest you, then visit the Delaware Water Gap in the northwest section of the state. They have hiking trails, boating, fishing, beautiful scenery, and more. If you head to the Skylands area in the northwest, be sure to visit in the winter. You'll find many skiing, snowboarding, and sledding areas where you can burn off some of that extra energy. Don't forget the reservoirs throughout the state that provide some of the same activities as the ones you can find in the Delaware Water Gap and the Skylands.

On a hot summer day, head for the Jersey Shore. Explore miles and miles of sandy beaches where you can swim or get a tan. Get a few friends and ride your boogie board. Take a walk and enjoy the shops, the saltwater taffy, the Italian ice treats, and the amusements on the boardwalk in Atlantic City. You can even take a ride on an old-fashioned paddlewheel boat in Tom's River, Beach Haven, and Point Pleasant Beach.

If you're into sports, New Jersey has the Meadowlands Complex. This is the home of various professional sports teams including football's Giants and Jets, basketball's Nets, hockey's Devils, and soccer's Red Bulls. Baseball fans can take in a game at eight different professional league parks. Some of the teams that play there include the Trenton Thunder, the Somerset Patriots, and the New Jersey Jackals. If you like auto racing, visit one of the auto racetracks that sponsor NASCAR and NHRA races in towns like New Egypt and Old Bridge. Throughout New Jersey, there are also many public parks that have sports fields and tennis courts for you to enjoy.

If you like history, there are many places to visit throughout the state. For example, in the northeast Gateway region, places of interest include the Edison National Historic Site in West Orange and President Grover Cleveland's birthplace in Caldwell. In the Skylands region, check out the Fosterfields Living History Farm in Morris Plains and the Elias Van Bunschooten (Colonial) Museum in Sussex. The Delaware region has Batsto (Colonial) Village in Batsto and the C. A. Nothnagle Log House in Gibbstown. Be sure to remember to check out the many lighthouses throughout the Shore regions. Finally, visit the NJ Vietnam Veterans' Memorial in Holmdel and pay tribute to our soldiers who lost their lives in defense of our country.

New Jersey provides a lot of variety for your vacations, and you never have to leave the state. Whether you're looking for amusement rides, majestic mountains, sandy beaches, sports, or history, you can find them in your own home state. Remember to think of New Jersey, your in-state vacation spot, when you're planning your next vacation.

Reading: Informational (Everyday) Text • 153

1. Which of these titles would relate more closely to the **central idea** or **theme**?
   - A. My Vacation
   - B. Where to Take a Vacation
   - C. New Jersey Vacations for New Jersey Residents
   - D. Vacations for All Seasons

2. What is the main point of the third paragraph?
   - A. It's hot at the seashore.
   - B. The New Jersey seashore has swimming, shopping, food, and more.
   - C. All of the historic areas are located at the New Jersey seashore.
   - D. The New Jersey seashore doesn't get many visitors in the winter.

3. Which one of these statements is a detail that does **not** support the central idea or theme in the fourth paragraph?
   - A. The Meadowlands Complex is the home of various professional sports teams.
   - B. There are eight different professional league parks for baseball.
   - C. There are swimming pools in many towns.
   - D. There are auto racetracks that sponsor NASCAR and NHRA races.

4. Which one of these statements is a detail that does **not** support the central idea or theme in the fifth paragraph?
   - A. The NJ Vietnam Veterans' Memorial is located near the Garden State Parkway.
   - B. The Edison National Historic Site in located in West Orange.
   - C. The Fosterfields Living History Farm is located in Morris Plains.
   - D. The C. A. Nothnagle Log House is located in Gibbstown.

Be sure to check your answers with those on pages 263–264.

Essay for Central Idea or Theme

State the **central idea** or **theme** of the entire article. Be sure to use specific examples to explain your answer.

PREWRITING SECTION
Use the empty space provided to make a writing plan for your essay before you begin writing.

ESSAY

Be sure to check your essay against the suggestions made on page 264.

Target Skills 4–6: Questioning, Clarifying, and Predicting

Questioning is the effective use of questions to gather information. **Clarifying** is the way to find out further information about a topic. **Predicting** is making educated guesses based on both the information that you have already found out and information that you already know.

Strategy

As you are doing your reading, use these strategies.

- [ ] For effective **Questioning**, make sure that your questions are designed to bring you the information that you seek. Be specific.
- [ ] Use specific questions when you need help **Clarifying** information.
- [ ] When you are **Predicting**, make sure that your predictions are based on logic and common sense.

Practice

The passage that you will read is a 7th grade student's journal entry entitled My First Day of School.

Read the passage thoroughly and answer the questions. **Be sure to:**

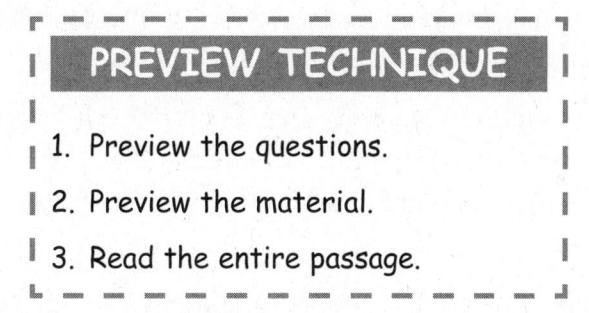

```
PREVIEW TECHNIQUE

1. Preview the questions.
2. Preview the material.
3. Read the entire passage.
```

My First Day of School
by Pat Cole

When I set my alarm last night, I realized that tomorrow I would be following a different routine for the next few months. Since school had let out last June, I suddenly had a lot more freedom. I could sleep a little later, eat lunch whenever I wanted to, watch my favorite daytime television programs, and just hang out with my friends. Tomorrow morning, it was time to go back to school.

The next morning, my mom woke me up even before my alarm rang. She told me that I had to make sure that I was awake. I couldn't go back to sleep.

If I did, I would be late for the first day of school. She said, "That's not the way you want to start out your school year, is it?" I just grumbled "No" and slid out of my bed.

I found my way to the bathroom and jumped in the shower. During the summer, I never had to take my shower before breakfast. I always made some cereal, poured a glass of juice, and settled in with my favorite television program on one of the music channels. Today, however, I had to finish my shower, dry my hair, and have a little breakfast. Oh, I couldn't do these things in slow motion. My mom kept reminded me to "Hurry up!" so I wouldn't be late. She also reminded me to wear the new outfit we had bought last week. "You should always make a good first impression, especially on the first day of school," she said. It would feel funny dressing up for breakfast after an entire summer of eating while wearing my pajamas.

My mom made me hot cereal, toast, and juice for breakfast. She also cut up some melon for me. I was still a little tired and didn't feel like eating much. My mom told me that I would be hungry before lunch if I didn't eat a good breakfast, but I just wasn't hungry. Besides, lunch was only a few hours away, wasn't it?

After I had finished my breakfast, I walked out the door. I noticed that my skateboard was hanging from the hook near the door. I wonder what would happen if I took my skateboard and rode it one last time down my driveway. The bus isn't due for another minute. Besides, aren't the buses always late on the first day? Oh, it's just my luck. Here's comes the bus—right on schedule.

Well, I least I'm getting to be with my friends on the ride to school. We talk about all the things we always talk about, but it's different today. Before we know it, the bus pulls up to the school. We all get off and head to our homerooms.

Classes aren't too bad. Miss Washington is still greeting every one of her students at her front door. Vice-Principal Palmer is disciplining a rowdy student for getting in trouble near the lockers. I only have to carry my math and public speaking textbooks this year because most of our classes let us keep an extra book at home.

Things actually didn't go too badly all throughout my day, but I did have one little problem. Around ten o'clock in the morning, I was hungry. Lunch wasn't on my schedule until noon. I had to sit in three different classes and listen to my stomach reminding me that I should have eaten my breakfast. What's worse is we had a discussion in English class of the ways fast food restaurants try to sell us their burgers, fries, tacos, and chicken. I could almost hear the food calling me by my name.

After I had lunch, the rest of the day seemed to fly by. I enjoyed my social studies class because Mr. Barns is a great guy. He doesn't hassle his students, and he never makes fun of anyone in his class. Gym was great because I got to blow off a little steam.

Miss Springer let us choose an activity today, so my friends and I played dodgeball.

When the day was over, I got on the bus and headed home. I didn't think it was fair that we were assigned a one-page journal entry in English class, but I guess I can finish by just writing about my day.

Boy, I hope the weekend gets here quickly. I'm going to sleep late on Saturday.

1. What was Pat's attitude after setting the alarm for the morning of the first day of school?

    ○ A. Happy because the summer was boring.
    ○ B. Afraid because the school was in a different town.
    ○ C. Upset because there would be less freedom in school.
    ○ D. Excited to be with friends again.

2. What could you predict was happening when Pat used the excuse "lunch was only a few hours away" when his mom wanted him to eat a good breakfast?

    ○ A. Pat's mom would be right.
    ○ B. Pat would be right.
    ○ C. Pat's brother would be right.
    ○ D. All of the above.

3. If Pat had taken his skateboard and ridden it "one last time down my (his) driveway" before the bus came, why might Pat's mom be upset?

    ○ A. Pat's new clothes might be ruined.
    ○ B. Pat might get hurt and miss the first day of school.
    ○ C. Pat might miss the bus.
    ○ D. All of the above.

4. During the morning of the second day of school, select what you think Pat is likely to do.

    ☐ A. Sleep late
    ☐ B. Eat breakfast while wearing pajamas and sitting in front of the television
    ☐ C. Eat a good breakfast
    ☐ D. Walk the dog
    ☐ E. Call his friends

Be sure to check your answers with those on page 264.

Essay for Questioning, Clarifying, and Predicting

Predict how the rest of the school year is expected to go for Pat. Use information from the essay to support your predictions.

PREWRITING SECTION
Use the empty space provided to make a writing plan for your essay before you begin writing.

ESSAY

Be sure to check your essay against the suggestions made on page 265.

Target Skill 7: Fact vs. Opinion

A **Fact** is information that can be measured and proven. An **Opinion** shows the way someone feels about a **Fact**.

Strategy

As you are doing your reading, use these strategies.

A fact is something that is easy to measure and prove.

- [ ] Look for measurements for proof (for example, *gallons*, *days*, and *inches*).
- [ ] Look for quotes and citations from books and newspapers.

An opinion is an interpretation.

- [ ] Look for key words or phrases, such as *Sometimes* or *As I see it*.

Practice

The passage that you will read is a 7th grade student's letter to the mayor of her town.

Read the passage thoroughly and then answer the questions that follow. **Be sure to:**

> **PREVIEW TECHNIQUE**
>
> 1. Preview the questions.
> 2. Preview the material.
> 3. Read the entire passage.

A Letter to the Mayor

14 Pleasant Avenue
Springtown, NJ 09151

March 25, 2007

Dear Mayor Patel,

I believe that we should have a place in town where all the kids can get together. The park near the river used to have a building where we could play games or just sit with our friends and talk. There was even some blacktop where we used to roller skate or ride our skateboards. Now, the building is closed because there's no one to take care of it. Mr. Ross used to volunteer his time on the weekends to make sure the building was kept up for us kids, but he retired and moved to Florida.

A meeting place for us kids is a great idea for our town. Right now, we have no place to go where we can be with our friends. When we go to the movies, the security guards are mean to us. They're always chasing us away. Sometimes, they even holler at us for laughing too loudly. How can we help it if something's funny? Don't you laugh out loud sometimes, too?

Every time we ask for a meeting place for us teens, we're told that large groups of teens cause trouble. Why do people say this to us? We don't look for trouble. Now, I know that some kids can cause problems, but that's why there are adults to watch us. If you put a large group of adults together, don't you think that some of them would get in trouble too? If you don't believe me, just look at the police records for the past month. Are teens the only ones causing trouble?

Last month when we came to a town council meeting to ask for a teen center, you became upset with us. You told us that there were too many kids hanging out in the Maple Grove Shopping Center parking lot behind the movie theater. You told us that you were concerned that nine teenagers had been arrested for fighting during the last month. That may be so, but those kids don't represent all of us in town who really want a place to go at night. If you gave us a teen center, there wouldn't be any more trouble in town because we'd be off the streets. We'd all want to be with our friends.

Please reconsider my request for a teen center in town. It's a place we really need. Without it, we'll probably just keep having trouble in town.

Sincerely,

Victoria Martinez

Reading: Informational (Everyday) Text • 165

1. Which of the following statements is a fact?

    - A. Victoria Martinez wrote the letter to Mayor Patel.
    - B. Victoria Martinez wrote the letter to her friends.
    - C. Mayor Patel wrote the letter to Victoria Martinez and her friends.
    - D. Mayor Patel wrote the letter to Victoria Martinez.

2. Choose the statement that is **not** a fact?

    - A. "I believe that we should have a place in town …"
    - B. "… the building is closed."
    - C. "Mr. Ross used to volunteer his time on the weekends."
    - D. Mr. Ross "retired and moved to Florida."

3. Which of these statements is a fact?

    - A. The security guards are "always chasing us away."
    - B. "… the security guards are mean to us."
    - C. "…we go to the movies."
    - D. "… large groups of teens cause trouble."

4. Which of these statements is an opinion?

    - A. "… we came to a town council meeting."
    - B. "… there were too many kids hanging out in the Maple Grove Shopping Center parking lot."
    - C. We asked "for a teen center."
    - D. "…nine teenagers had been arrested for fighting during the last month."

Be sure to check your answers with those on page 265.

Essay for Fact vs. Opinion

Victoria asks for a meeting place where she and her friends can go. She says, "If you (Mayor Patel) gave us a teen center, there wouldn't be any more trouble in town because we'd be off the streets. We'd all want to be with our friends." Is this an example of **Fact** or **Opinion**? Please explain in detail.

PREWRITING SECTION
Use the empty space provided to make a writing plan for your essay before you begin writing.

ESSAY

Be sure to check your essay against the suggestions made on page 266.

Target Skill 8: Following Directions

To do something well, we should make sure that we follow directions carefully. These are our guides for success.

Strategy

As you are doing your reading, use these strategies.

Directions are given in order. We must follow the order to get the desired result.

- [ ] Look for key words and phrases—for example, *First*, *Next*, and *After completing Step 1*.

- [ ] Look for warning phrases—for example, *Before continuing* and *Be sure to*.

- [ ] Only use the directions that are given to write your essay. Do not wander from the topic.

Practice

The passage that you will read contains the guidelines to a Guided-Book Report.

Read the passage thoroughly and then answer the questions. **Be sure to:**

```
PREVIEW TECHNIQUE

1. Preview the questions.
2. Preview the material.
3. Read the entire passage.
```

Guided-Reading Book Report—Guidelines
Free—Choice Fiction

Reading a good novel can be exciting. Finding out about the different characters and learning how the author blends each action and scene together are only some of the thrills you can have while reading. This experience can be a good one. If you read your book with a friend, you can discuss the book together. That means that it's OK to pick out a book to read with a friend, read the book together, and then discuss it too.

Once you select your book, you will need to follow these steps.

1. Find a friend who also wants to read the same book.
2. Have your parent/guardian sign your book permission slip.
3. Return your slip to Mr. Rhoades by February 26.
4. Write down the following information in your personal guided reading log:
    a. Your name.
    b. Your reading partner's name.
    c. The title and author of the book that you and your partner are reading.
5. Divide your book into three sections. Enter the page numbers into your reading log.
6. Write down the dates that you plan to discuss each section of your book. Be sure to schedule a meeting at least once a week so you and your partner can complete the assignment no later than March 18.

You will be expected to finish reading the book and complete all the discussions with your partner. If you wish to read more quickly than the rest of the class, you may do so without worrying about discussing sections that you were not yet assigned to read. Sometimes when you are really interested in a book, you want to read ahead. This unit has been designed to encourage you to do that.

Once a week, you and your partner will form a guided reading small discussion group. You will meet for no more than 20 minutes with another pair of students who are reading a different book. One of you will serve as a group facilitator who will keep the discussion "on track." You will also select a recorder who will take notes that will be signed by all group members and submitted to Mr. Rhoades. Your group must answer the following questions each time you meet:

- What are the major events that have happened in this section of the novel?
- Who are the major characters, and what are their roles?
- What conflicts are occurring?
- What is the biggest change you have observed from the beginning to the end of the section?
- Who is your favorite character in this section and why?
- What advice would you give to the main characters at this stage of the book?
- What grade (A, B, etc.) would you give this section of the book and why?

Reading: Informational (Everyday) Text • 171

When you finish your student meetings, you will then share your responses with Mr. Rhoades. You must complete all three sessions by the March 18 deadline stated to receive two "A+" grades. Completing two sessions will earn you two "C" grades. Completing one session will earn you two "D" grades. A failure to complete any sessions will result in two "0" grades.

If you have any questions during this unit, please ask Mr. Rhoades at once. Also, please share with Mr. Rhoades any difficulties and successes that you may have.

1. What type of book is being assigned for the Guided-Reading Book Report?
   - A. Free-Choice
   - B. Free-Choice Fiction
   - C. Free-Choice Non-fiction
   - D. Free-Choice Biography

2. Select the next step after "Have your parent/guardian sign your book permission slip." Highlight the step below.

A.	Find a friend who also wants to read the same book.
B.	Ask a parent/guardian to help you to select a book.
C.	Have your partner sign your book permission slip.
D.	Return your book permission slip to Mr. Rhoades by February 26.

3. Which of the following information does **not** need to be included "in your personal guided-reading log"?
   - A. your name
   - B. your reading partner's name
   - C. your parent/guardian's signature
   - D. the title and author of the book that you and your partner are reading

4. Which of these grades will a student earn by completing two guided reading sessions?
   - A. two "A+" grades
   - B. two "C+" grades
   - C. two "C" grades
   - D. two "D" grades

Be sure to check your answers with those on page 266.

Essay for Following Directions

Describe the steps needed to form a guided-reading small discussion group. You do not need to discuss the questions that will be asked.

PREWRITING SECTION
Use the empty space provided to make a writing plan for your essay before you begin writing.

ESSAY

Be sure to check your essay against the suggestions made on page 266.

Target Skill 9: Recognizing Literary Forms and Information Sources

There are many types of literary forms, including novels, short stories, and poetry. There are also many information sources such as books, magazines, and Internet sites.

Strategy
As you read literature:

- Always look for the theme, the main character(s), the setting, and the conflict/resolution. These have been covered in the previous chapter.

As you read information sources:

- Always look for the main idea and supporting details.

Practice
Read the passage thoroughly and then answer the questions. **Be sure to:**

PREVIEW TECHNIQUE

1. Preview the questions.
2. Preview the material.
3. Read the entire passage.

Professional Sports Broadcasting—My Dream Job
by Philip Cheung

I've always wanted to be a professional sports broadcaster. That's all I've ever wanted to be. While my friends talk about their dreams of becoming movie stars, hip hop artists, fashion designers, or chefs, I just smile. While all of those career choices might be exciting, they don't get me personally excited. If the conversation happened to turn to sports broadcasting, however, then I would join right in and tell everybody about my plans.

You see, I've never wanted to do anything else. Becoming a professional sports broadcaster is my dream job. Whenever my friends and I would play ball, I would think about what it would be like to be sitting in a booth with the TV cameras pointed directly at me. I would talk about my team's record, our recent successes and failures, and our strategy for winning today's game.

Then I would call over my friend Karl and interview him about the great catches he's been making all year. If there was time, I would interview a player from the opposing team to discuss their recent progress.

Most people might say that I wouldn't be able to play the game and announce it at the same time. I disagree. I plan to introduce a whole new way to broadcast a game. Sometimes the manager of a team is "hooked up" to a microphone during a game. I've even seen this done with certain star players. Why couldn't I do the same thing? I could describe the game and give my commentary right from the playing field. Who would be better to describe the game than somebody who's right in the middle of the game? Yes, that "somebody" would be me.

Now I know that I have to go to school "to learn my trade," as my dad is always telling me. That's not a problem. I'm willing to work hard to realize this dream. I won't give up until I make it.

I'm already reading a lot of books about famous sports broadcasters. Right now, I'm reading books about Mel Allen, Red Barber, Howard Cosell, Jon Miller, and Jim McKay. I've written a short story for my English class. It involves my meeting with Phil Rizzuto, the Hall of Fame player and former broadcaster. I've even written a song about becoming a sports broadcaster. It's called "My Search for Air Time." I played it during our school's talent show, and I won third place.

My favorite sports poem is "Casey at the Bat." The main character, Casey, had a lot of confidence. He probably had too much because he didn't even swing at the first two strikes. What a great interview I could have with Casey. I would run over to him and ask him about his decision not to swing at the first two pitches. I'd also ask him if he felt that he tried his best to hit the last pitch. Then I would probably have to stop the interview because Casey might be angry with me.

I'm only in seventh grade now, but it's not too early to start preparing for my dream career. I've already joined the school newspaper to help me with my writing skills. I've volunteered to be a helper at the broadcasts of our high school's soccer games, as long as I'm not playing a game myself that day. I've also called our local cable television station and asked if I could maybe have a tour of the studio. If I'm lucky and my dream comes true, maybe I'll be a famous broadcaster and some seventh graders will call my station to ask for a tour. I'll gladly show him or her around.

1. What is the main idea of Philip's essay?

    - ○ A. Phil's struggles in seventh grade
    - ○ B. Phil's dream to be a professional sports manager
    - ○ C. Phil's dream to be a professional sports announcer
    - ○ D. Phil's dream to be a hip hop artist

2. Philip's piece deals directly with his own life. What type of essay would it be?

    - ○ A. Autobiographical
    - ○ B. Biographical
    - ○ C. Fictional
    - ○ D. Poetic

3. Which of these statements would most likely **not** be true about books that feature famous sportscasters?

    - ○ A. The books feature sportscasters who enjoy sports.
    - ○ B. The books feature sportscasters who have received training before they began to broadcast.
    - ○ C. The books feature sportscasters who enjoy working with people.
    - ○ D. The books feature sportscasters who never cared about playing the game.

4. If Philip's piece were to be published, in which type of publication would it most likely be found?

    - ○ A. A professional broadcasting magazine.
    - ○ B. A school literary magazine.
    - ○ C. A university literary magazine.
    - ○ D. A national weekly sports magazine.

Be sure to check your answers with those on page 267.

Essay for Recognizing Literary Forms and Information Sources

Describe how this student's written work would be different if it were written as a short story.

PREWRITING SECTION
Use the empty space provided to make a writing plan for your essay before you begin writing.

ESSAY

Be sure to check your essay against the suggestions made on page 267.

Target Skill 10: Finding Information and Answering with Prior Knowledge

Whenever you are reading textbooks, magazines, or other information sources, the material that you may be learning is blended with the material that you already know. For example, the guidelines that you are given to write a science report are combined with your prior knowledge about writing effective reports.

Strategy
As you read:

- [ ] Always find the main idea(s).
- [ ] Follow all the directions that you are given.
- [ ] Use the knowledge that you know to make your efforts even more effective.

Practice
Read the passage thoroughly and then answer the questions. **Be sure to:**

PREVIEW TECHNIQUE

1. Preview the questions.
2. Preview the material.
3. Read the entire passage.

Guidelines for Making a Class Presentation
by Miss Ostrovsky

Your major assignment for this marking period is a five-minute presentation to the class. You will select any of the major topics that we have covered in our class and then re-teach that material to the other students in our class. You will be graded for your coverage of the material, your use of media, your platform (presenting) skills, and your professionalism. Remember that your information and the way you present it are both important. You will be graded on both areas.

Let's look at each of the categories on which you will be graded.

Coverage of Material

You must select a major concept from our unit dealing with verbs. Please choose one of the following main divisions.

For Transitive Verbs:

- ☐ Direct Objects
- ☐ Indirect Objects

For Intransitive and Linking Verbs:

- ☐ Predicate Complements
- ☐ Predicate Nouns (and pronouns)
- ☐ Predicate Adjectives

For Subject/Verb Agreement:

- ☐ Singular
- ☐ Plural

For Helping (Auxiliary) Verbs:

- ☐ Part of a Verb Phrase
- ☐ Part of a Contraction

For Verb Modifiers:

- ☐ Adverbs
- ☐ Adverb Phrases

You must provide the following information:

- Definitions
- Rules
- Examples
- Exceptions (if any)

Your Use of Media

Choose at least two of the following media options.

For Computer Slide Show:

- ☒ Laptop Computer
- ☐ LCD Projector

For Flip Chart and Easel:
- ☐ White Board
- ☑ Posters

Follow our Classroom Guidelines for Graphics.

- Clarity
- Legibility
- Color
- Size
- Shapes

Give your media a test run a day or more before you present the lesson.

Your Platform (Presenting) Skills

Please speak effectively. Watch your:

- Volume
- Pace
- Inflection
- Use some gestures appropriately.
- Stand up straight.
- Make good eye contact.

Your Professionalism

- Stay in control at all times.
- Don't laugh or act silly with your friends.

1. Which of the following is **not** a major verb division for Miss Ostrovsky's class?

    - A. Transitive Verbs
    - B. Intransitive and Linking Verbs
    - C. Helping (Auxiliary) Verbs
    - ⊘ D. Conjugating Verbs

2. Besides using a laptop computer and an LCD projector for a computer slide show, what other piece of equipment would be the most useful for the slide show?

    - A. Audio Headset
    - ⊘ B. Movie Screen
    - C. Spiral Notebook
    - D. Chalk Eraser

3. Choose the likely result for a student who does not follow the "Classroom Guidelines for Graphics."

   - A. No one will notice because the information is the most important part of the presentation.
   - B. Miss Ostrovsky will give the student one more chance to do better.
   - C. The student will receive a lower grade.
   - D. The student will receive a detention.

4. What would be the most unlikely reason for Miss Ostrovsky to assign this project?

   - A. She just bought a new computer.
   - B. She's punishing the students for misbehaving.
   - C. She's going on maternity leave.
   - D. She understands that teaching with media helps to improve learning.

Be sure to check your answers with those on pages 267–268.

Reading: Informational (Everyday) Text • 185

Essay for Finding Information and Answering with Prior Knowledge

When Miss Ostrovsky's students give their lessons about verbs, they must provide four different types of information. Explain why this information is important.

PREWRITING SECTION
Use the empty space provided to make a writing plan for your essay before you begin writing.

ESSAY

Be sure to check your essay against the suggestions made on page 268.

CHAPTER 5

Writing

GRAMMAR GUIDE: USING GRAMMAR CORRECTLY IN YOUR WRITING

As we have already mentioned, the grammar that you use in your writing on the Grade 7 ELA/Literacy Test must be correct. The score for your argumentative essay and your short and long essays uses grammar as one of the elements being graded. That's the reason why you must write sentences that do not have grammar mistakes.

Strategy

When you write for any standardized test like the NJ PARCC Grade 7 Language Arts Test, you always need to proofread your work. Checking the content of the essays that you write is important. It is also important to check your grammar.

Be sure to:

1. Read each essay to yourself. Make sure that your sentences sound right.
2. Be sure that you have not broken any of the grammar rules that we are going to review together.

Let's do some practice exercises so we can improve your chances of doing well on this test. Let's practice by concentrating on some of the most common areas that can cause you major problems with your grammar.

PRACTICE FOR TARGET SKILLS

Target Skill 1: Agreement—Number, Case, and Gender

There are three major points of agreement in your sentences.

1. Number—Singular or Plural
2. Case—Subject or Object
3. Gender—Masculine, Feminine, or Neuter (Neither Masculine nor Feminine)

Please note that when considering case, the noun may be the simplest one to deal with.

For pronouns, which by definition take the place of nouns, there are actually three cases. The first is the subjective (nominative) case, which applies when a noun is either used as a subject or as the complement of a linking (copulative) verb. For example, the sentence "She is the President" may also be written as "The President is she" since the linking verb "is" allows the subject "She" and the predicate complement "**President**" to change places without changing the meaning of the sentence.

The second case is possessive (genitive), and the same explanation for nouns applies to pronouns as well since pronouns act as noun replacements. For example, consider the sentence: "**The actor in the play gave his soliloquy at the end of the first act.**" The pronoun "**his**" reflects the fact that the soliloquy is the actor's and not someone else's.

The third type of case is objective (accusative). Consider these sentences: "**Concerning my sister Alisha, I saw her at the beach yesterday with her boyfriend. When Alisha saw me walking home later that day, she gave me a ride. Since it began to rain soon after I got into Alisha's car, I was very grateful that she gave a ride to me.**" In the first sentence, "**her**" is a direct object (I saw whom? I saw "**her.**"). In the second sentence, "**me**" is an indirect object (Alisha gave a ride to whom? Alisha gave a ride to "**me.**"). In the third sentence, "**me**" is an object of the preposition in the phrase "**to me.**" Remember, an object of a preposition is always in the objective (accusative) case.

Number

1. Make sure that your subjects agree in number with your verbs.

    a. When a noun is singular, the verb should also be singular.
    b. When a noun is plural, then the verb should also be plural.
    c. When there is more than one noun, then the verb is automatically plural.

2. Remember that singular verbs may end in "s" but plural verbs do not. This rule is the opposite of the one for nouns: "Use '-s' or '-es' at the end of many plural nouns."

Practice

First, read the paragraph below and answer the questions. Then underline the three verbs that are incorrect. Finally, write the correct form of the verb above the incorrect ones.

My Friend and I Is Going to the Video Game Store

After school today, my friend Sam and I don't plan to go straight home. Instead, we plan to go to the video game store. We is going to walk down Main Street and then turn right on Maple Avenue. There are three new games being released today, and we're going to be at the store to try them out with our friends.

1. Select the statement(s) that contain a subject-verb agreement mistake.
   - ☑ A. "My Friend and I Is Going to the Video Game Store."
   - ☐ B. "After school today, my friend Sam and I don't plan to go straight home."
   - ☐ C. "Instead, we plan to go to the video game store."
   - ☑ D. "We is going to walk down Main Street and then turn right on Maple Avenue."
   - ☑ E. "There are three new games being released today, and we're going to be at the store to try them out with our friends."

2. Which of the pronouns are in the genitive case?
   - ☐ A. "My"
   - ☐ B. "I"
   - ☑ C. "We"
   - ☑ D. "We're"
   - ☑ E. "Our"

Answer Explanations

1. The correct answers are **A. My Friend and I Is Going to the Video Game Store**, and **D. We is going to walk down Main Street and then turn right on Maple**. First of all, remember that you are looking to find the sentences that have subject-verb agreement mistakes and not the ones that do not. In response A. the compound subjects **Friend** and **I** require the plural verb **Are** and not the singular verb **Is**. Answer **D. We is going to walk down Main Street and then turn right on Maple Avenue** also contains a subject-verb agreement mistake since the subject **We** requires the plural verb *are*. Answer **B. After school today, my friend Sam and I don't plan to go straight home** is not incorrect since the subjects **Sam and I** are correctly agreed by the verb **don't plan** (actually **do not plan** since n't is an abbreviated form of not, which is an adverb and therefore not part of the verb). Answer **C. Instead, we plan to go to the video game store** is selected since **we** and **plan** agree perfectly. Answer **E. There are three new games being released today, and we're going to be at the store to try them out** is correct, but tricky. While **we're going** follows the pattern of a subject coming before a verb and thereby making it easier to solve the subject-verb agreement puzzle, the first part of the sentence may be puzzling. The subject of the phrase **There are three new games being released today** is the plural noun **games** and not the adverb **new**.

Be sure to check your answers for the incorrect verbs with those on page 269.

2. The correct answers are **A. My** and **E. Our**. These two pronouns are in the genitive (possessive) case. Answers **B. I, C. We,** and **D. We're (We are)** are all in the nominative case.

Case

Make sure that your sentences use the right case.

1. There are two ways to use Subject Pronouns.
   a. Subject of the sentence; for example, "*I* am the President."
   b. Predicate Complement; for example, "The President is *I*."

2. There are three ways to use Object Pronouns.
   a. Direct Object (answers "Whom" or "What" is receiving the action of the verb); for example, "Mom will take *me* to the skate park."
   b. Indirect Object (answers "To whom?" "To what?" "For whom?" or "For what?" the action of the verb is being done); for example, "Dad will make *us* dinner later."
   c. Object of the Preposition (the noun or pronoun that ends the prepositional phrase); for example, "Give your ticket to *her*."

Practice

Read the following paragraph. Then, select the pronouns that are used incorrectly and list them in the space(s) provided. (For practice, write the correct form of the pronoun above the incorrect one.)

Our Test Review Was a Game!

(1) Mr. Bogosian tried something new in class today: he played a review game to give we a chance to get ready for ours test. (2) Us kids actually had fun playing the game with him. (3) Francisco answered the most questions so we clapped for he. (4) Even so, we were the real winners since more than half of us earned ours best test score of the year.

Sentence 1

Mr. B tried something new in class today; he played a review game to give us a chance to get ready for our test.

Sentence 2

We kids actually had fun playing game with him.

Sentence 3

Francisco answered most questions so we clapped for him.

Sentence 4

Even so, we were the real winners since more than half of us earned our best test score of this year.

Answer Explanations

Our Test Review Was a Game!

Mr. Bogosian tried something new in class today: he played a review game to give **we** a chance to get ready for ours test. **Us** kids actually had fun playing the game. Francisco answered the most questions so we clapped for **he**. Even so, we were the real winners since more than half of us earned ours best test score of the year.

1. us
1. our 2. We
3. him
4. our

Gender

When your subjects are pronouns, make sure they agree in gender with your verbs.

1. Masculine (Male), Feminine (Female), and Neutral (neither Masculine nor Feminine) pronouns need the same gender for the nouns they are replacing.

    a. Masculine—Man ⇒ *He*, *Him*, and *His*.
    b. Feminine—Female ⇒ *She*, *Her*, and *Hers*.
    c. Neutral—neither Masculine nor Feminine ⇒ *It* and *Its*

2. Gender only matters with third person singular pronouns.
3. Don't forget this important fact: whenever you refer to yourself **and** one or more other people, you always mention yourself last. That is polite. For example, "Please meet my friend and me at the mall tomorrow after school" is correct. However, "Please meet me and my friend" is incorrect since you always come last if you are being referred to with one or more others.

194 • New Jersey Grade 7 ELA/Literacy Test

Practice

Part A
For the following sentences, underline the correct answers.

1. Mrs. Cairo asked Mary to pick up (her, its) books.

2. Jackson took (his, its) brother to the movies.

3. The table can hold (her, its) own weight.

Be sure to check your answers with those on page 270.

Part B
For the following paragraph, list the pronouns in each sentence on the blank lines below. For the ones that are used incorrectly, change them to the correct pronoun and write them next to the incorrect ones.

(1) On a cool day in November, Mary saw her best friend Kemisha walking down her street. (2) Before she could get to the door to wave to ~~she~~ [her], the phone rang. (3) ~~Its~~ [It] seems that Mary's Aunt Belinda was calling to tell ~~hers~~ [her] some good news. (4) Mary's brother Carlos was going to ~~be~~ coming home from college next week, and ~~him~~ [he] and his friend were going to stay at Aunt Belinda's house for a day. (5) When asked if Mary would like to visit also, Mary asked, "Would it be okay if me and my best friend ~~Kemisha~~ both came to visit?" (6) As long as ~~her~~ [she] and her mom talked first, Aunt Belinda would have no problem with Mary bringing Kemisha too.

Sentence 1

Sentence 2

Sentence 3

Sentence 4

Sentence 5

Sentence 6

Answer Explanations

Part B

In Sentence 1, "**her** (best)" and "**her** (street)" are both used correctly. In Sentence 2, "**she** (could)" is used correctly but "(wave to) **she**" should be "(wave to) **her**" since the second "**her**"—(wave to) **her**—is the object of the preposition "**to**." In Sentence 3, "**Its** seems" should be "**It** seems" since "**Its**" is a possessive. Also, "(to tell) **hers**" should be "(to tell) **her**" since a personal pronoun rather than a possessive pronoun is needed here. In Sentence 4, the two pronouns are "**him**" and "**his**." The phrase should read "**he** (and) **his** (friend)" since "**he**" is part of a compound subject and therefore needs to be a subject pronoun. In Sentence 5, the two pronouns are "**me** (and) **my** (best friend)." The phrase should read "**my best friend and me**" since the speaker always goes last in a series. In Sentence 6, the pronouns are "**her**" and "**her** (mom)." The phrase should read, "**As long as she and her mom talked first.**" This substitution can easily be checked by simply substituting "**she**" for "**her**."

Target Skill 2: Structure—Sentence Types (4 Major)

1. **Simple Sentence**

    The major elements of a simple sentence are the subject and the verb.

    Here's an example of a simple sentence:

    In the woods, the bear (subject) slept (verb) *in a cave.*

2. Compound Sentence

Major Elements of a Compound Sentence—Simple Sentence (Independent Clause) + Simple Sentence (Independent Clause) connected by one of the FANBOYS ("For," "And," "Nor," "But," "Or," "Yet," and "So")

Here's an example of a Compound Sentence.

- I (Subject) wished (Verb) for a warm day last Saturday, yet my sister (Subject) wished (Verb) for a cold day.

3. Complex Sentence

Major Elements of a Complex Sentence—Simple Sentence (Independent Clause) + Subordinating Conjunction ("While," "Throughout," and "Whenever," for example) + Simple Sentence (Dependent Clause)

Here's an example of a Complex Sentence.

I studied for my test on Monday since my game was cancelled by the heavy rain.

> Please note: It is the Subordinating Conjunction (in this case, "since") that causes the Independent Clause to become a Dependent Clause. The Subordinating Conjunction ("Because," "Despite," or "While," for example) attaches on to the Simple Sentence and thereby prevents it from standing alone as an Independent Clause. It can also appear at the front of the sentence and do the same work. For example, "Since my game was cancelled by the heavy rain, I studied for my test on Monday" is also a Complex Sentence.

4. Compound-Complex Sentence

Major Elements of a Compound-Complex Sentence—Simple Sentence (Independent Clause) + Simple Sentence (Independent Clause) + Subordinating Conjunction + Simple Sentence (Dependent Clause)

Here's an example of a Compound-Complex Sentence.

I came home from the park yesterday and I immediately took the dog for a walk because I had forgotten earlier.

> Please note: The Subordinating Conjunction works the same way here as it does in the Complex Sentence. Furthermore, it may also appear at different places in the sentence. For example, "I came home yesterday, and since I had forgotten earlier, I immediately took the dog for a walk.

Practice
Read the following passage and then answer the questions.

When I set my alarm last night, I realized that today I would be following a different routine for the next few months. When school let out in June, I had a lot more freedom. I slept a little later, ate lunch whenever I wanted to, watched my favorite daytime television programs, and just hung out with my friends. This morning, my summer will come to an end and I shall get on the bus for school.

My mom woke me up even before my alarm rang. She told me that I had to make sure that I was awake. I couldn't go back to sleep. If I did, I would be late for the first day of school. She said, "That's not the way you want to start out your school year, is it?" I just grumbled "No" and slid out of my bed.

I found my way to the bathroom, and I jumped in the shower because it was already 7:00 AM. During the summer, I never had to take my shower before breakfast. I always made some cereal, poured a glass of juice, and settled in with my favorite television program or one of the music channels. Today, however, I am finishing my shower, drying my hair, and having a little breakfast. Oh, I couldn't do these things in slow motion. My mom kept reminding me to "Hurry up!" so I wouldn't be late. She also reminded me to wear the new outfit we had bought last week. "You should always make a good first impression, especially on the first day of school," she said. It would feel funny dressing up for breakfast after an entire summer of eating while wearing my pajamas.

198 • New Jersey Grade 7 ELA/Literacy Test

Match the sentence types with the appropriate sentences by clicking on the correct labeled box.

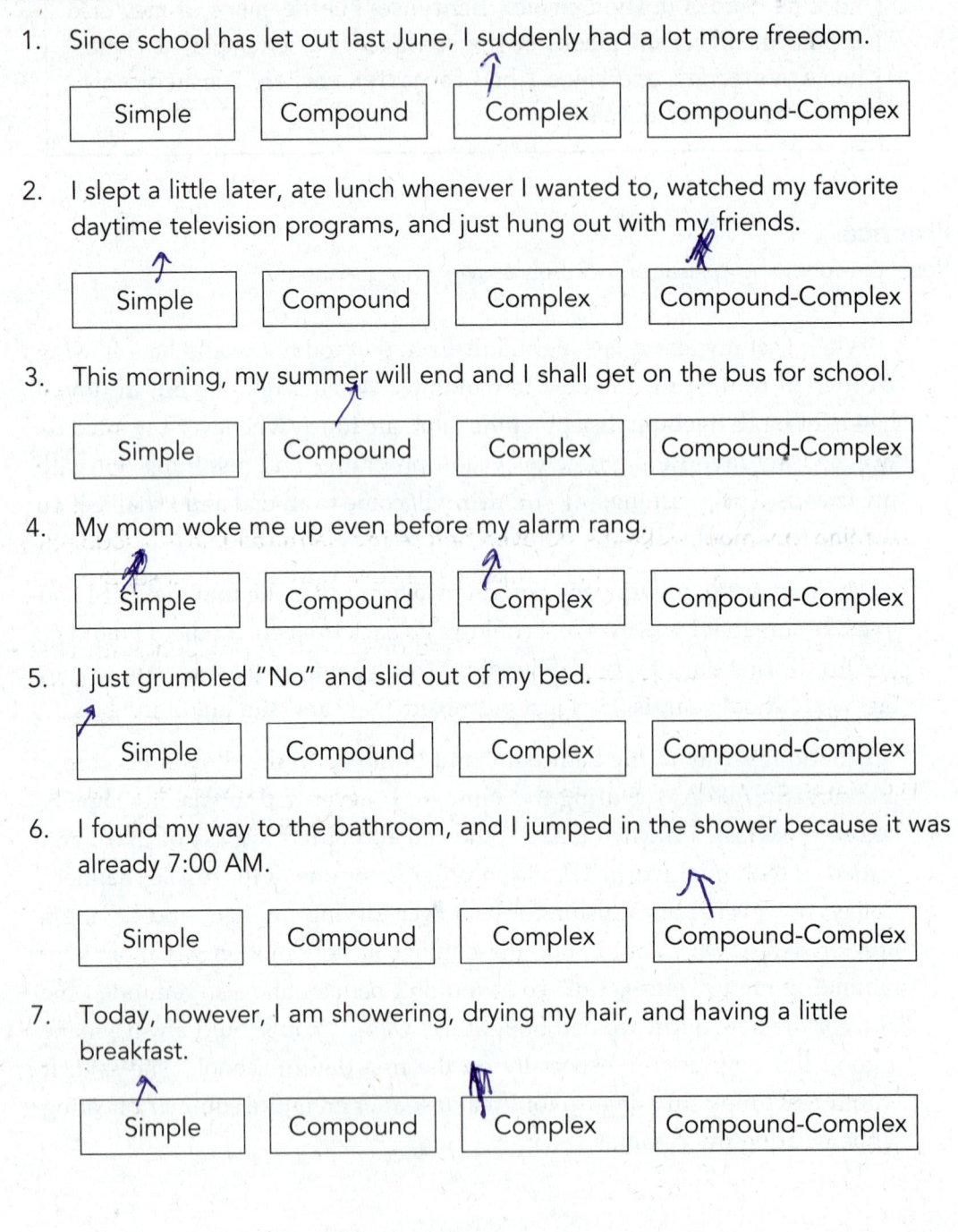

1. Since school has let out last June, I suddenly had a lot more freedom.

   | Simple | Compound | Complex | Compound-Complex |

2. I slept a little later, ate lunch whenever I wanted to, watched my favorite daytime television programs, and just hung out with my friends.

   | Simple | Compound | Complex | Compound-Complex |

3. This morning, my summer will end and I shall get on the bus for school.

   | Simple | Compound | Complex | Compound-Complex |

4. My mom woke me up even before my alarm rang.

   | Simple | Compound | Complex | Compound-Complex |

5. I just grumbled "No" and slid out of my bed.

   | Simple | Compound | Complex | Compound-Complex |

6. I found my way to the bathroom, and I jumped in the shower because it was already 7:00 AM.

   | Simple | Compound | Complex | Compound-Complex |

7. Today, however, I am showering, drying my hair, and having a little breakfast.

   | Simple | Compound | Complex | Compound-Complex |

Answer Explanations

1. The correct answers for **Simple** are 2. I could sleep a little later, eat lunch whenever I wanted to, watch my favorite daytime television programs, and just hang out with my friends, 5. I just grumbled "No and slid out of my bed," and 7. Today, however, I am showering, drying my hair, and having a little breakfast. In 2, there is one subject (I) with four verbs (**slept, ate, watched,** and **hung [out]**. This is an example of a simple subject with a compound (more than one) predicate. Also, the helping verb **could** is unstated for the other three verbs. In 5, the simple subject I has two verbs: **grumbled** and **slid**. In 7, the subject I has three verbs: **am showering, drying,** and **having**. Similar to 5, the helping verb **am** is unstated for the other two verbs. The correct answer for **Compound** is 3. **Tomorrow my summer will have ended, and I shall get on the bus for school.** The two simple sentences (independent clauses) **Tomorrow my summer will have ended** and **I shall get on the bus for school** are joined by a comma preceding the coordinating conjunction **and**. The correct answers for **Complex** are 1. **Since school had let out last June, I suddenly had a lot more freedom** and 4. **The next morning, my mom woke me up even before my alarm rang.** In 1, I suddenly had a lot more freedom is the simple sentence (independent clause) preceded by the phrase (dependent or subordinate clause) "**Since school had let out last June.**" The dependent clause cannot stand on its own as a dependent clause and is therefore subordinate to the independent clause. In 4, the independent clause is "**The next morning, my mom woke me up**" while the dependent clause is "even before my alarm rang." The correct answer for **Compound-Complex** is 6. **I found my way to the bathroom, and I jumped in the shower because it was beginning to get late."** The two independent clauses are **I found my way to the bathroom, and I jumped in the shower"** and "**I jumped in the shower.**" These two sentences are joined by a comma and the word **and**. In addition, the "complex" piece of the answer is the phrase "**because it was already 7:00 AM**" is a dependent clause that cannot stand alone.

Target Skill 3: Misplaced Modifiers

A misplaced modifier is simply one or more words that don't refer directly to the word(s) being modified. Instead, they refer to the wrong word(s). The result is confusion.

Strategy

1. Keep your word(s) next to or very close to the word(s) being modified.
2. If the meaning of your sentence is misleading, then rewrite it so it's clear.

Practice

Part A
Rewrite the following sentences correctly.

1. In her desk, Savannah found a blue lady's bracelet.

   Savannah found a blue lady's bracelet, in her desk.

2. I once met a man with one arm named Rashawn.

   I once met a man with one arm, his name was Rashawn.

3. I heard that the burglar has been captured on the evening news.

   On the evening news I heard that the burglar was captured.

Be sure to check your answers with those on page 270.

Part B
Read the following passage. Review the sentences that have misplaced modifiers. Then, rewrite the sentences correctly on the lines below the passage. If no correction is needed, simply do not write an answer on the line corresponding to the sentence.

(1) When I woke up this morning, I heard my silly dog Sparky barking at the traffic near my refrigerator [while she was sitting next to my]. (2) It seems that the traffic somehow gets more congested as soon as Sparky prepares to take his morning nap beside my bed. (3) I try to calm Sparky down, but sometimes I'm just not able to do so. (4) Sometimes I'll walk Sparky to my neighbor's house to visit with their pet dog Ruffian. (5) Distracted by Ruffian, the time seems to pass quickly. (6) Soon [And when Sparky is], Sparky isn't angry anymore.

Sentence 1

Sentence 2

Sentence 3

Sentence 4

Sentence 5

Sentence 6

Answer Explanations

Part B

1. When I woke up this morning, I heard my silly dog barking at the traffic while she was sitting next to my refrigerator. (The "traffic" was not near the refrigerator.)

2. It seems that the traffic somehow gets more congested as soon as Sparky prepares to take his morning nap beside my bed. (The "morning" is not near the bed.)

3. (Leave this line blank.)

4. (Leave this line blank.)

5. The time seems to pass quickly when Sparky is distracted by Ruffian. (The "time" is not being distracted by Ruffian.)

6. (Leave this line blank.)

Target Skill 4: Voice

There are two kinds of voice in all sentences.

1. **Active Voice**—The subject does the action in the sentence. *Example:* "The girls' twirling squad won the first place trophy in the county tournament."
2. **Passive Voice**—The subject does not do the action in the sentence. *Example:* "The first place trophy in the county tournament was won by the girls' twirling squad."

The active voice is preferred. Use it especially for standardized tests like the NJ PARCC.

Strategy

1. Use the active voice to give your sentences a little more energy. Also, remember that the evaluators of standardized tests like the NJ PARCC prefer the active voice.
2. Use the passive voice as little as you can on the test.

Practice

Part A
Read the following passage. Identify the sentences written in the passive voice. Write those sentences in the correct spaces below the passage. If the sentence is written in the active voice, then leave the space blank.

(1) Yesterday my best friend Kenny and I were planning to go to a professional soccer game. (2) We planned to see our favorite team the Smithville Screaming Hawks play the Mountain Ridge Rebels. (3) Getting tickets to the game was not an easy task. (4) A call to the Screaming Hawks was made by my Uncle Sanjay. (5) He hoped that his friend, who is an assistant coach for the team, could get us some tickets. (6) Rooting for the "Hawks" would be a thrill for us. (7) When my cell phone rang, Kenny and I held our breaths in anticipation. (8) The suspense was getting to be too much for us. (9) I begged my Uncle Sanjay to tell us if he was able to get the tickets. (10) The news of having sideline passes was almost too much for us. (11) We jumped up and down and made so much noise that Uncle Rajah teased us that we were going to have to become the "Hawks" newest cheering squad members.

Sentence 3

We did not have an easy task getting tickits for the game

Sentence 2

Sentence 3

Sentence 4

My uncle Sanjay made a call to screaming hawks

Sentence 5

Sentence 6

We would be thirlled to be Rooting for hawks

Sentence 7

Sentence 8

Sentence 9

Sentence 10

We were thrilled to have side line passes
We couldnt contsool our exitment.

Sentence 11

Answer Explanations

Sentences 3, 4, 6, and 10 are passive voice sentences. Sentence 3 ("**Getting tickets to the game was not an easy task**") may be rewritten as "We did not have an easy task when we wanted to get tickets to the game." Sentence 4 ("**A call to the Screaming Hawks was made by my Uncle Sanjay**") may be rewritten as "My Uncle Sanjay made a call to the Screaming Hawks. Sentence 6 ("**Rooting for the 'Hawks' would be a thrill for us**") may be rewritten as "We would be thrilled to be rooting for the 'Hawks.'" Sentence 10 ("**The news of having sideline passes was almost too much for us**") may be rewritten as "We were overwhelmed to hear that we would be getting sideline passes, and we almost couldn't handle our excitement."

Part B
Read the following sentences and rewrite them correctly in the active voice.

1. Every desk in the library was filled with students yesterday.

   Every desk was filled with students In the library yesterday

2. At my favorite ice cream store, my sundae was prepared by the new owner.

   My sundae was prepared by the new owner at my favourite ice cream store

3. I was scolded by my parents when I didn't do all my chores yesterday.

   I was scolded by my parents because I didn't do my chores yesterday

Be sure to check your answers with those on page 270.

Target Skill 5: Sentence Variety

When you write, your sentences should not follow the same pattern. Otherwise, they become very boring and difficult to read. The solution is to add variety when you write.

Strategy

1. Avoid starting every sentence with the subject and verb.

    a. Use a prepositional phrase or two to begin your sentence.

    Example: In the middle of the day, I usually eat my lunch.

    b. Use a prepositional phrase or two to end your sentence.

    Example: I usually eat my lunch in the middle of the day.

2. Combine two sentences to make a compound or complex sentence.

    a. Compound Sentence: Two sentences joined by adding a comma and the words "and," "or," or "but" to connect two sentences.

    Example: I went to the game, but my sister went to the park.

    b. Complex Sentence: A sentence that has one part that is a sentence and one that is not.

    Example: I went to the game while my sister went to the park.

3. Vary the length of each sentence.

    Example: I walked my dog yesterday. Because it was such a nice day, I went to my friend's house after I had my lunch.

4. Change the order of one or more adverbs, as long as the meaning stays the same.

    Example: Change "Tomorrow I will go home" to "I will go home tomorrow."

Practice

Rewrite the paragraph on the lines below. Try to include the skills that have just been covered in this section.

Getting in Trouble

I got in trouble yesterday. My friends and I cut across our neighbor's lawn. He became very upset. He yelled at us. We said we weren't hurting anything. He said that somebody stole his lawn chair as a prank. Now he's blaming us. We're innocent. I guess we shouldn't have walked on his lawn.

We got in trouble yesterday. Me and my friends walked across our neighbor's lawn. He became very upset. He yelled at us. I said, "We weren't hurting anything." He said that somebody stole his chair as a prank. Now he's blaming us. We said were innocent. I guess we shouldn't have walked on his lawn.

Be sure to check your essay against the sample response and explanation on pages 270–271.

Writing • 207

Target Skills 6 and 7: Fragments and Run-ons

A **fragment** is a piece of a sentence. It cannot stand alone as a sentence.

Example: Hassan from the school around the corner.

A **run-on** is more than one sentence that is joined incorrectly.

Example: Francesca was bored she went to the movies.

Strategy

1. Change a fragment into a full sentence.

    Example: Hassan from the school around the corner is on my soccer team.

2. Here are two ways to fix a run-on.

    a. Separate the run-on into two different sentences.

      Example: Francesca was bored. Therefore, she went to the movies.

    b. Combine the run-on into one sentence.

      Example: Since Francesca was bored, she went to the movies.

Practice—Fragments

Rewrite the following sentences correctly to eliminate fragments.

1. Through the park.

    Killian walked through the park.

2. My best friend from Vineland.

    My best friend is from Vineland

3. Exercising every morning.

    ~~I Emma~~ I noticed Emma Exercising every morning.

Practice—Run-ons

Rewrite the following sentences correctly to eliminate run-ons.

1. Come to my birthday party it will be fun.

   ----

2. I'm doing my homework now I can't talk to you

   ----

3. I'll take out the trash I'll walk the dog.

Be sure to check your answers with those on page 271.

Practice—Prepositional Phrases, Compound and Complex Sentences, Fragments, and Run-ons

Read the following passage. On the lines below, write the number of each sentence that contains: a prepositional phrase, a compound sentence, a complex sentence, a sentence fragment, or a run-on sentence. Once you write down the sentence number, you must also write down the answer.

(1) While I was sending a text message to my best friend, I heard a strange noise in my backyard. (2) I ignored the noise at first. (3) Since I was so busy. (4) The noise soon became louder, so I went on the porch to investigate. (5) At first, I couldn't discover the source of the noise. (6) Because I was curious, I stepped onto the patio. (7) Something came dashing across the sidewalk, I yelled for help. (8) Dumb move. (9) It was only the neighbor's dog, and it was chasing a squirrel.

Prepositional Phrase(s)

Sentence Numbers and Phrases (Listed by number and separated by a semicolon)

Compound Sentence(s)

Sentence Number and Sentence

Complex Sentence(s)

Sentence Number and Sentence

Sentence Fragment(s)

Run-on Sentence(s)

----

(1) While I was sending a text message to my best friend, I heard a strange noise in my backyard. (2) I ignored the noise at first. (3) Since I was so busy. (4) The noise soon became louder, so I went on the porch to investigate. (5) At first, I couldn't discover the source of the noise. (6) Because I was curious, I stepped onto the patio. (7) Something came dashing across the sidewalk, I yelled for help. (8) Dumb move. (9) It was only the neighbor's dog, and it was chasing a squirrel.

Answer Explanations

"(1) While I was sending a text message *to my best friend*, I heard a strange noise *in my backyard*," "(2) I ignored the noise *at first*," "(4) The noise soon became louder, so I went *on the porch* to investigate," "(5) At first, I couldn't discover the source *of the noise*," "(6) Because I was curious, I stepped *onto the patio*," and "(7) Something came dashing *across the sidewalk*, I yelled *for help*" contain prepositional phrases (noted with *italics*). The compound sentences are "**(4) The noise soon became louder, so I went on the porch to investigate**" and "**(9) It was only the neighbor's dog, and it was chasing a squirrel.**" The coordinating conjunction in #4 is "**so**" while the coordinating conjunction in #9 is "**and.**" The complex sentences are "**(1)** *While* **I was sending a text message to my best friend, I heard a strange noise in my backyard**" and "**(6)** *Because* **I was curious, I stepped onto the patio.**" The subordinating conjunctions are noted in italics. The sentence fragments are "**(3) Since I was so busy**" and "**(8) Dumb move.**" The run-on sentence is "**(7) Something came dashing across the sidewalk, I yelled for help,**" since a coordinating conjunction such as "and," a semicolon, or a period separating the two clauses is needed.

Target Skills 8 and 9: Punctuation with Commas and End Marks

1. A **comma** has a few basic purposes in a sentence.

    a. It combines with the words "and," "or," or "but" to make a compound sentence.

    Example: I ran, but you walked.

    b. It separates more than two items in a series.

    Example: We ate, played games, and rode the rides at the amusement park.

    c. It's used when the first part of a complex sentence isn't a full sentence.

    Example: When we played video games yesterday, we had fun.

d. It separates the name of a city from the name of a state.

   Example: Linden, New Jersey.

e. It's used after greetings and closings in letters.

   Example: "Dear Moira," and "Sincerely yours,"

f. It's used after introductory words and phrases.

   Example: "Yes, I'm coming now," "During the winter, I like to ice skate," and "Nevertheless, we shall be completing our review of our homework assignment before we dismiss for recess today."

g. It's used with an appositive (a word that further explains another word).

   Example: My brother, a hard worker, was voted captain of the team.

h. It's used before a quotation.

   Example: I heard my teacher say, "Class, open your books to page 47."

2. There are four basic **end marks** used for sentences.

   a. Period
      i. Declarative Sentence (Statement).

         Example: I like ice cream.

      ii. Imperative Sentence (Command or Request).

         Example: Come here.

   b. Question Mark—Interrogative Sentence (Question).

      Example: Can you help me?

   c. Exclamation Mark—Exclamatory Sentence (Strong Feeling or Emotion).

      Example: We won the city championship!

Strategy

1. Learn the rules.
2. Follow the rules.

Practice—Commas

Punctuate the following sentences correctly by using commas correctly.

1. I had a hamburger and you had pizza.

2. My mom asked me to go to the store mail a letter and put my dirty clothes in the wash.

3. Because I earned all "A's" and "B's" on my report card I'm getting a reward.

4. We moved to New Jersey from Springfield Ohio.

5. "Sincerely yours Allen" is the ending I used for my letter.

6. No I won't make fun of the new student in our class.

7. The winner of the fund-raising challenge was Nicole a student from my class.

Practice—Punctuating Sentences
Punctuate the following sentences by adding the correct end marks.

1. I just won a million dollars

2. Please take care of yourself

3. Did you eat the last piece of cake

4. The class project will be due on March 3

Be sure to check your answers with those on page 271.

Read the following passage. Next, circle any punctuation and end marks that are either misused or omitted. Finally, write in what each correct punctuation mark or end mark should be if it has been either misused or omitted. If no additional mark is needed in a sentence, write the sentence number and "No mark" in the margin.

(1) Neither Constantine my best friend nor I could remember the three items that my mom had told us to pick up at the supermarket. (2) We know that she was going to prepare Texas-style chili for us for dinner and we were very excited. (3) The last time she made Texas-style chili, my uncle my brother, and my older sister all complained that it was too spicy. (4) Nevertheless, I like spicy foods. (5) For me Texas-style chili needs to be spicy. (6) Don't you agree?

(7) When Constantine, and I arrived at the store, we still couldn't remember all three items. (8) Constantine said "We need ground beef, and cans of tomato sauce!" (9) However, that's only two items. (10) I knew there had to be a third but I just couldn't remember it. (11) This was so embarrassing?

(12) Feeling a bit despondent, Constantine and I decided to return home! (13) When we arrived, we had to admit to my mom that we couldn't remember the third ingredient she had asked us to buy? (14) Imagine the looks on our faces when she took the ground beef and tomato sauce from us and asked "Where's the chili powder." (15) That was so embarrassing.

Answer Explanations

The answers are listed in order.

1. "...Constantine, my best friend, nor I..."—Commas are needed for the appositive.
2. "...for dinner, and we were..."—A comma is needed for the compound sentence.
3. "...my uncle, my brother, and..."—A comma is needed since there are more than two items in a series.
4. " However, I like..."—A comma is used after an introductory word.
5. "For me, Texas-style..."—See previous reason.
6. "No mark"
7. "When Constantine and I..."—No comma is needed after "Constantine," since there are only two items in the series.
8. "Constantine said, 'We..."—A comma is needed before the quotation.
9. No mark"
10. "...a third, but I..."—A comma is needed before the coordinating conjunction "but" in this compound sentence.
11. "This was so embarrassing!"—This sentence is an exclamation, not a question, and it therefore requires an exclamation mark.
12. "...to return home."—This is a statement, not an exclamation.
13. "...she had asked us to buy."—This is a statement, not an question.
14. "...and asked, "Where's the chili powder?"—The comma is needed before the quotation, and the question mark is needed for the question being posed."
15. "That was so embarrassing!"—The statement is an exclamation.

Target Skills 10 and 11: Homophones and Homographs

1. **Homophones** are words that sound alike and may be spelled alike or differently. Each set of homophones has the same pronunciation.

   Example: You can **pare** ("cut off") the limb of a **pear** ("fruit") tree. Then you can cut the limb into two equal pieces to make a **pair** ("set of two").

2. **Homographs** share the same spelling, but each has a different meaning.

   Example: The campers could not **bear** ("support") to think that a **bear** ("wild animal") might be wandering outside their tents.

3. **Homographs** may also have different pronunciations. For example, **"bow"** (to bend forward at the waist) and **"bow"** (the front of a ship) are pronounced differently than **"bow"** (a way to knot material like string and cloth).

Strategy
Make sure that you know the appropriate meaning of the homophones and homographs that you wish to use. Spelling and word choice do count on the test. For more examples of homophones and homographs, you can search an online dictionary or thesaurus.

Practice—Homophones

Part A
Underline the correct homophones in the following sentences.

1. I had to (so, sew) a button on my coat yesterday.

2. (Their, There, They're) not the same desserts that we had at the party last week.

3. Please hand in your homework (to, too, two) the teacher.

4. When you don't speak up, I can't (hear, here) you.

5. The petals on this lovely (flour, flower) have a pleasant aroma.

Part B
Read the following passage. Circle the misused homophones and write above them the correct answer for each.

(1) Eye want ewe to no that I am going to fix our clock in the kitchen so it will keep the write thyme. (2) It seams that it has knot bin accurate fore the last weak. (3) That fact is not easy four me to except. (4) I wood fix the clock if aye could. (5) Even after I tried to reed the part of the instructions that explain how two repair the clock, I still was sew confused.

Answer Explanations

1. In this sentence, "**Eye**" sould be "**I**," "**ewe**" should be "**you**," "**no**" should be "**know**," "**write**" should be "**right**," and "**thyme**" should be "**time**."

2. In this sentence, "**seams**" should be "**seems**," "**knot**" should be "**not**," "**fore**" should be "**for**," and "**weak**" should be "**week**."

3. In this sentence, "**four**" should be "**for**" and "**except**" should be "**accept**."

4. In this sentence, "**wood**" should be "**would**" and "**aye**" should be "**I**."

5. In this sentence, "**reed**" should be "**read**," "**two**" should be "**to**," and "**sew**" should be "**so**."

Practice—Homographs

Part A
Choose the correct meaning of each homograph.

1. This tea was made from an exotic **bark**.
   - A. an animal's cry
   - B. the covering of a tree

2. My backpack was very **light** today.
   - A. not heavy
   - B. not dark

3. Of which local team are you a **fan**?
   - A. admirer
   - B. cooling device

Writing • 215

4. Before you put on a bandage, be sure to clean your **wound**.
   - A. turning in a circular way
   - B. skin cut

5. Is this television program **live** or pre-recorded?
   - A. residing in a place
   - B. happening in the present time

Part B
Read the following passage. Next, note all the words that are homographs.

(1) When I went to see my favorite band playing live in concert, I was hoping to get a picture of the lead singer. (2) I couldn't believe that I would be present to listen to my favorite singer in person. (3) My sister told me that the concert promoter had arranged to record the entire show. (4) Since I had been lucky enough to win front row seats that put me very close to the stage, I was able to give my favorite lead singer a high five as she took her bow.

Answer Explanations

1. In this sentence, the homographs are "**live**" and "**lead**."

2. In this sentence, the homograph is "**present**."

3. In this sentence, the homograph is "**record**."

4. In this sentence, the homographs are "**close**" and "**bow**."

Be sure to check your answers for Part A: Homophones and Homographs on page 272.

> After you review the answers, be sure to go back and review any areas that gave you problems.

Target Skill 12: Grammar Demons

Unusual Order

Some sentences have an unusual order.

1. **Inverted Order** sentences have their subjects placed after the verb.

    a. Some sentences that begin with **"Here"** or **"There."**

    Example: **Here** is the desk. **There** are the notebooks.

    b. Some declarative sentences are **Inverted Declaratives**.

    Example: In my classroom is my bag. Nearby are my shoes.

Strategy

1. Be sure that the subject and the verb agree in number in an **Inverted Order** sentence. As mentioned, look for the subject after the verb.
2. Use the same strategy for **Inverted Declaratives**.

Practice—Unusual Order

Part A
Underline the correct verbs in the following sentences.

1. Here (is, are) four tickets to the movies.

2. Upstairs (is, are) your new outfit.

3. There (is, are) a rip in the carpet.

4. In the garage (is, are) your two baseball gloves.

Be sure to check your answers for Part A with those on page 272.

Part B
Read the following paragraph. Highlight only the sentences that are written in inverted order.

   (1) When I left for school this morning, everything seemed to be fine. (2) There were birds chirping in the trees as I strolled along the sidewalk. (3) When I rounded the corner, I said hello to Mrs. Gabilli as she was preparing to paint the new bird house that she had built. (4) In my hand was the set of study cards I had made last week to prepare for my art history test today. (5)

Even though there was a small cloud in the sky, I knew that it wasn't going to rain later. (6) My baseball team would be playing in our first playoff game, and I was chosen to be the starting pitcher. (7) There are many honors I could have received, but this was the most important one for me right now. (8) On my dresser was my lucky coin that I would place in my pocket whenever I would pitch. (9) I would have to make sure that I put the coin in the top pocket of my warm-up jacket for good luck.

Answer Explanations

The sentences that are written in Inverted Order are "(2) There were birds chirping in the trees as I strolled along the sidewalk," "(4) In my hand was the set of study cards I had made last week to prepare for my art history test today," "(7) There are many honors I could have received, but this was the most important one for me right now, " and "(8) On my dresser was my lucky coin that I would place in my pocket whenever I would pitch."

Adjective or Adverb

Adjectives and **Adverbs** are both modifiers.

1. **Adjectives** modify nouns and pronouns.
2. **Adverbs** modify verbs, adjectives, and other adverbs.

Strategy

1. Remember that many, but **not** all adverbs end in *-ly*.
2. In the sentence "**You ran well,**" the word **"well"** is an adverb. You cannot use the word **"good,"** which is an adjective.
3. In the sentence "**You look well,**" the word **"well"** is an adjective that is used instead of the adjective **"good"** because the sentence refers to health. Also, please note that you may refer to someone's appearance with the word "good": "That suit looks good on you."), but you when you tell someone that he/she looks healthy, you say, "You look well."
4. When a verb is linking the subject with a predicate complement, the complement may be an adjective but never an adverb. For example, you may say "The flowers smell nice" since nice is an adjective. You may not say "The flowers smell nicely," however, since "nicely is an adverb. Linking verbs are forms of "be" (*is, am, are, was,* and *were*) and the sensate verbs that refer to the five senses (sight, smell, taste, touch, and hear). These verbs include *looks, smells, tastes, feels,* and *sounds*. Appropriate sentences would include "I was happy," "The food on my dinner plate looks delicious," and "The cotton blanket feels very soft."

Practice—Adjective or Adverb

Part A
Underline the correct words in the following sentences.

1. That was a (good, well) meal.

2. Now that I have eaten, I feel (good, well).

3. I feel (bad, badly) about doing poorly on my science test.

4. The coach ended practice when we all performed (bad, badly).

5. I earned a (real, really) good grade on my English test.

6. My wish to be a singer someday is (real, really).

Be sure to check your answers for Part A with those on page 272.

Part B
Read the following passage. Next, circle all of the adjectives and adverbs that are misused. Then, write the correct answer above the mistakes. If there are no mistakes in a sentence, then write the number of the sentence and "No mistakes" in the margin.

(1) Last summer, my friends and I promised ourselves that we were going to have the best summer ever. (2) The previous summer had been badly for us. (3) It rained all the time, or so it seemed. (4) Anyway, we all were real excited to be getting out of school on the last day, but our friend Harry did something crazy. (5) He tried to be really cool, so he called the principal by her first name. (6) Didn't he realize that he was not acting correct? (7) The principal called his parents, and Harry had to serve detention for a full day—after school was already over!

Answer Explanations

1. In this sentence, there are no mistakes.
2. In this sentence, "**badly**" should be "**bad.**"
3. In this sentence, there are no mistakes.
4. In this sentence, "**real**" should be "**really.**"
5. In this sentence, there are no mistakes.
6. In this sentence, "**correct**" should be "**correctly.**"
7. In this sentence, there are no mistakes.

Quotations

There are two types of **Quotations**: **Direct** and **Indirect**.

1. **Direct Quotations** contain the exact words that someone has said.

   Example: "Bring me the newspaper, please," said my uncle.

2. **Indirect Quotations** give the idea behind what someone has said, rather than the exact words.

   Example: My uncle asked me to bring the newspaper to him.

Strategy

1. Capitalize the first word of a **Direct Quotation**.

   Example: Mom asked, "Are you coming?"

2. Separate a quotation from the rest of the sentence by using a comma.

   Example: "I'm going to the video game store now," I said to my mom.

3. Do not use a comma to separate a quotation if there is an end punctuation mark (period, exclamation mark, or question mark) in the place where the comma would go.

   Example: "May I go to the video game store now?" I asked my mom.

4. For a divided quotation, don't start the second part with a capital letter unless it starts a sentence.

   Example: "Are you coming," Mom asked, "or are you staying home?"

   Example: "I'm not coming," I answered. "My report for health class is due tomorrow."

5. For quotations that have many sentences that follow one after the other, use one set of quotation marks only.

   Example: I told Kirsten, "Don't forget to bring the sunscreen to the beach. The last time we went, you forgot to bring the sunscreen. We don't want to get sunburned."

6. Periods go inside the closing quotation marks. Question marks and exclamation marks go outside the closing quotation marks **unless** the quotation is a question or an exclamation.

   Example: My brother said, "Let's go home."

   Example: My brother yelled, "Don't go in my room!"

   Example: Did Sarah really say, "I don't care"?

7. In a dialogue, start a new paragraph each time the speaker changes.

   Example: "Can you help me with my homework?" I asked my cousin Fred.
   "I'll be happy to help you," answered Fred.
   "If we finish early, we'll go to the mall," I said.
   "That's great!" he replied.

Practice—Quotations

Add the correct capital letters and punctuation marks to the following sentences.

1. The principal said over the intercom students, please report to the cafeteria at the end of second period today

2. Write your homework assignment in your notebooks said Mrs. Hudson

3. Are we there yet said my brother after every five minutes of our trip

4. Should we go to the park said Carrie or should we go to ball field

5. I answered we should go to the park they're having a special program there besides, all our friends will be there too

6. That's sounds great said Carrie

Underlining or Quotation Marks?

Titles of works are punctuated two ways.

1. **Underlining** is used for long works including books, newspapers, magazines, movies, plays, TV series, musical compositions, art works, and certain transportation (specific planes, trains, and spacecraft). Please note that italics can be used instead of underlining when you are typing.

    Example: <u>The Pearl</u>, <u>The Star-Ledger</u>, *The Sound of Music*, and the <u>USS Missouri</u>.

2. **Quotation Marks** are used for short works including poems, short stories, articles, chapters of books, and songs.

    Example: "The Road Not Taken," "The Raven," and "Oh, Susannah."

3. Use underlines for complete works that are long. **Direct Quotation**.

    Example: Last month, we read <u>Animal Farm</u> in our English class.

4. Use quotations for shorter works since they may actually be a part of a larger work.

    Example: We watched "The Confrontation," which is episode three of our favorite TV show.

5. Only use italics when you are typing on the computer. Do **not** try to write in italics.

Practice—Underlining or Quotation Marks?

Part A
Add the correct underlines or quotes to the following sentences.

1. My sister is reading Great Expectations, a novel by Charles Dickens.

2. In class we read Dream Deferred, a poem by Langston Hughes.

3. Before the play-off game, we stood and took off our caps as the loudspeakers played God Bless America.

4. In class today, Mr. Porter read an article from The New York Times.

Be sure to check your answers with those on page 273.

Part B

Read the following passage. When you see quotation marks, related capitalization or punctuation marks, or underlines being used incorrectly, correct the mistake on the lines provided. If there are no mistakes, then simply write "No mistakes."

(1) As the bell rang on the last day of school, I thought to myself, What am I going to do this summer? (2) Last summer, I read the Jack London classic entitled "The Call of the Wild." (3) I thought to myself, It's so hot that if I read a book about the Klondike, then I should be able to cool off. (4) Well, I didn't get any cooler, but I did especially enjoy the characters Hal, Mercedes, and Charles. (5) In fact, I've signed up this summer for a summer reading contest with <u>The Shore Sentinel</u>, our local newspaper. (6) I'm hoping to read Robert Frost's <u>Stopping by the Woods on a Snowy Evening</u>. (7) Maybe this one will help me cool off a bit.

(8) I'm finally going to be able to stay up late on occasion (with mom and dad's permission, of course) to watch my favorite team when they play the West Coast teams. (9) I'm going to re-read Alex Haley's article <u>Thank You</u>. (10) It tells about the importance of saying those two words, and I fully agree with him. (11) I hope to go to one of the large concert halls to listen to some live music. (12) It's always better to go to a place like the PNC Arts center to listen to a band than it is to listen to a recording. (13) The recording is great, but attending a concert is unforgettable. (14) My plans sound great, but I keep telling myself, "Don't forget to take a little time to relax.

Sentence 1

Sentence 2

Sentence 3

Sentence 4

Sentence 5

Sentence 6

Sentence 7

Sentence 8

Sentence 9

Sentence 10

Sentence 11

Sentence 12

Sentence 13

Sentence 14

Answer Explanations

1. In this sentence, it should read: ...myself, "What am...summer?"
2. In this sentence, it should read: ...entitled <u>The Call of the Wild.</u>
3. In this sentence, it should read: "...myself, It's so hot...cool off."
4. In this sentence, there are no mistakes.
5. In this sentence, there are no mistakes.
6. In this sentence, it should read: ...Frost's "Stopping by...Evening."
7. In this sentence, there are no mistakes.
8. In this sentence, there are no mistakes.
9. In this sentence, it should read: ...article "Thank You."
10. In this sentence, there are no mistakes.
11. In this sentence, there are no mistakes.
12. In this sentence, it should read: ...PNC Arts Center
13. In this sentence, there are no mistakes.
14. In this sentence, it should read: ..."Don't forget...to relax."

Target Skill 13: Spelling Demons

Definitions

There are many **spelling demons** that we have trouble spelling correctly. Even adults struggle with these words.

Strategy

1. Learn how to spell correctly as many of these **Spelling Demons** as you possibly can. Remember, spelling and word choice count on the NJ PARCC.
2. If you are unsure of the spelling of a word while you are taking the test, use a different word that you know how to spell correctly.
3. Go on the Internet and conduct a search for misspelled words. You'll find a number of lists that you can use to help you avoid these **spelling demons**.
4. Keep a personal spelling list. Write down any words are that difficult to spell. Check your list at least once a week to review these words.
5. Be sure to check the list in the **Appendix**. Feel free to add to this list as you find other word demons.

Practice—Spelling

Part A
Write the correct spelling of each misspelled word. There may be more than one misspelling.

1. If you don't bring a note to excuse your abscence from school, you'll get a detention.

   ----

2. Let's buy some baloons for hour party.

   ----

3. I am assigned the job of changing the date on the Class calender.

   ----

4. The month after January is Febuary.

   ----

5. Do we have any grammer homework tonite?

   ----

6. Oops, my shoelaces are lose.

   ----

7. Our town's parade ocurred last weakend.

   ----

8. Mom ask me to get the butter for the mashed potatos.

   ----

9. Our music Class is studying rythm and blues artists from the 1970s.

   ----

10. I used the vaccuum to pick up the dirt that spill on the rug.

Be sure to check your answers for Part A with those on page 273.

Part B
Read the following paragraph, then use the lines below to rewrite any of the italicized words that are spelled incorrectly. Please note that number three is a two-word title. You do not need to do anything for the words that are spelled correctly.

While I was preparing to study for my test in my Libary Basicks course last nite, my cell phone started buzzing. I was recieving a text message from my new friend sandy, who had just moved here from a foriegn country, Whales. Sandy thought that she had left her study notes at her neighbors house when she babysat while they went to a local restarant to have diner. Sandy didnt want to faile the test because her Aunt works in a book store in her home country. Luckily, I was abel to take a pickture of my notes and send them as an atachment. Snady thanked me and told me that it is a priviledge to know me, which caused a noticable blush to appear on my face.

Answer Explanations

Phrase 3 should be "*Library Basics.*" The words that are incorrect should be written in the following way: 4. "*night,*" 7. "*receiving,*" 10. "*Sandy,*" 11. "*foreign,*" 12. "*Wales* (the country, not the mammal)," 16. "*neighbor's*" (singular possessive), 18. "*restaurant,*" 19. "*dinner,*" 20. "*didn't,*" 21. "*fail,*" 23. "*aunt*" (only capitalized when used either as part of a name or a substitute for a name as in "May I have your permission, Aunt, to go to the park?"), 26. "*able,*" 27. "*picture,*" 28. "*attachment,*" 29. "*Sandy*" (Be careful not to let your brain get used to seeing the word *Sandy* spelled correctly so it automatically changes the mistake to the correct spelling while you are reading.), 30. "*privilege,*" and 32. "*noticeable.*"

The words that are spelled correctly (and which you were not required to write down) are as follows: 1. "*While,*" 2. "*preparing,*" 5. "*cell,*" 6. "*buzzing,*" 8. "*text,*" 9. "*friend,*" 13. "*Sandy,*" 14. "*thought,*" 15. "*study,*" 17. "*babysat,*" 22. "*because,*" 24. "*country,*" 25. "*Luckily,*" 31. "*know,*" 33. "*blush,*" and 34. "*appear.*"

Answers and Explanations for Practice Exercises, Chapters 1–5

Chapter 1

Sample Argumentative Essay and Corrections

We Need Healthier Foods and Drinks at My School (1)

If our school gave grades for the meals and drinks that many of us are (2) eating and drinking in school, would we get a lot of failing grades? It seems that many of us students aren't eating healthy lunches and snacks, and (3) these poor choices are harmful ones. Our general health and concentration is being affected negatively (4). In addition (5), our families can't always provide us with the right nutritional choices. Therefore (6), we should eliminate the serving of unhealthy meals and snacks in our school.

By making better nutritional choices, we can increase our chances of focusing more directly on our lessons. Sugar and caffeine, which are common ingredients in many snack foods and drinks, have an adverse (7) effect (8) on our ability to maintain our concentration. We can pay attention in class and ask more thoughtful questions when we are not being distracted by the "rush" and the "slump" we get from these snacks. When we learn more, we can have a better chance to get higher scores on our quizzes, tests, and projects.

Eliminating unhealthy meals and snacks in school will help our bodies to develop (9) more properly. We should avoid foods and snacks that are not only high in sugar and caffeine, but also (10) in fats and salt. We need to stay strong to fight off and prevent various diseases like the common cold and the flu (11). We should try to stay healthy in our young years to battle various diseases including high blood pressure, diabetes, bone diseases, and heart problems. The habits we establish now most likely will be the ones we will follow when we get older.

There are those who believe that us **(12)** students should be allowed to make hour **(13)** own choices. How are we ever going to become responsible? While becoming responsible is a necessary skill for us to learn, we are to **(14)** young to be aloud **(15)** to make decisions that are gonna effect **(16)** us in the future. If we are permitted to make silly **(17)** choices, then who will ensure that we do well in school, remain healthy, and grow up to have good health and function as productive members of our society? Going on the internet **(18)** may be entertaining , but letting our time on the computer take away time from our studies is wrong. The same is true with our wish to make our own food choices. So, **(19)** the freedom to decide is only preferable when we can show that we are responsible enough to make these important, critical **(20)** decisions for ourselves.

By not eating the right foods and snacks in school, we are potentially causing ourselves a great deal of harm. We are hurting ourselves in the classroom by affecting our ability not only to concentrate, but also to do our best work. We are hurting our bodies by weakening our defenses **(15)** against everyday problems like colds and flu and more severe problems including diabetes and heart disease. We are hurting our parents' or guardians' **(16)** chances of helping us to be healthy since we are all following busy and hectic schedules that do not always allow us time to make the best food choices. We often choose the most convenient choices instead. I therefore believe that eliminating unhealthy meals and snacks in school is an idea that should be adopted today. Shouldn't we all strive **(17)** to receive a passing grade for our food choices as we grow up to be reasonable, intelligent, and healthy adults?

Independent Writing Practice Argumentative Writing/Letter

Suggested Main Points

Check each correction and reason for the correction by line number.

1. This change provides a more specific title that better fits the essay.
2. *Many of us* is a better choice since not all students are making poor choices. Also, we should change *food and snack* to *food and drink* choices.
3. Creating a compound sentence by combining the two sentences with a comma and the coordinating conjunction *and* adds sentence variety.
4. Adding the word *negatively* shows specifically the writer's position. Otherwise, the effect may actually be positive.
5. Never begin a sentence with *And*. It is too casual. Use a transition like *In addition*, *Moreover*, or *Also*.
6. Never begin a sentence with *So*. It is also too casual. Use a transition like *Consequently*, *Therefore*, or *As a result*.
7. The power word *adverse* is a better choice than the weaker word *bad*.
8. The word *effect* should be used here as a noun (a naming word), not a verb (a word showing action or state of being).
9. The word *develop* is commonly misspelled with an e at the end.
10. When you use the phrase *not only*, it is strongly suggested that you also use the phrase *but also*. Even so, try not to overuse this pairing by placing it no more than once in a paragraph.
11. The words *flu* and *flew* are common homophones that can be misused. Remember, *flu* is a medical condition and *flew* is the past tense form of *fly*.
12. The choice here is simple: just get to the point.
13. The word *Internet* is always capitalized.
14. The phrase *is why* is incorrect grammatically. You must say *is the reason why* instead.
15. The correct spelling is *defenses*.
16. For plurals that end in "-s" like the words *parents* and *guardians*, add an apostrophe at the end of each word: *parents'* and *guardians'*.
17. The power word *strive* is a better choice than the weaker word *try*.

Chapter 2

Sample Speculative Essay Response

Frisky Saves the Day

As the sun came up, JJ looked at the alarm clock as she lay in bed. She had been asleep when she was woken up by the music from her clock radio and some other noise. The noise was coming from downstairs, and it seemed to be loud. She figured her mom would take care of it, but the noise kept going. How would JJ be able to sleep with all that noise?

JJ was known as being trustworthy. She always helped out people who needed help. She had stopped some kids at school from bullying another kid one time. She had taken care of a neighbor's dog while the neighbor was away. "I probably should help out in my house, too," she thought.

As she walked out of her room, she was able to tell that the noise that she had been hearing was coming from Frisky, her puppy. Frisky sounded excited, but JJ figured that her puppy was acting the way it always did. This puppy would run around non-stop for almost ten minutes at a time. The barking was probably just Frisky's way of being excited.

When JJ got downstairs, however, she noticed that it smelled as if something was burning. JJ called to her mom to ask if anything was wrong, but her mom didn't answer since she had just stepped outside for a moment. JJ called again, but still didn't get an answer. "Maybe something really is wrong," she said.

As JJ opened the door to the kitchen, the sun that would usually be in JJ's eyes was blocked since her mom had pulled down the shade. At once, JJ noticed that Frisky was barking and running around in circles. Before she could try to calm down her puppy, JJ noticed that there was smoke coming from the oven. JJ had to act quickly.

She started to fill up a bucket with water, but then JJ remembered a conversation she had last week with her Uncle Ralph.

JJ asked him, "'Should you throw water on a fire?"

Her Uncle Ralph had replied, "Not if the fire is a grease fire—you know, like the ones in a kitchen. Then you should open a box of salt and throw the salt on the fire."

Luckily, the muffins hadn't caught fire yet. JJ was able to take a box of salt, look through the oven door to make sure the fire hadn't started yet, cautiously open the door, and remove the muffins before they caught fire. JJ turned off the oven as her mom raced into the kitchen.

"What happened, JJ?"

"Frisky's barking woke me up, and I came down just in time to turn off the oven and prevent a fire. Frisky's a hero, mom," JJ said with relief.

"You're a hero too, JJ. You may have saved our lives."

"Mom, please don't go outside again if the oven is on. It's dangerous."

"I promise," said JJ's mom.

Both JJ and her mom learned a valuable safety lesson that morning: never leave the stove or the oven unattended.

Notice that in this essay, the writer made the following improvements. The title relates directly to the main event in the story, and **the essay opens with two compositional risks.**

- There is more detailed description.
    - "As the sun came up, JJ looked at the alarm clock as she lay in bed."
    - "She had taken care of a neighbor's dog while the neighbor was away."

- The entire "scene" is painted completely.
    - "JJ was known as being trustworthy. She always helped out people who needed help. She had stopped some kids at school from bullying another kid one time. She had taken care of a neighbor's dog while the neighbor was away. "I probably should help out in my house, too," she thought."

- There is dialogue.
    - "What happened, JJ?"
      "Frisky's barking woke me up, and I came down just in time to turn off the oven and prevent a fire. Frisky's a hero, mom," JJ said with relief.

- There are specifics.
  - "JJ was able to take as box of salt, make sure the fire hadn't started, open the door, and take out the muffins. JJ's mom raced into the kitchen." Was the original sentence.
  - It has been replaced by "JJ was able to take a box of salt, look through the oven door to make sure the fire hadn't started yet, cautiously open the door, and remove the muffins before they caught fire."
- There is a lesson that JJ and her mom both learn: "never leave the stove or the oven unattended." (Insight)

Independent Writing Practice/Speculative Essay

Suggested Main Points

Possible information to include in your essay.

- The main conflict deals with the following problem: should the narrator Jean take the present and keep it, or should Jean try to find the person whose name is on the present?
- The plot (story line) deals with Jean walking down the street on the way to the store on Saturday morning around 10:00 AM. Jean turns a corner and sees the wrapped birthday present. There is no one around on this clear summer morning.
- The setting is a small town in the summer. There is no one on the street where Jean finds the present. In the town, most people know each other. However, even this fact doesn't help Jean to know for whom the present is intended since the name on the tag has been smeared by the moisture from the morning dew.
- Jean is an honest seventh grader who always tries to do the right thing. She is a member of the student council at school, and she has been a girl scout since she was eight years old. She also won the award for most reliable student at school last year when she was in sixth grade.
- Jean tries to find someone to ask for advice about whether or not she should try to find the owner of the present. She first meets Harriet from school, who advises Jean to keep the present. Jean's too honest and doesn't think that Harriet's advice is good.
- Jean's best friend Miriam comes by and tells her that Jean should follow the advice she always gives to Miriam: "Honesty is the best policy." Jean agrees with Miriam, and the two girls walk one block to the police station to turn in the present they have found.

- The working title for the story is "Jean Finds a Present." The final title is "Jean Takes Her Own Advice."

Chapter 3

Practice—My First Day of School

1. The correct answer is D. "**Upset because there would be less freedom in school.** This answer is supported in lines 2–3: "Since school had let out last June, I suddenly had a lot more freedom." Answer A. "**Happy because the summer was boring**" is countered by answer D. None of the other answers is supported in the text.

2. The correct answer is A. "**Pat's mom would be right**" since the text says in lines 20–21, "My mom told me that I would be hungry before lunch if I didn't eat a good breakfast." Yet, he didn't heed her advice. Answer E. A and C is only partially correct since C. "**Pat's brother would be right**" is neither supported in the text nor is a brother mentioned at all. Answer B. "**Pat would be right**" must be incorrect since A is the correct answer. Answer D. "**Pat wanted to watch TV**" is incorrect since he usually watched TV while he ate his breakfast in the summer. This would not be possible if F. "**Pat's family didn't own a TV.**"

3. The correct answers are B. "**Pat's new clothes might be ruined,**" C. "**Pat might get hurt and miss the first day of school,**" and E. "**Pat might miss the bus.**" Answer A. "**Pat had never ridden a skateboard before**" is countered by the statement from lines 24–25: "I wonder what would happen if I took my skateboard and rode it one last time down my driveway." Answer D. "**Pat might have to stay away from the class bully on the bus**" has no support in the text. Since there are three correct responses, answers F. "**None of the above**" and G. "**All of the above**" are not possible.

4. The correct answers are B. "**Eat the breakfast Pat's mother has made**" (supported by lines 20–22: "My mom told me that I would be hungry before lunch if I didn't eat a good breakfast, but I just wasn't hungry") and D. "**Remember to put the completed diary assignment in the school bag**" (supported by lines 45–47: "I didn't think it was fair that we were assigned a one-page journal entry in English class, but I guess I can finish by just writing about my day."). Answer A. "**Sleep late**" is wrong since line 48 states: "Boy, I hope the weekend gets here quickly. I'm going to sleep late on Saturday." There is no text evidence to support answers C. "**Send a message on social media to his girlfriend,**" E. "**Walk the dog,**" and F. "**Go to the local store and get the morning newspaper.**"

5. The correct answer is F. "**Have an effect.**" The other answers all are part of the advertising process, but they do not reflect the word "influence."

Practice—A Letter to the Mayor

1. The correct answers are B. "Victoria Martinez wrote the letter to Mayor Patel and requested a new teen center" (line 18: "Last month when we came to a town council meeting to ask for a teen center" and line 25: "Please reconsider my request for a teen center in town.") and E. "Mayor Patel believes that there is already a problem with 'too many kids hanging out in the Maple Grove Shopping Center parking lot behind the movie theater.'" (lines 19–20: "You told us that there were too many kids hanging out in the Maple Grove Shopping Center parking lot behind the movie theater." Answer A. "Mr. Ross continues to volunteer his time so the building where the kids would skate and skateboard is 'kept up for us kids'" is incorrect since in lines 5–6 Victoria says," Mr. Ross used to volunteer his time on the weekends to make sure the building was kept up for us kids, but he retired and moved to Florida." Answers C. "Victoria Martinez tells Mayor Patel that she has also written a letter to her friends to ask for their support" and F. "Mayor Patel once agreed to build a new teen center, but the request was not able to be realized because of a budget deficit" have no basis in the text. Answer D. "Mayor Patel is hearing for the first time, this request from Victoria Martinez and her friends for a new teen center" is countered by Victoria's statement in lines 18–19 when she says "Last month when we came to a town council meeting to ask for a teen center, you became upset with us."

2. Statements A. "I *believe* that we should have a place in town where all the kids can get together," D. "A meeting place for us kids is a *great* idea for our town," E. "When we go to the movies, the security guards are *mean* to us," and F. "We don't *look for trouble*" are opinion statements with the key words in italics. Statements B. "The park near the river used to have a building where we could play games or just sit with our friends and talk" and C. "There was even some blacktop where we used to roller skate or ride our skateboards" contain facts that can be pointed to and measured. They are not opinions.

Practice—Guided-Reading Book Report Guidelines

1. The correct answers are C. "If you read your book with a friend, then you may discuss the book together," D. "Have your parent/guardian sign your book permission slip," and F. "Once a week, you and your partner will form a guided reading small discussion group" since they reflect measurable fact. The incorrect answers that contain opinions (with the opinions in italics) are A. "Reading a good novel *can be exciting*," B. "Finding out about the different characters and learning how the author blends each action and scene together *are only some of the thrills you can have* while reading," and E. "Sometimes when you are really interested in a book, you want to read ahead."

Answers and Explanations for Practice Exercises, Chapters 1-5 · 237

2. **Part A:** The correct answer is **B. Free Choice Fiction**, which is noted in the title. Do not skip over the title when you read a piece, whether it is fictional or informational. The title holds key information that sets the direction of the entire piece.

   Part B: Answer **D. The story contains a fictional main plot, conflict, and a resolution** is the correct answer because the question asked for the "qualities that are **not** generic to the type of genre being assigned." Always read test questions thoroughly and accurately. When rushed, you could make a mistake by presuming that the information is one way while it is actually being portrayed another way.

3. Answers **E. "Your homeroom teacher's name"** and **F. "The amount of books you have read during the marking period"** do not need to be included in the log. All the other information is required and supported in the text.

4. The correct answers are **D. "You must keep a reading log"** ("*Enter the page numbers into your reading log*") and **F. "For each session, you must discuss with your group the conflicts in the book."**

Practice—*The Wonderful Wizard of Oz*

1. The correct answers are **B. "Uncle Henry always laughed"** and **E. "The tornado ripped through the house, destroying everything."** Sentence #1 in paragraph 3 tells us **"Uncle Henry never laughed."** The last sentence of the passage has Aunt Em state, "'Quick, Dorothy!' she screamed. 'Run for the cellar!'" It does not mention what happened when the tornado hit. In paragraph #1, we learned that **A. "Dorothy lived with her Uncle Henry and Aunt Em."** In paragraph 5, **C. "Uncle Henry and Dorothy heard 'a low wail of the wind' that came from the south."** In paragraph 8, **D. "Aunt Em warned Dorothy to go in the cellar to protect herself from the cyclone that was expected to arrive."**

2. The correct answers are **C. "Toto always made Dorothy laugh" D. "Dorothy loved Toto dearly."** These answers are found in paragraph #3. Answer **A. "Dorothy adopted Toto from a shelter, and he never left her side."** is incorrect. Although Dorothy did indeed love Toto "dearly," there is no evidence to prove that he was adopted from a shelter or that Toto never left Dorothy's side." The same reasoning can be used to find answer **B. "Uncle Henry and Aunt Em gave Toto to Dorothy, and now Dorothy and Toto are always together"** to be incorrect. Answer **E. "Dorothy loved Toto even more than she loved Uncle Henry and Aunt Em"** is never addressed in the passage.

3. The events that are "out of sequence" are **B. "Aunt Em warned Dorothy to 'Run for the cellar!'"** and **E. "Uncle Henry said to his wife, 'There's a cyclone coming, Em.'"** Answer B is the last action in paragraph #8 while E is mentioned

in paragraph #6. Answers A. "Dorothy saw nothing but the great gray prairie on every side" found in paragraph 2, C. "Uncle Henry sat on the doorstep and looked anxiously at the sky" found in paragraph 4, and D. "Uncle Henry ran toward the shed where the cows and horses were kept" found in paragraph 6 occur both in sequence and before answers B and E. Please note that Uncle Henry warns his wife of the approaching tornado **before** he runs "toward the shed" in paragraph 6.

4. **Part A:** The correct answers are A. "Austere" and E. "Seldom amused." The first line in paragraph 3 states, "Uncle Henry never laughed." In the next sentence, the author says of Uncle Henry, "he looked stern and solemn, and rarely spoke." There is nothing in the passage to describe Uncle Henry's behavior as B. "out of control" since in paragraph 6 when "he ran toward the sheds where the cows and horses were kept," he did so with a purpose in mind. Answer C. "Filled with laughter" is incorrect since the statement "It was Toto that made Dorothy laugh" is mentioned right after the first two lines in paragraph three to show a contrast of Dorothy's personality with that of Uncle Henry. Answer D. "Sincere" has no basis in the paragraph and has nothing to do with Uncle Henry being "stern."

    Part B: The correct answers are B. "Uncle Henry seldom laughed" and F. "He did not know what joy was." These are the traits of someone who is "austere" and "Seldom amused." All the other answers are story details that do not match the meanings of the correct answers.

5. **Part A:** The correct answer is D. "A storm with swirling winds." In paragraph #1, the "cyclone cellar" is described as the place "where the family could go in case one of those great whirlwinds arose." Answer A. "A weather map" is not a weather event. Answer B. "A heat wave" is a likely condition for a cyclone, but there may or may not be swirling winds at that time. Answer C. "A desert breeze" would not be common in Kansas, even though the ground is dry. Answer E. "Heavy fog" is uncommon in a cyclone since the winds would blow it away.

    Part B: The first correct answer is A. "…the sky, which was grayer than usual" since this grayish sky is one of the early signs of a cyclone, therefore necessitating the need for a "cyclone cellar." It is mentioned in paragraph #4. The second correct answer is "…a small hole dug in the ground…" because in paragraph #2, that is the definition the author uses to describe the "cyclone cellar." Answer B. "…she could see nothing but the great gray prairie on every side" refers to the dryness of the prairie and not the approaching cyclone. Answers D. "The sun had baked the plowed land into a gray mass…" and E. "…the sun blistered the paint and the rains washed it away…" refer to the harshness of the climate and its effects on the land and the house in the story.

6. **Part A:** The story is set in D. "A farm on the prairies in Kansas." Dorothy did originally come from A. "An orphanage," but she lived there before arriving on the farm. Answer B. "The mountains and prairies in Kansas" is only partly correct since there are no mountains being mentioned. This is the type of tricky response that is typical of a standardized test. Remember, an answer is correct **only** when it is completely correct. Answer C. "The eastern coast of the United States" is wrong because Kansas is in the Midwest. Answer E. "A wagon train" is incorrect because a wagon train is never mentioned in the passage.

   Part B: The first correct answer is D. "'I'll go look after the stock.' Then he ran toward the sheds where the cows and horses were kept" since the term "stock" refers to the "cows and horses" that are kept on the farm. The second correct answer is E. "...the lumber to build it had to be carried by wagon many miles" since the lumber was brought in to build Uncle Henry and Aunt Em's farm house. Answer A. "When Dorothy, who was an orphan ..." refers not to the farm, but to Dorothy's background. Answers B. "...the broad sweep of flat country that reached to the edge of the sky in all directions" and C. "...she could see nothing but the great gray prairie on every side" refer to the land in general, not necessarily to a farm.

Practice—Tornadoes—The Facts

1. The first correct answer B. "The winds of the most powerful tornadoes have been known to reach speeds of 200 miles an hour" is found in paragraph #1 of question 1. The second correct answer is C. "Tornadoes are common in Kansas" is found in paragraph #1 of question 5. Answer A. "Tornadoes have the potential to be dangerous" is inaccurate since tornadoes are dangerous because they are severe storms. No mention of D. "The United States has the highest incidence of tornadoes" or E. "Some tornadoes have been known to travel along the ground for 50 miles" is mentioned in *The Wonderful Wizard of Oz.*

2. The first correct answer is C. "*The Wonderful Wizard of Oz* refers to the weather phenomenon as a cyclone while 'Tornadoes—The Facts' refers to the weather phenomenon as a tornado." The term "cyclone cellar" is used in paragraph #1 of *The Wonderful Wizard of Oz* while the term "tornado" is pluralized as part of the title of the informational piece, "Tornadoes—The Facts." The second correct answer is D. "*The Wonderful Wizard of Oz* portrays a set of fictional characters who are dealing with a cyclone and 'Tornadoes—The Facts' contains advice but no characters." The characters in *The Wonderful Wizard of Oz* are Uncle Henry, Aunt Em, Dorothy, and Toto. The piece "Tornadoes—The Facts" is informational and therefore does not

feature characters. Answer A. "*The Wonderful Wizard of Oz* is written to inform and "Tornadoes—The Facts" is written to entertain" if the two titles switched places. Answer B. "*The Wonderful Wizard of Oz* gives advice for anyone who sees a cyclone approaching and "Tornadoes—The Facts" does not" also does just the opposite. Answer E. "*The Wonderful Wizard of Oz* is non-fictional, and "Tornadoes—The Facts" is fictional" is also guilty of switching the facts.

3. The first correct answer A. **"Tornadoes make contact with a cloud and the surface of the earth over which they are traveling"** is contained in paragraph #1 of question #1. The second correct answer D. **"More tornadoes occur in the United States than they do in any other part of the world"** appears in the answer to question #4. The third correct answer F. **"Even though tornadoes generally move from the southwest to the northeast, they have been known to travel in every direction"** is found in the answer to question #3.

4. The first correct answer **"The pattern of a tornado is at times unpredictable and variable"** is found in the paragraph following question #2. The second correct answer is D. **"The Enhanced Fujita Scale, used to measure the strength of tornadoes, assigns a rating of five to the most powerful tornadoes"** found in paragraph #2 of question #1. The third correct answer **"When a tornado watch is announced, it is wise to take shelter"** is found in paragraph #3 of question #5. Answer A. **"Every tornado is almost completely transparent as it travels across the ground"** is disproved in the paragraph following question #3 when it is stated that "As these (dust and debris) begin to accumulate inside the tunnels of the tornadoes, the transparency lessens considerably." Answer B. **"The winds of a tornado are seldom more than 125 miles per hour"** is disproved in the paragraph following question #1: "The winds of the most powerful tornadoes have been known to reach speeds of 200 miles an hour… (and) have even been measured at more than 250 miles an hour." Answer E. **"Opening your windows during a tornado will help to equalize the pressure in your house and thereby help to keep it safe"** is disproved in the paragraph #3 following question #5: "Do not open your windows to alleviate the pressure from the tornado because you may be injured by flying glass while you are opening the windows. Besides, there is no advantage gained by opening the windows."

5. The correct answer is C. **"Description"** because in our explanation of description, we have said, "…your major task is to paint a clear word picture. You must give the details in such a way that those who have little experience in the area can still understand your point clearly." Answer A. **"Cause and effect"** is incorrect since specific causes of tornadoes are not followed by the specific events resulting from each one. Answer B. **"Compare and contrast"** is incorrect

because we are neither comparing nor contrasting tornadoes with any other weather phenomena. Answer **D.** "Problem/Solution" is incorrect since general questions about tornadoes and strategies for dealing with them are covered. Solutions are one focus, not the main focus of "Tornadoes—The Facts."

Sample Response 1/Essay for Plot, Character, and Setting

Severe weather can be a strong attention getter itself, but L. Frank Baum in *The Wonderful Wizard of Oz* uses the title of his first chapter "The Cyclone" not only to catch the reader's attention, but also to prepare the reader for the difficulties the characters must face.

In the second sentence, Baum establishes a depressing mood by mentioning that Dorothy lives with her Uncle Henry and Aunt Em not in a comfortable house, but rather in a "small" one. Although the term "home" would connote more of a comfortable feeling, Baum uses the term "house" to distance the characters from that feeling. The fact that the lumber "had to be carried by wagon many miles" reinforces the idea of hardship. The "one room" containing "four walls, a floor and a roof," a "rusty looking cookstove," and no evidence of anything elegant or comforting serves to reinforce a somber tone to the piece. The house lacked a garret and a cellar, but it did have "a small hole dug in the ground called a cyclone cellar, where the family could go" for protection during cyclone. In the second paragraph, Baum adds that the prairie was "gray," the land was "baked," and "Even the grass was not green." The paint on the house was "blistered" and "washed away." Unfortunately, so was the red from Aunt Em's cheeks and lips."

This ominous and depressing setting establishes Baum's intention to introduce the devastation of the approaching cyclone (which is actually "a hurricane and not a tornado" as "Tornadoes—The Facts" points out). Baum understands a cyclone's power. According to "Tornadoes—The Facts," these phenomena "have been known to reach speeds of 200 miles an hour" and can even exceed 250 miles per hour. Imagine being an orphan who moves to a simple farm house to be raised by an "Uncle" and "Aunt" with your only laughter coming from your pet dog Toto.

When Dorothy laughed, however, Aunt Em "would scream and press her hand upon her (own) heart." As the hurricane approached, Aunt Em reacted in a similar fashion. "Quick, Dorothy!" she screamed. "Run for the cellar!"

The depressing atmosphere is further reinforced by Baum in the fourth and fifth paragraphs. In paragraph 4, Uncle Henry "sat upon the doorstep and looked anxiously at the sky, which was even grayer than usual." Dorothy wasn't laughing a child-like laugh nor was she "playing" with Toto. Rather, she was standing "in the door with Toto in her arms (while) she looked at the sky too," awaiting the storm. Baum mentioned how "the long grass bowed in waves before the coming storm" and how "There now came a sharp whistling in the air from the south" along with the "ripples in the grass." These facts build suspense before the approaching cyclone would arrive.

Aunt Em recognized that as "Tornadoes . . ." points out, a cyclone has the "potential to wreak havoc and cause devastation to homes, farms, buildings, and any edifice and area in their paths." Unwittingly, she was also heeding their advice that when a cyclone approaches, "it is wise to take shelter" and to "Find a safe, solid shelter and go there if you have time." Remember, "Tornadoes . . ." point out that Kansas and Florida have the third most tornadoes ("cyclones") with "an average of 55 a year" so this type of devastation is common to Uncle Henry and Aunt Em. Sadly, it may become common to Dorothy and Toto as well.

Dorothy dealt with a lack of laughter, drab surroundings, and two overworked and dour surrogate parents, along with an approaching cyclone. In eight short paragraphs, Baum artistically blends the playfulness of youth, the difficulty of being raised by surrogate parents, the combination of the drab existence and harsh realities of life on Uncle Henry's farm, and the inevitable havoc to be caused by an approaching cyclone to create a somber portrait of life on Uncle Henry's farm.

This essay probably earns a "4" because it:

- Begins with a compositional risk: "Severe weather can be a strong attention getter itself…"
- Addresses each question directly and thoroughly.
- Uses text-based references to both texts: "The 'one room' containing 'four walls, a floor and a roof', a 'rusty looking cookstove' in *The Wonderful Wizard of Oz* and cyclones 'have been known to reach speeds of 200 miles an hour' in 'Tornadoes—The Facts.'"
- Has great length and insight (Ex. "Although the term 'home' would connote more of a comfortable feeling, Baum uses the term 'house' to distance the characters from that feeling.")
- Uses good essay construction with varied sentence structure and length.
- Adds examples of "how difficult it must be to live" on the farm.
- Mentions the farm's physical traits and Uncle Henry, Aunt Em, and Dorothy's personalities.
- Adds insight by connecting the dullness of both the setting and the characters.
- Uses appropriate grammar, spelling, and vocabulary and academic vocabulary ("connote," "ominous," and "phenomena," for example).
- Demonstrates a strong focus and sense of unity and coherence.

Sample Response 2/Essay for Plot, Character, and Setting

L. Frank Baum in *The Wonderful Wizard of Oz* called his first Chapter The Cyclone, and it got my attention. What about you?

Uncle Henry and Aunt Em adopt Dorothy since she was an orphan. The author Baum writes some depressing things. Uncle Henry and Aunt Em live in a "small" house built by lumber that was "carried by wagon many miles." There wasn't much that was happy in this piece. The house was "one room," and they used a "rusty looking cookstove" to make their meals. Just in case a cyclone swept down on them, the family would run to the "cyclone cellar" to be safe from the storm. There were prairies, but they weren't green like they are in that Zane Grey book I read last week in the library. In *The Wonderful Wizard of Oz*, their prairie was "gray" and the land was "baked."

In the fourth paragraph, we find out that a big cyclone is headed toward the farm. We know this because the author says "the long grass bowed in waves before the coming storm" and there was "a sharp whistling in the air from the south." Even the grass had "ripples." Uncle Henry, Aunt Em, Dorothy, and Toto would be in big trouble if the storm came and they were standing around and waiting for it.

In "Tornadoes—The Facts," they have all this really cool stuff about tornadoes. They say that tornadoes can usually go about 200 miles an hour. Some can even go faster than 250 miles an hour. If Dorothy and her family knew that, then maybe they would have really been scared. They might have panicked and not gone into the "cyclone cellar" like the article says to do. They probably know what to do, however, since they live in Kansas. They have a lot of cyclones in Kansas. Well, they're really tornadoes. Baum called them cyclones by mistake. Anyway, they said in "Tornadoes—The Facts" that a cyclone can "wreak havoc and cause devastation to homes, farms" and lots of other stuff. They tell you to "take shelter . . . if you have time."

So, Dorothy had to put up with no laughs except from Toto, a dull place to live, two dull people to raise her, and a big cyclone coming her way. Wow, that L. Frank Baum sure knows how to use some details to make his audience feel sorry for Dorothy. As they said in "Tornadoes—The Facts," "take shelter . . . if you have time."

This essay probably earns a "2" because it:
- Unsuccessfully attempts to begin with a compositional risk: "L. Frank Baum in *The Wonderful Wizard of Oz* called his first Chapter The Cyclone, and it got my attention. What about you?"
- Addresses each question, but the way it does so is neither direct nor thorough.
- Uses text-based references to both texts: "The "one room" containing "four walls, a floor and a roof," a "rusty looking cookstove" in *The Wonderful Wizard of Oz* and cyclones ""wreak havoc and cause devastation to homes, farms," but the references are brief.
- Has some length, but the insight has very little academic feel to it (Ex. "So, Dorothy had to put up with no laughs except from Toto, a dull place to live, two dull people to raise her, and a big cyclone coming her way.")
- Uses simple essay construction with little variation of sentence structure and length.
- Tries to explain the difficulty of living on the farm.

- Fails to connect the farm's physical traits with Uncle Henry, Aunt Em, and Dorothy's personalities.
- Attempts to make a literary allusion ("There were prairies, but they weren't green like they are in that Zane Grey book I read last week in the library.")
- Uses simple grammar and accurate spelling.
- Uses vocabulary that lacks an academic flavor ("happy," "big," "go," and "says to do," for example).
- Demonstrates an inconsistent focus and an attempt at unity and coherence.

Practice—The Road Not Taken

1. The correct answer is A. "First person" because the author uses "I" often. Answers B. "Second person" and C. "Third person" are not used when "I" is used. Answer D. "Both A and C" is incorrect because the poem is only written in one voice. Answers E. "All of the above" and F. "None of the above" is incorrect because the poem has to be told in one of the three persons mentioned.

2. **Part A:** The correct answer is D. **"The traveler was sad that he couldn't travel both roads."** Sentence #2 in stanza #1 (line 2) says that the traveler was **"sorry I (he) could not travel both."** Answers A. "The traveler was lost" and B. "The traveler was hungry" aren't mentioned in the poem. Answer C. "The traveler was happy that he could travel both roads" is the opposite of the correct answer D.
   Part B: The correct answer is **"And sorry I could not travel both"** (line 2). The other answers do not reflect the correct answer in Part A.

3. The correct answer is A. **"The traveler hoped but doubted he would take the other road some day."** Answer B. "The traveler was sure he would take the other road some day" is disproved by answer A. Answers C. "The traveler was paralyzed with fear," D. "The traveler was encouraged by his friend to take the other road," and E. "The traveler was addled" do not appear in the poem.

4. **Part A:** The details that do not appear in the poem are A. **"Two roads ran parallel in the woods"** (since they actually "diverged"), B. **"The narrator took the more traveled road by,"** C. **"The narrator couldn't decide which road to travel and thus took neither,"** E. **"The narrator walked down each road before he made a decision about which one to travel,"** F. **"Each road was used about the same amount,"** and I. **"The narrator consulted with a good friend before deciding which road to take."** Answer D. "The narrator took the road that had not been traveled as much as the other road" appears in line 19: "I took the one less traveled by." Answer G. "The narrator believes that the course he chose to take has made a significant difference in his own life" is supported by lines

19–20: "I took the one less traveled by / And that has made all the difference." Answer H. "The narrator isn't sure if he'll ever return to the road he has not taken" is supported by line 20: "I doubted if I should ever come back."
Part B: The order of appearance in the poem is H. "The narrator isn't sure if he'll ever return to the road he had not taken" (line 15), D. "The narrator took the road that had not been traveled as much as the other road" (line 19), and "The narrator believes that the course he chose to take has made a significant difference in his own life" (line 20).

5. The correct answer is C. "The choice of the road taken changes the traveler's life" (line 20). The remaining answers have no basis in the text.
6. The correct answer is D. "abaab." In the first stanza, for example, the last words are "wood," "both," "stood," "could," and "undergrowth. Hence, lines 1, 3, and 4 (represented by A) rhyme as do lines 2 and 5 (represented by B).

Practice—How Do We Handle a Challenge?

1. The correct answer is D. "Facing these challenges is never easy, but we must ultimately face these challenges ourselves." In this paragraph, the topic sentence actually concludes the paragraph. Answers A. "Our lives are often filled with many challenges," B. "There are problems that we need to solve, difficult questions that we need to answer, and obstacles that we have to overcome," and C. "We can either face those challenges or give in to them" are statements that lead up to the theme.
2. Statements A. "Our lives are often filled with many challenges," B. "Both options, however, can lead us in different directions in our lives," E. "If we haven't worked hard so far, then we have placed ourselves in an unenviable position," and G. "The answer is not a simple one." These answers are all contingent upon perception, rather than fact. Statement C. "The assignment will count for one-third of our grade" is a basic statement of fact. Statement D. "…the time will come to pass when our assignment will be due" is supported by the previous statement made in lines 7–8: "proceed to complete the task both well and on time." Statement F. "He says that he can have someone get him a completed assignment" is a typically misleading type of statement that requires careful thought to be answered correctly. While the friend's statement that "**he can have someone get him a completed assignment**" is an opinion statement, it is embedded in the larger statement that reports that the friend "**says**" this. That the friend made this statement is a fact, and that is the basis for this answer.

3. **Part A:** The correct answer is D. "Problem/Solution" since the author is posing a problem and encouraging us to solve the problem "ourselves." Answer A. "Cause and effect" is incorrect because the major focus is solving a problem, not looking at the causes of it. For answer B. "Compare and contrast" to be true, the main focus again would need to be on these techniques (comparing and contrasting different alternatives). Answer C. "Description" would be correct only if the problem itself were being described in detail. Answer E. "Chronological" would be correct only if a timeline were being followed.
    Part B: Answer B. "challenges" is a word common in Problem/Solution essays. Answers A. "often," C. "imagine," and D. "assignment" may appear in any of the text patterns.
4. Answer D. "What should we do?" captures the main idea of the narrator struggling with a decision he needs to make for himself. Answer A. "Take, for example, an important assignment that we have been given" would be correct only if the narrator had been given the task of making this decision. Answer B. "If we haven't worked hard so far, then we have placed ourselves in an unenviable position" presumes that someone has placed the narrator in a position of having to make his decision. Answer C. "Do we give in, knowing that there's a chance that we could get caught cheating?" is incorrect because there is no reference to cheating in the poem. Answer D. "We are definitely in a bind" presumes that the narrator is in trouble, which he is not. Answer E. "That will get us in trouble" is incorrect because there is no mention of trouble being connected with the decision the narrator must make.
5. The word "unenviable" means A. "difficult." Answer B. "inane" means "senseless," answer C. "complicated" means "complex," answer D. "advantageous" means "providing a favorable position," and E. "partial" means "not entirely."

Sample Response/Paired Passage/Essay for Theme, Cause and Effect, Point of View, Details, Sequence, and Fact vs. Opinion

Both Robert Frost and Philip Postrun speak of making a decision. Frost takes a more personalized approach while Postrun gives advice directly. Frost doesn't seem to speak directly to everyone, which is something that Postrun does. While Postrun gives everyone a challenge by saying that everyone of us must each decide ourselfes what to do, Frost tells the story from his own eyes. Frost wants the reader to take his advice just because it's their. But Postrun says that we all have to "decide ourselves" what to do.

This essay is weak because:

- There is little to grab the reader's attention in the opening.
- The reader should restate the question somewhere in the opening, rather than saying the authors "speak of making a decision" rather than restating the phrase "deal(ing) with the concept of "facing a challenge."
- There are no direct citations from the text to expand the points being made.
- Frost's personalized approach is actually personalized to him, not the audience. That needs to be explained the way it is with Postrun giving "advice directly."
- The lack of academic vocabulary helps to keep this score low. For example, "gives" could be "presents, "what to do" could be "what action to take," "his own eyes" could be "his own point of view" or "his own perspective,"and "But" should be replaced with "However," "Nonetheless," or "In contrast."
- The spelling and grammar mistakes do not help to raise the score. "...everyone of us" needs to be "every one of us," "ourselfes" should be "ourselves," and "their" should be "there."

An essay that would receive a higher score:

- catches the reader's attention with a brief compositional risk: "Facing a challenge can be a challenge in itself, and both Robert Frost and Philip Postrun seem to realize this.:
- The question is directly stated when the passage states that the authors are dealing with "the concept of facing a challenge.".
- Citations are made directly from the text: "While Frost uses the vivid imagery of 'Two roads (that) diverged in a yellow wood'" and "Postrun states very matter-of-factly that 'We can either face those challenges or give in to them'" for example.
- The main idea in Frost's piece is "And sorry I could not travel both (line 2)," as he speaks of a personal decision. In contrast, Postrun feels that when handling a challenge, "we must each decide ourselves (line 26)."
- There is good length to the essay. Two well-developed paragraphs is a reasonably good length for this type of piece.
- Academic vocabulary is evident throughout as the writer uses phrases including "vivid imagery," "significant," "personalized," and "scenario."
- Transitions including "While" and "Furthermore" are used.
- There are no grammar or spelling mistakes.

Answers and Explanations for Practice Exercises, Chapters 1–5 · 249

Practice—The Queen Bee

1. The correct answer is **A. "The youngest (the dwarf)"** Answers **B. "Second oldest"** and **C. "Oldest"** are incorrect because they wanted to tear down the anthill, kill the ducks to "roast them," and "kill the bees so they could get their honey." Answer **D. "All of the above"** cannot be correct since it would have to include answers B and C.

2. Part A: The correct answer is **A. "unimportant."** Answer **B. "important"** is an antonym while the other definitions are simply incorrect. Please note that answer **D. "precocious"** means advanced beyond one's years and is a solid academic vocabulary word.
   Part B: The correct answers are **C. "Let the pretty insects enjoy themselves; I cannot let you burn them"** (line 18) and **"the dwarf married the youngest and the best of the princesses"** (lines 17–18). Remember, the question has asked you to find the "phrases/sentences (that) refer to the opposite of the king's younger son's insignificance," not the same. Answer **B. "when he had found them they only laughed at him"** indicates the son's insignificance while the other answers do not support the question.

3. The correct answer is **B. "Find the first hundred pearls or be turned into marble."** This is supported by lines 35–36: "In the wood, under the moss, lie the thousand pearls belonging to the king's daughter; they must all be found: and if one be missing by set of sun, he who seeks them will be turned into marble." The other responses have no basis in the text. Please note that answer **A. "Find the first hundred pearls or be turned into stone"** sounds correct since the oldest brother **did not** find even 100 pearls. If you had read the fable too quickly, you might have made this mistake. Answers **C. "Find the dwarf or be turned into stone"** and **D. "Find the princess or be turned into stone"** are not accurate. Only those who were unable to complete the challenges were turned into stone.

4. The correct answer is **D. "Accepted the challenge and failed, also getting turned into marble"** Answers **A. "Ran away"** and **B. "Locked the old man in a prison and escaped with his brothers"** Do not happen in the story. Answer **C. "Accepted the challenge and succeeded"** is true only for the little dwarf.

5. The correct answer is **D. "They would help him later in the story."** Answers **A. "They would attack him because he's a dwarf,"** **B. "They would pay him money,"** **C. "They would run away because they're afraid of dwarfs,"** and **E. "They would help him to steal the treasure from the queen"** have no basis in the story.

Practice—"Friends, Romans, and Countrymen . . ."

1. **Part A:** The correct answer is E. "greatly desirous." While the traits of all the other suggested definitions may in small part be related to "ambitious," only answer E is the exact definition.
   Part B: Answer A. "There was a conflict between Caesar and Brutus caused by Brutus's ambition" is correct since it states the main conflict of the speech. Answers B. "There was a conflict between Caesar and Brutus caused by Antony's ambition" and C. "There was a conflict between Caesar and Brutus caused by Caesar's ambition" have mixed up the roles in the conflict. Answer D. "The implied conflict is between Caesar and Antony" is illogical since Antony is speaking to defend the honor of Caesar.

2. **Part A:** The correct answer is C. "Marc Antony disliked Caesar." The two key phrases in the question are "From the opening two lines" and "one could infer." At the beginning of the speech, it was Marc Antony's intent to seem as if he was coming to "bury Caesar, not to praise him." Marc Antony's true intent came later in the speech, not in the opening. This is the reason answer A. "Marc Antony wished to portray Caesar as a hero" is incorrect. Answers B. "Marc Antony was not liked by the citizens of Rome," D. "Marc Antony was related to Caesar," and E. "Marc Antony didn't even know Caesar, but he made this statement to help out Brutus" have no basis in the opening two lines.
   Part B: The correct answer is D. "Caesar was honorable, and Brutus was not." The quote "Ambition should be made of sterner stuff" is saying that Caesar wasn't ambitious at all. Answer B. "Brutus was honorable, and Caesar was not" is the opposite of the truth and therefore incorrect. Answers A. "Caesar was overly emotional, and stress had caused his death," C. "Caesar was a poor man when he died."

3. **Part A:** The correct answer is A. "more serious." Answers B. "more intelligent," C. "more imaginative," "more creative," and E. "more thorough" are not synonyms.
   Part B: The correct answer is B. "Marc Antony says that Brutus's accusation that Caesar was 'ambitious'" is false. When Marc Antony says, "Ambition should be made of sterner stuff," he is using irony to show that Caesar would have needed to be much more serious about being ambitious if he were indeed ambitious at all. Answers A. "Marc Antony is falsely accusing Brutus of stealing gold from Caesar's treasury," C. "Marc Antony is glad that Caesar has been killed so he (Antony) can ascend to the throne," D. "Marc Antony is angry that he has not received any praise for killing Caesar.

Sample Response 1/Essay for Conflict/Resolution and Making Predictions

Predictability in a story is not always an easy thing—unless one begins to act as a detective would and searches for clues. In the fable "The Queen Bee" by the Brothers Grimm and Marc Antony's speech in Shakespeare's *Julius Caesar*, the authors blend a bit of irony to achieve a purpose.

"The Queen Bee" takes the reader through a series of events in which the king's two older sons are out to "seek their fortunes" in whatever way suits them. They are willing to do that which is easy for them, even though their actions will impact negatively. Furthermore, they are not apologetic in the least. In Marc Antony's speech, however, Antony is using a bit of irony when he states, "I come to bury Caesar, not to praise him." His intention is take suspicion away from him so he can cleverly change the notion of Caesar from an enemy to a hero.

The youngest son, known as the dwarf, serves as the foil to his two older brothers in "The Queen Bee. He tells his brothers to let the ants and ducks "enjoy themselves" rather than harm them. When the older brothers later fail in their quest to find "the thousand pearls belonging to the king's daughter," the dwarf is successful because he is helped by those who received mercy through his kindness. The story instructs the reader to understand that good deeds do not go unrewarded.

Antony in *Julius Caesar* also achieves success, but his success was unforeseen by the audience he's addressing and not by Brutus's supporters. Why, he begins by addressing the audience not as enemies but as "Friends, Romans, (and countrymen)." He then proceeds cleverly to take statements Brutus had made against Caesar and ironically minimize their impact. Brutus is described as "noble" while Antony keeps repeating the phrase that Caesar is "ambitious" and then disproving the accusation. He notes that Caesar "brought many captives home to Rome," wept with the poor, and even refused "a kingly crown" three times.

Moreover, Antony ends by contrasting his own statement of "I speak not to disprove what Brutus spoke" with "You all did love him once, not without cause" so "What cause withholds you then, to mourn for him?" The dwarf in "The Queen Bee" gained his reward as a result of his good deeds. Antony, however, faced his enemies squarely and through powerful rhetoric and irony, he used comparison and contrast to change the image of Brutus from an "honourable man" to one who was not.

This essay

- catches the reader's attention with a brief compositional risk: It addresses both authors' use of making predictions and irony.
- The student wisely looks at the way the authors "Compare and contrast the challenge that each of these two individuals faced" and states this in the opening paragraph.
- The characters in "The Queen Bee" take action while Marc Antony uses irony in his speech.
- Citations are made directly from the text. For example, the two older brothers in "The Queen Bee" "are out to 'seek their fortunes' in whatever way suits them" while Marc Antony states, ""I come to bury Caesar, not to praise him." And "While Frost uses the vivid imagery of 'Two roads (that) diverged in a yellow wood'" and "Postrun states very matter-of-factly that 'We can either face those challenges or give in to them'" for example.
- There is good length to the essay. One brief and three well-developed paragraphs is an extraordinarily good length for this type of piece. Remember, length is rewarded on these standardized tests.
- Academic vocabulary is evident throughout as the writer uses phrases including "predictability," "suspicion," and "unforeseen."
- Transitions including "unless," "Furthermore," and "Moreover" are used.
- There are no grammar or spelling mistakes.

Sample Response 2/Essay for Conflict/Resolution and Making Predictions

In the story "The Queen Bee," these two brothers who are the king's son want to be on easy street so they go out to find some serious money. They have this dwarf character with them, and he's actually their younger brother. Because they wanted to pull down an ant hill as a prank and cook the ducks for food, the authors show that these guys are cruel. They show the dwarf as being much kinder, however, since he tells his brothers not to do this harmful stuff. They are complete opposites.

Marc Antony in *Julius Caesar* is an opposite too, but his opposite is Brutus. Antony tries to show up Brutus by telling all the "Friends, Romans, countrymen" that Caesar wasn't such a bad guy, but Brutus said he was ambitious and Brutus would know. You see, Antony is hinting that Brutus wasn't a good guy for killing Caesar. Caesar did good stuff like bringing back soldiers and saying three times that he didn't want to be king. Unfortunately, he got killed because Brutus said he was "ambitious." That's kind of ironic, isn't it?

This essay is weak because:

- it has no compositional risk and no restatement of the question.
- There is little if any comparison or contrast in the essay.
- The language is much too casual: "easy street," "serious money," and "stuff," for example.
- The brevity of the piece contributes to the low score attained. There need to be more thought and more examples presented.
- The Brothers Grimm's work should be referred to as a fable, not a "story."
- There are no spelling and grammar mistakes, but the use of phrases like "good stuff" are not appropriate in an academic exercise.
- The essay writer actually uses text references and the literary term "irony," but these are not properly showcased in a mindful essay.
- There are transitional phrases ("Because" and "Unfortunately," for example) used, but they need to be used in a stronger essay context.

Practice—"The Children's Hour"

1. The correct answer is **D. "abcb."** The words "lower" and "Hour" are known as near rhymes. The other answers are incorrect.
2. The correct answer is **D. "gloomy"** and **E. "insincere."** There are no signs of doom or despair, nor is there anything that could be deemed to be "insincere." Answer **A. "formal"** is acceptable since the language is standard and polite, not slang. Answer **B. "clear"** is correct since the message is stated clearly. Answer **C. "realistic"** is acceptable since Longfellow speaks of "the Children's Hour," a chance to spend time with his children.

3. The correct answer is B. "playful as noted in the children's merry eyes as they look to take Longfellow 'by surprise.'" Answers A. "nasty, C. "angry," and D. "sad" are not typical emotions of children with "merry eyes."
4. Part A: The correct answers are A. "a small tower" and F. "a gunner's enclosure." None of the other answers fits the definition of a "turret." Answer C. "a tank missile" could be misleading if one does not read the answers carefully and hastily concludes that all of the answers with a military connection are correct.
   Part B: The correct answers are A. "climb," D. "escape," E. "surround," and F. "everywhere" since they all deal with the children's playful invasion of the father's chair, which is portrayed as a turret. Answer B. "arms" is not correct since the reference in the poem is to the arms of a chair, not the arms carried by military personnel. Answer D. "back" refers to part of the chair.
5. The correct answer is D. "challenging" Answer A. "angry" belies the poem's playful mood. Answer B. "Pompous" is wrong since the poet is not arrogant. Answer C. "sad" is the opposite of the playful tone of this poem.
6. The correct answer is C. "Serious" since Longfellow's words are similar to those in a news report. There's no evidence to support Answers A. "Worried," B. "Sad," and D. "Humorous."

Practice—"We Shall Fight on the Beaches"

1. Part A: The correct answers are D. "England would not be an easy target for any invaders" and F. "England was prepared to defend itself aggressively as it had done in the past" since they both reflect the phrase "bitter weeds." Answer A. "England could not defend itself" is wrong because it is the opposite of the correct answer. Answers B. "England was in the midst of a drought" and C. "England was a country known for its farms" are not mentioned in the speech. Answer E. "England was prepared to defend itself, but it would prefer a peaceful solution" is only partially correct since the option of a peaceful solution runs counter to the phrase "bitter weeds."
   Part B: The correct answer is C. "Determined" since he used the phrase "bitter weeds" to show that England has been a strong force in the past and will continue to be one in the future, as well. Answer A. "Timid" is wrong because it runs counter to being "determined." Answer B. "Inconsistent" does the same. Answer D. "Light-hearted" does not reflect a determined tone.

Answers and Explanations for Practice Exercises, Chapters 1–5 • 255

2. The correct answer is **A. "Rigor."** Answer **C. "Mildness"** is wrong because it has the opposite meaning. Answers **B. "Exhaustion," D. "Creativity"** are wrong because they are not synonyms.

3. **Part A:** The correct answers are **A. "Espionage"** and **E. "Sabotage"** since they both deal with activities that look to undermine England. Answers **B. "Patriotism"** and **C. "Loyalty"** are traits that are not typical of fifth column actions. Answers **D. "Oratory"** is a skill practiced by people with various beliefs, and Answer **F. "Faith-based"** is a trait that is also practiced by many.
   Part B: The correct answer is **D. "Fifth Columnists"** since they would look to overthrow England. Answer **A. "Napolean's army"** is wrong since they were involved in a different war. Answers **B. "The British Expeditionary Force"** and **C. "British subjects (citizens)"** are wrong since they all are on the side of the British.

4. **Part A:** The correct answers are **A. "Reassuring"** and **F. "Hopeful."** The British are soothed by the reference to the thwarting of Napolean's invasion that demonstrated "There are bitter weeds in England." Answers **B. "Irate," C. "Insensitive," D. "Vengeful,"** and **E. "Aggressive"** all do not reflect the attempt by Churchill to reassure his nation that success was indeed in their future.
   Part B: The correct answers are **C. "Determined"** and **F. "Uplifting."** Answers **A. "Timid," B. "Inconsistent," D. "Light-hearted,"** and **E. "Antagonistic"** are wrong since they reflect the wrong emotions.

5. The correct answer is **D. "Repetition for effect"** since the phrase "We shall fight" is repeated by Churchill. Answers **A. "Simile," B. "Metaphor,"** and **C. "Personification"** are not used here by Churchill.

Sample Response 1/Essay for Mood and Tone

For Winston Churchill, the British Prime Minister during WWII, a battle meant a serious encounter between his Allied forces and the Axis forces. For Henry Wadsworth Longfellow, however, he compares a battle to a playful game in which he participates with his young children.

Churchill speaks of Hitler's plan "for invading the British Isles" and Napoleon's unsuccessful invasion. Churchill states, "There are bitter weeds in England," a metaphor of the British forces' toughness. Longfellow, on the other hand, speaks of "a pause in the day's occupations (routines)" which is referred to "as the Children's Hour." Next, Longfellow describes the children's mischievous invasion by using the onomatopoeia of the "patter of little feet". In addition, the suspense created by "The sound of a door that is opened," and the contrast of this so-called invasion by children with "voices soft and sweet" emphasizes a light-hearted mood. This pleasant, yet mischievous invasion is furthered by the cute, simple rhyme of "feet" and "sweet."

The mood of Churchill's speech becomes gloomy and quite serious as he speaks of "increasing stringency," "enemy aliens and suspicious characters," and "British subjects who may become a danger or a nuisance'. The alliteration in the phrases "fierce fighting" and "not the slightest sympathy" further emphasize the goal of eliminating "this malignancy in our midst," another example of alliteration. In contrast, Longfellow uses alliteration in the phrase "plotting and planning" to highlight the playfulness of the children. As the children unleash "A sudden rush from the stairway, A sudden raid from the hall!" one can almost anticipate the onrush of awaiting laughter.

Churchill contrasts the next to the last paragraph with his final one. He sees no "absolute guarantee against invasion," but states that "we shall prove ourselves once again able to defend our Island home, to ride out the storm of war, and to outlive the menace of tyranny, if necessary for years, if necessary alone." The grouping of the three actions "defend," "ride," and "outlive" add both emphasis and confidence. He ends his speech by repeating the phrase "we shall" eleven times with seven of those being "we shall fight," thus changing the serious, somber mood to one of energized hope and determination. Longfellow's battle is more playful as the children "climb up into (his) turret" and "seem to be everywhere," almost devouring him "with (playful)kisses." The literary allusion to "the Bishop of Bingen/ In his Mouse-Tower on the Rhine!" refers to a Bishop who was kept in a tower and eaten by the mice, a tale told likely to frighten little children. These threats, nonetheless, are unlike Churchill's since Longfellow vows to keep the children "fast in (his) fortress" and "in the round tower of (his) heart." The mood here is playful and mischievous, which is different than Churchill's somber mood that changes to hope.

Answers and Explanations for Practice Exercises, Chapters 1–5 · 257

This essay
- catches the reader's attention by contrasting Winston Churchill's serious battle with Henry Wadsworth Longfellow's playful battle..
- The student methodically alternates the serious tone of Churchill with the playful one of Longfellow.
- The literary analysis reflects higher-order thinking and insight.
- The use of literary devices by both authors is mindfully included: Churchill's use of metaphor and repetition for effect and Longfellow's use of onomatopoeia and alliteration, for example.
- Citations are made directly from the text. For example, Churchill notes "There are bitter weeds in England" while Longfellow speaks of impish youngsters with ""voices soft and sweet."
- There is excellent length to the essay.
- Academic vocabulary is evident throughout as the writer uses phrases including "participates," "emphasizes," and "malignancy."
- Transitions including "on the other hand," "In addition," and "In contrast" are used.
- There are no grammar or spelling mistakes.

Sample Response 2/Essay for Mood and Tone

    Winston Churchill gives this speech to fire up his people against Hilter's Nazi invasion while Longfellow, a poet, talks about these kids who are goofing around to try to invade his privacy.

    Churchill talked about Hitler "invading the British Isles." He also talked about Napoleon, who wasn't successful with his invasion. I guess Churchill is trying to fire up his people. But Longfellow isn't. You see, he has these silly kids who are driving him crazy. He hears the kids' "patter of little feat," and "The sound of a door" opening. So you know that something's going down real soon! I guess the poet rhymes "feet" and "sweet" so this stuff sounds cute or something.

    Churchill gets all serious when he talks "enemy aliens and suspicious characters." He uses some alliteration when he say "fierce fighting." But Longfellow tries alliteration when he says "plotting and planning" to attack him to play fight.

    At the end of the speech, Churchill starts firing up everybody. He tells them "we shall prove ourselves once again able to defend our

Island home, to ride out the storm of war, and to outlive the menace of tyranny, if necessary for years, if necessary alone." But Longfellow's invading kids "seem to be everywhere." Yeah, but he'll handle them. He'll threaten to put them "down into the dungeon." That should frighten them off.

This essay

- has a weak opening, and the language is a bit unfocused. Phrases such as "fire up his people" and "kids who are goofing around" can be phrased a little bit better.
- The comparison and contrast in the essay is weakened by the use of a conversational tone that sometimes includes slang.
- There are no spelling and grammar mistakes.
- The essay writer actually uses text references but no literary terms.
- There are basic transitional phrases ("also," "So," and "But," for example) used.

Practice—"Trees"

1. The correct answer is **A. "A tree."** Answer **B. "Grass"** is neither mentioned nor hinted at. Answer **C. "A mouth"** is part of the personified tree, and it's mentioned in line three and not line two. Answer **D. "Robins"** is wrong because they lived in the tree. Also, they're mentioned in line eight, not line two.
2. The correct answer is **C. "Get nourishment."** Answers **A. "Speak,"** **B. "Cry,"** and **D. "Yawn"** are incorrect because they're never mentioned. Answers **E. "Shelter the birds"** and **F. "Play with the rain"** do not relate to the metaphor of the "hungry mouth" of the tree.
3. Part A: The correct answers are **B. "Metaphor,"** **C. "Personification,"** and **D. "Alliteration"** because the tree is compared to a person with arms (metaphor and personification). Also, the "l" sound is repeated in the words "lifts" and "leafy." Answer **A. "Simile"** is incorrect because the comparison does not use "like" or "as." Answer **E. "Rhyme scheme"** is incorrect because this refers to the pattern of rhyming at the end of each poetic line.
   Part B: The correct answer is **F.** because the reader is using literary devices to imagine the tree as a real person.
4. The correct answer is **B. "A living form of shelter."** Answer **A. "A hungry predator"** is wrong since the tree is doing the opposite of preying by giving shelter. While some high-fashion models may wear creative hats, the tree is in no way serving in that capacity so Answer **C. "A fashion model"** is wrong. Answer **D. "The poet"** is wrong since he is not the tree.

5. The correct answers are C. "Trees are a beautiful part of nature" and G. "Trees can figuratively pray. This sentiment of Answer C. is reflected in the first two lines of the poem: "I think that I shall never see / A poem lovely as a tree." Answer G. is reflected in lines 5 and 6: "A tree that looks at God all day, And lifts her leafy arms to pray" since Kilmer is envisioning the tree's upward branches as a sign of prayer. Answer A. "Trees exhaust all the nutrients from the earth" is incorrect since lines 3 and 4 in the poem ("A tree whose hungry mouth is prest (pressed) / Against the earth's sweet flowing breast" do not address the concept of "exhaust(ing) the nutrients." Answer B. "Trees are nice until they have to be cut down" is never addressed. Answer D. "Trees are a beautiful part of nature, but they can be dangerous for birds" runs counter to the idea that the tree wears "A nest of robins in her hair." Answer E. "Trees like the snow, but they don't enjoy the rain because it washes away the soil" is wrong since the trees live "intimately...with rain." Answer F. "Trees think that Joyce Kilmer is foolish" has no evidence in the poem to support it.

Practice—Forest Trees of Wisconsin: How to Know Them

1. Part A: The correct answers are D. "Forests are communities, and trees are not" and F. "Trees and forests have different lifespans." These answers are contained in the Introduction: "Trees, like all living things, grow and mature and die while the forest, which is a community of trees, may live indefinitely because the trees reproduce before they die." Answers A. "Trees and forests are both communities," B. "Neither trees nor forests are communities," C. "Trees are communities, and forests are not," and E. "Trees and forests have the same lifespan" are not supported by the text.
Part B: The correct answer is D. "Compare and contrast" since the Introduction speaks of the differences between trees and the forest itself.
2. The statements that are true about vegetative reproduction: B. "Cuttings are used in vegetative reproduction" and F. "Most trees in the forest grow from seeds, not vegetative reproduction" are found in the second (Vegetative Reproduction) and the third (Reproduction by Seed) sections of the text. Statements A. "Seeds or nuts from the trees are used in vegetative reproduction," C. "All conifers reproduce vegetatively by sprouting," D. "Regardless of age, most conifers reproduce vegetatively by sprouting," and E. "Baldwin apple trees can grow from seeds and not from grafting" are statements that are not supported by the text: they state the opposite of the true facts.

3. The correct answers are A. "The acorn is considered to be a botanical fruit" and D. "The Lombardy poplar bears no staminate flowers since it was developed as a mutation." Answers B. "The corn plant reproduces vegetatively, not by seed" and C. "For trees like the ashes and the poplars, 'the female trees will not bear seed' unless there are pistillate trees 'in the vicinity'" are wrong because the opposite is true. Answer E. "The Lombardy poplar can reproduce both vegetatively and through the formation of seed" is wrong because it "is always reproduced vegetatively."

4. The correct answer is D. "Prevails." Answer A. "Grows" is wrong because the Norway or white pine can grow without flourishing. Answers B. "Simplifies" and C. "Explores" are wrong because they are not synonyms.

5. The correct answers are B. "After birds eat pin cherries, they "may drop the seed far from the parent tree" and thereby help to reforest areas "after forest fires," D. "Since the jack pine "protects its seeds from fire," it is a good reforestation tree "following a forest fire," and E. "The 'growing space' for trees has a direct effect on the 'form of trees.'" The first two answers (B. and D.) are supported in the Distribution of Seed section while answer E. is supported in the How Trees Grow section. Answer A. "Since seeds from the aspen "are very light and so perishable" and their "cottony down covers" make them easy to be "carried by the wind," they are able to reforest any area that is not "burned over" is incorrect since these trees are good at reforestation after a fire. Answers C. "Seeds of pine, maple and basswood have wings so that they are carried farther by wind, thereby hindering the reproduction process" and E. "When looking at 'the trees at the edge of the forest,' notice that the side that is 'towards the open' part of the forest is free of branches" are wrong since the opposite is true for both responses.

Sample Response 1/Essay for Poetic Devices

Joyce Kilmer's poem *Trees* and the informational text from the Wisconsin Division of Forestry clearly indicate the difference between poetry and prose. In *Trees*, Kilmer paints a heartfelt picture of the beauty of a tree when he mentions that it pales in comparison to a poem: "I think that I shall never see / A poem lovely as a tree." In contrast, the Wisconsin Division of Forestry makes a matter-of-fact statement about trees: "Trees, like all living things, grow and mature and die while the forest, which is a community of trees, may live indefinitely because the trees reproduce before they die." The soft, pleasant tone in Kilmer's piece is replaced by the naturally unemotional tone of "textbook" prose in the Division's piece.

While Kilmer creates his image of trees by using personification with phrases including "A hungry mouth," "leafy arms," and "hair," the Division's piece factually states that "some trees like basswood will sprout regardless of age," "the way the seeds are produced is the basis for classifying plants," and "Jack pine is especially interesting because it protects its seeds from fire." Both authors divide their work into smaller sections. Nonetheless, Kilmer's couplets are small packages of delicate thought while the Division's heading represent different characteristics of forest trees. It may have been possible for Kilmer to categorize each of his couplets. However, that would have taken away the rhythm and the flow of his poem. The Division's categories allow the reader to divide the information into more manageable pieces. Kilmer's poem is meant to inspire while the Division's prose is meant to inform.

This essay

- catches the reader's attention by directly addressing the prompt's statement that "Joyce Kilmer and the Wisconsin Division of Forestry had a different purpose in mind when writing about trees."
- The student contrasts Kilmer's "heartfelt picture" of the tree that "pales in comparison to a poem" with the Division's factual statements about the trees.
- Tone is contrasted with Kilmer's soft style running counter to the Division's unemotional prose.
- Citations are made directly from the text throughout both paragraphs: "A poem lovely as a tree" from Kilmer and "Trees...grow mature and die..." in the Division's work.
- There is good length to the essay. The paragraphs contain sufficient examples to support each point being raised.
- Academic vocabulary is evident throughout as the writer uses phrases including "heartfelt," "unemotional," "regardless," and "couplets."
- Transitions including "In contrast," "While," and "However" are used.
- There are no grammar or spelling mistakes.

Sample Response 2/Essay for Poetic Devices

Joyce Kilmer in *Trees* wrote a poem, but the guys in the Wisconsin Division didn't. Kilmer used poetry language like "hungry mouth" and "leafy arms." Nobody has leafy arms. Anyway, the Division uses phrases like "Cuttings from small branches" and "Seeds of pine, maple and basswood have wings." That last phrase actually sounds a little like poetry. Anyway, Kilmer gets all romantic while the Division is serious at all times.

Kilmer makes his tree sound like a human. That's personification. He says phrases like "A poem lovely as a tree." That's a simile! He also says "A tree that may in Summer wear / A nest of robins in her hair." That's personification. The Division doesn't do any of that. Besides, Kilmer's poem isn't a fable with a moral. It's a short statement with lots of description. But the Division writes stuff that might be in a textbook so they're not going to use poetry. That wouldn't make sense.

This essay
- shows that the prompt is weakly addressed.
- The contrast in the two styles of writing considers each style separately rather than in contrast.
- The language is much too casual, rather than academic: "Kilmer gets all romantic" rather than "Kilmer's images generate a sense of romanticism."
- The author makes some good points about the Division's unintended poetry: "Seeds of pine, maple and basswood have wings" and Kilmer's use of personification and simile.
- There are no spelling and grammar mistakes, but the use of phrases like "guys" and "stuff" are not appropriate in an academic piece.
- The essay writer actually uses text references, but these are not properly showcased in a mindful essay.
- There is an attempt to use transitional phrases ("Anyway" and "Besides," for example), but they need to be used in a stronger essay context.

Chapter 4

Practice—Things Had Really Changed

1. The correct answer is D. "All events are listed in sequence" since Answers A. "First, Jonathan had quickly written a note in his planner as he sat down at his desk," B. "Second, Jonathan "was assigned to cover the school's wrestling matches'," and C. "Third, Jonathan "had received the highest grade in the class on the last test" all follow the correct sequence.
2. The correct answer is A. "None." Answers B. "One," C. "Two," and D. "Five" do not appear in the text.

3. The correct answer is B. "He thought his friends wouldn't think he was 'cool'." Answer A. "His best friend had been thrown off the team" is not mentioned in the text. Answers C. "He thought Katie wouldn't think he was 'cool'," and D. "He thought his teachers wouldn't think he was 'cool'," are proven wrong by Answer A. "road" do not appear in the poem.
4. The correct answer is D. "The school newspaper." Answers A. "principal's newsletter" and B. "The parent-teacher's group's newsletter" are wrong because he writes for a newspaper, not a newsletter. Don't be fooled by Answer C. "The class newspaper." Even though Miss Rumson supported Jonathan, there is no mention of a class newspaper.

Suggestions for Essay for Details and Sequence of Events

You should mention that things in school "really began to change for Jonathan" after he had joined the school newspaper. Point out that when he began to study, "he received the second highest grade on Miss Rumson's test." Mention that the head cheerleader "Katie asked him if he would study with her for the next test." Explain that his friends didn't tease him for being on the school newspaper because the "older brother of one of his friends was on the team." Add that Miss Rumson had called Jonathan's mom to tell her "that he had received the highest grade in the class on the last test" and that she had recommended him to the editor of the local newspaper. Be sure to conclude by stating that through hard work, things in school indeed had "really began to change for Jonathan."

Practice—Vacation

1. The correct answer is C. "New Jersey Vacations for New Jersey Residents" since it reflects the **central idea or theme**. D. "Miss Rumson." Answers A. "My Vacation," B. "Where to Take a Vacation," and D. "Vacations for All Seasons" are incorrect because none of them mentions New Jersey.
2. The correct answer is B. "The New Jersey seashore has swimming, shopping, food, and more." Answer A. "It's hot at the seashore" is wrong because it's not the main point. Answer C. "All of the historic areas are located at the New Jersey seashore" is not true. Answer D. "The New Jersey seashore doesn't get many visitors in the winter" is not mentioned anywhere in the passage and is not a main point.
3. The correct answer is C. "There are swimming pools in many towns" because it is not included in the paragraph. Answers A. ""The Meadowlands Complex is the home of various professional sports teams," B. "There are eight different professional league parks for baseball" and D. "There are auto racetracks that sponsor NASCAR and NHRA races" are mentioned in the paragraph.

4. The correct answer is A. "The NJ Vietnam Veterans' Memorial is located near the Garden State Parkway." Answers B. "The Edison National Historic Site is located in West Orange," C. "The Fosterfields Living History Farm is located in Morris Plains," and D. "The C. A. Nothnagle Log House is located in Gibbstown" are all included as supporting details in the paragraph.

Essay for Central Idea or Theme

You should mention that as someone who lives in New Jersey, "you could take a vacation without leaving our state." Be sure that you include the mountains, the seashore, and the areas of sports and history" as vacation options. Also, mention some of the activities and places of interest in these areas.

Practice—My First Day of School

1. The correct answer is C. "Upset because there would be less freedom in school." This information contrasts the sentence "Since school had let out last June, I suddenly had a lot more freedom." Answer A. "Happy because the summer was boring" is incorrect because Pat was enjoying the summer. There is no evidence to support answer B. "Afraid because the school was in a different town." Answer D. "Excited to be with friends again" is wrong since Pat hung out with friends during the summer.
2. The correct answer is A. "Pat's mom would be right" since a mom's advice is usually good advice. Besides, Pat's mom was already making sure that Pat made it to school on time. Answer B. "Pat would be right" is incorrect because Pat is thinking about how much fun summer has been rather than how important it is to get ready for school. Answer C. "Pat's brother would be right" is not right because no mention is made of a brother. Answer D. "All of the above" is wrong, especially because it is disproved by Answer C. "Pat's brother would be right."
3. The correct answer is D. "All of the above." Answers A. "Pat's new clothes might be ruined," B. "Pat might get hurt and miss the first day of school," and C. "Pat might miss the bus" are concerns for Pat's mom. Remember, Pat's mom wakes Pat early because being late is " the way you (Pat) want to start out your school year, is it?"
4. The correct answer is C. "Eat a good breakfast" because Pat was hungry around 10 AM on the first day of school and "Lunch wasn't on my (Pat's) schedule until noon." Answer B. "Sleep late" is wrong because Pat won't sleep late until the weekend. Answer C. "Eat breakfast while wearing pajamas and sitting in front of the television" was possible only during the summer. Answer D. "Walk the dog" is wrong because there is no mention of a dog in the entire essay.

Suggestions for Essay for Questioning, Clarifying, and Predicting

You should mention the following:

- Pat's year will probably be a good one.
- Pat's mother cares because she wakes Pat up before the alarm rings. She reminds Pat to "Hurry up!" and not be late for the first day of school. She also says that being late would not be the way "to start out your (Pat's) school year."
- Having a caring parent or guardian is helpful for any student, especially one who doesn't eat enough breakfast on the first day of school.
- Pat seems to enjoy some classes and teachers.
- The only textbooks Pat has to carry home are for "math and public speaking."
- Pat thinks that social studies teacher "Mr. Barns is a great guy."
- "Gym was great because I (Pat) got to blow off a little steam."

Practice—A Letter to the Mayor

1. The correct answer is A. "Victoria Martinez wrote the letter to Mayor Patel." Answer B. "Victoria Martinez wrote the letter to her friends" is incorrect because Victoria talked about her friends but she didn't write them a letter. Answers C. "Mayor Patel wrote the letter to Victoria Martinez and her friends" and D. "Mayor Patel wrote the letter to Victoria Martinez" are wrong because Victoria wrote the letter.
2. The correct answer is A. "I believe that we should have a place in town …." The word believe is an opinion word. Answers B. "'… the building is closed'," C. "Mr. Ross used to volunteer his time on the weekends," and D. "Mr. Ross 'retired and moved to Florida'" are all facts that can be proven.
3. The correct answer is C. "… we go to the movies." Answers A. "The security guards are always chasing us away" and B. "… the security guards are mean to us" are Victoria's opinions. Answer D. "… large groups of teens cause trouble" is not always true and is therefore an opinion.
4. The correct answer is B. "… there were too many kids hanging out in the Maple Grove Shopping Center parking lot." Answers A. "'… we came to a town council meeting'," C. "'We asked 'for a teen center'," and D. "'…nine teenagers had been arrested for fighting during the last month'" are all facts that can be proven.

Suggestions for Essay for Fact vs. Opinion

You should mention the following:

- Victoria is giving an opinion.
- Her promise that "there wouldn't be any more trouble in town" can't be guaranteed because she doesn't control the behavior of all the teens in town.
- Her statement that "we'd be off the streets" is an opinion for the same reason.
- Victoria's statement that she and the teens in town would "all want to be with our friends" is her perception rather than fact.

Practice—Guided-Reading Book Report, Choice Fiction

1. The correct answer is B. "Free Choice Fiction." Answer A. "Free Choice" is incorrect because the word "Fiction" is not included. Answers C. "Free Choice Non-fiction" and D. "Free Choice Biography" are wrong. Even though they contain the phrase "Free Choice," the genres (types) are wrong.
2. The correct answer is D. "Return your book permission slip to Mr. Rhoades by February 26." Answer A. "Find a friend who also wants to read the same book" is wrong because it is the step before, not after, the second one. Answers B. "Ask a parent/guardian to help you to select a book" and C. "Have your partner sign your book permission slip" are not part of the list of steps.
3. The correct answer is C. "Your parent/guardian's signature." Answers A. "Your name," B. "Your reading partner's name," and D. "The title and author of the book that you and your partner are reading" all need to be included in the reading log.
4. The correct answer is C. "Two 'C' grades." Answer A. "Two 'A+' grades" is assigned for the completion of all three sections, not two. Answer B. "Two 'C+' grades" is not a grade option. Answer D. "Two 'D' grades" is assigned if only one section is completed.

Suggestions for Essay for Following Directions

You should mention the following:

- The student and his/her partner meet "for no more than 20 minutes with another pair of students who are reading a different book."
- One student "will serve as a group facilitator who will keep the discussion 'on track'."
- A recorder will also be chosen to "take notes that will be signed by all group members and submitted to Mr. Rhoades."

Practice—Professional Sports Broadcasting, My Dream Job

1. The correct answer is C. "Phil's dream to be a professional sports announcer." Answers A. "Free Choice" is incorrect because the word "Fiction" is not included. Answers C. "Free Choice Non-fiction" and D. "Free Choice Biography" are wrong. Even though they contain the phrase "Free Choice," the genres (types) are wrong.
2. The correct answer is A. "Autobiographical" because it is written by Philip about himself. Answer B. "Biographical" is incorrect because someone else didn't write about Philip's life. Answer C. "Fictional" is incorrect because the information is factual. Answer D. "Poetic" is wrong because the structure does not follow poetic structure.
3. The correct answer is D. "The books feature sportscasters who never cared about playing the game." Answers A. "The sportscasters enjoy sports," B. "The sportscasters received training before they began to broadcast," and C. "The sportscasters enjoy working with people" are all traits of successful sportscasters.
4. The correct answer is B. "A school literary magazine." Answer A. "A professional broadcasting magazine" is not possible since the piece would not have enough interest for a professional audience. Answer C. "A university literary magazine" is not the place a seventh grader's essay would be published. Answer D. "A national weekly sports magazine" is wrong for the same reason.

Suggestions for Essay for Recognizing Literary Forms and Informational Sources

You should mention the following:

- A short story could be fictional, but that is an option.
- There needs to be at least one main character who's facing a conflict.
- This conflict needs to be resolved.
- There will be a theme (main idea), which may actually teach a lesson.

Practice—Guidelines for Making a Class Presentation

1. The correct answer is D. "Conjugating Verbs" since it was not included in the list. Answers A. "Transitive Verbs," B. "Intransitive and Linking Verbs," and C. "Helping (Auxiliary) Verbs" are all part of the list.
2. The correct answer is B. "Movie Screen" because slides are shown on a screen. Answer A. "Audio Headset" is incorrect because it is not necessary. Answers C. "Spiral Notebook" and D. "Chalk Eraser" are wrong because they have no direct use for a computer slide show.

3. The correct answer is C. "The student will receive a lower grade." Answer A. "No one will notice since the information is the most important part of the presentation" is wrong since Miss Ostrovsky has said that "your information and the way you present it are both important." There is neither evidence nor prior knowledge to lead one to conclude that answers B. "Miss Ostrovsky will give the student one more chance to do better" and D. "The student will receive a detention" are anything but incorrect.

4. The correct answer is D. "She understands that teaching with media helps to improve learning." Answer A. "She just bought a new computer" is wrong because the entire class could not complete their projects by using only Miss Ostrovsky's computer. Answer B. "She's punishing the students for misbehaving" is incorrect because this lesson is designed to help the students with their learning. Answer C. "She's going on maternity leave" is wrong because there is no connection between the assignment and a maternity leave.

Suggestions for Essay on Finding Information and Answering with Prior Knowledge

You should mention the following:

- The definitions of the verb concepts being covered will give the students the basic information they will need to understand the concepts.
- The rules will help the students to learn the right way to use the concepts.
- The use of examples will provide the students with the chance to practice the concepts.
- Looking at exceptions will help the students to avoid making mistakes in the future.

Chapter 5

Practice—Number, Case, and Gender

Number

1. Are
My Friend and I <u>Is</u> Going to the Video Game Store

After school today, my friend Sam and I don't plan to go straight home. Instead,

2. *plan*   3. *are*

we <u>plans</u> to go to the video game store. We <u>is</u> going to walk down Main Street and then turn right on Maple Avenue. There are three new games being released today, and we're going to be at the store to try them out.

Explanation
1. The subject "My friend and I" is plural so the verb must also be plural: "**Are**."
2. The subject "we" is plural so the verb must also be plural: "**plan**."
3. Again, the subject "we" is plural so the verb must also be plural: "**are**."

Case

Our Test Review Was a Game!

Mr. Bogosian tried something new in class today: he played a review game to

1. *us*   2. *We*

give <u>we</u> a chance to get ready for our test. <u>Us</u> kids actually had fun playing the

3. *him*

game. Francisco answered the most questions so we clapped for <u>he</u>. Even so, we were the real winners since more than half of us earned our best test score of the year.

Explanation
1. The object pronoun "**us**" is correct since it is the indirect object.
2. The subject pronoun "**We**" is correct since it is used in the subject position.
3. The object pronoun "**him**" is correct since it is the object of the preposition "**for**."

Part A: Gender
1. Mrs. Cairo asked Mary to pick up (**her**, its) books.
2. Jackson took (**his**, its) brother to the movies.
3. The table can hold (her, **its**) own weight.

Explanation
1. The correct answer is **"her"** since Mary is a girl.
2. The correct answer is **"his"** since Jackson is a boy.
3. The correct answer is **"its"** since the table is neuter: neither a girl nor a boy.

Practice—Misplaced Modifiers
Part A
1. A suggested answer is **"In her desk, Savannah found a lady's blue bracelet."** The bracelet is blue, not the lady.
2. A suggested answer is **"I once met a one-armed man named Rashawn."** The man is named Rashawn, not his arm.
3. A suggested answer is **"I heard on the evening news that the burglar has been captured."** The evening news is the place where the news was heard, not the location where the capture took place.

Practice—Voice
Part B
1. A suggested answer is **"Students filled every desk in the library yesterday."** The students do the action in an active voice sentence.
2. A suggested answer is **"At my favorite ice cream store, the new owner prepared my sundae."** The new owner is doing the action.
3. A suggested answer is **"My parents scolded me when I didn't do all my chores yesterday."** The parents are doing the scolding.

Practice—Sentence Variety
The following is one sample of the way this paragraph could have used more sentence variety.

Getting in Trouble

<u>1.</u> <u>2.</u>
Yesterday I unexpectedly got into some trouble. My friends and I forgot our
<u>3.</u>
manners, and we cut across our neighbor's lawn. He became very upset, and then
<u>4.</u> <u>5.</u>
he started yelling at us. We tried to explain to him that we weren't hurting anything.
<u>6.</u>
He said that somebody stole his lawn chair as a prank. Now he's blaming us, even
<u>7.</u>
though we're innocent. I guess we shouldn't have walked on his lawn.

Explanation

1. Change the position of the adverb **"Yesterday"** and add the word **"unexpectedly."**
2. Change the sentence to a compound sentence.
3. Combine the next two sentences into a compound sentence.
4. Change the simple sentence into a complex one ("… that we weren't hurting anything" can't stand alone as a sentence because of the word **"that."**)
5. No change was made.
6. Combine the next two sentences to make a complex sentence.
7. No change was made.

(Remember that these changes are suggestions. Your answers may be different.)

Practice—Fragments and Run-ons

Fragments

1. A suggested answer is "My cousin and I walked through the park."
2. A suggested answer is "My best friend from Vineland is visiting me today."
3. A suggested answer is "Exercising every morning keeps me in shape."

Run-ons

1. A suggested answer is "Come to my birthday party because it will be fun."
2. A suggested answer is "Because I'm doing my homework now, I can't talk to you."
3. A suggested answer is "I'll take out the trash, and then I'll walk the dog."

Practice—Punctuation with Commas and End Marks

Commas

1. I had a hamburger, and you had pizza.
2. My mom asked me to go to the store, mail a letter, and put my dirty clothes in the wash.
3. Because I earned all "A's" and "B's" on my report card, I'm getting a reward.
4. We moved to New Jersey from Springfield, Ohio.
5. "Sincerely yours, Allen" is the ending I used for my letter.
6. No, I won't make fun of the new student in our class.
7. The winner of the fund raising challenge was Nicole, a student from my class.

Punctuating Sentences

1. I just won a million dollars! (Exclamatory Sentence)
2. Please take care of yourself. (Imperative Sentence)
3. Did you eat the last piece of cake? (Interrogative Sentence)
4. The class project will be due on March 3. (Declarative Sentence)

Practice—Homophones and Homographs

Homophones

Part A
1. The correct answer is **"sew,"** which means to use "a needle and thread to join together cloth or other similar material. The homonym **"so"** means "thus" or "therefore."
2. The correct answer is **"They're,"** which is the contraction of "They are." **"Their"** is a pronoun showing ownership by more than one person, and **"There"** refers to a direction that is usually not close by.
3. The correct answer is **"to,"** which is a preposition usually meaning a direction. **"Too"** means "also," and **"Two"** is the number following one.
4. The correct answer is **"hear,"** which means receiving communication through the ear. **"Here"** means a nearby location.
5. The correct answer is **"flower,"** which is the blossom of a plant. **"Flour"** is grain that is very finely milled (ground).

Homographs

Part A
1. The correct answer is B. "The covering of a tree."
2. The correct answer is A. "Not heavy."
3. The correct answer is A. "Admirer."
4. The correct answer is B. "Skin cut."
5. The correct answer is B. "Happening in the present time."

Practice—Grammar Demons

Unusual Order

Part A
1. The correct answer is **"are"** since the subject is **"tickets."**
2. The correct answer is **"is"** since the subject is **"outfit."**
3. The correct answer is **"is"** since the subject is **"rip."**
4. The correct answer is **"are"** since the subject is **"gloves."**

Adjective or Adverb

Part A
1. The correct answer is **"good"** since this adjective modifies the noun **"meal."**
2. The correct answer is **"well"** since we are referring to health.

Answers and Explanations for Practice Exercises, Chapters 1–5 • 273

3. The correct answer is **"bad"** since this adjective modifies the noun **"meal."**
4. The correct answer is **"badly"** since this adverb modifies the verb **"performed."**
5. The correct answer is **"really"** since this adverb modifies the adjective **"good."**
6. The correct answer is **"real"** since this predicate adjective follows the linking verb **"is"** and modifies the subject **"wish."**

Quotations

1. The correct answer is: The principal said over the intercom, "Students, please report to the cafeteria at the end of second period today."
2. The correct answer is: "Write your homework assignment in your notebooks,"said Mrs. Hudson.
3. The correct answer is: "Are we there yet?" said my brother after every five minutes of our trip.
4. The correct answer is: "Should we go to the park?" said Carrie, "or should we go to ball field?"
5. The correct answer is: I answered, "We should go to the park. They're having a special program there. Besides, all our friends will be there too."
6. The correct answer is: "That's sounds great!" said Carrie.

Underlining or Quotation Marks

Part A

1. The correct answer is: My sister is reading <u>Great Expectations</u>, a novel by Charles Dickens.
2. The correct answer is: In class we read "Dream Deferred," a poem by Langston Hughes.
3. The correct answer is: Before the play-off game, we stood and took off our caps as the loudspeakers played "God Bless America."
4. The correct answer is: In class today, Mr. Porter read an article from <u>The New York Times</u>.

Practice—Spelling Demons

Part A

1. The correct answer is "If you don't bring a note to excuse your absence from school, you'll get a detention."
2. The correct answer is "Let's buy some balloons for our party."
3. The correct answer is "I am assigned the job of changing the date on the class calendar."
4. The correct answer is "The month after January is February."
5. The correct answer is "Do we have any grammar homework tonight?"

6. The correct answer is "Oops, my shoelaces are loose."
7. The correct answer is "Our town's parade occurred last weekend."
8. The correct answer is "Mom asked me to get the butter for the mashed potatoes."
9. The correct answer is "Our music class is studying rhythm and blues artists from the 1970s."
10. The correct answer is "I used the vacuum to pick up the dirt that spilled on the rug."

Practice Test—Performance-Based Assessment

CHAPTER 6

> **Please note:** We have included additional questions to the Performance-Based Assessment for extra practice.

Argumentative Writing Task (Analysis of Argument)

In this section, you'll be asked to write argumentatively.

Imagine that your school has been chosen to become an online school. Your classes will be offered through the Internet right on the laptop computer that the school will provide for you. You will be expected to log on to your classes and spend a certain amount of time doing research on the Internet. Chat rooms, blogs, and e-mails will be common ways to communicate. You will never have to leave your home to attend a class.

Write a letter to your principal and explain whether or not you think this idea is a good one.

Speculative Writing Task (Narrative Writing)

You are visiting an amusement park and getting ready to board one of the exciting rides. You are with a family member or friend. Think about which exciting ride you might be getting ready to board. Write a story based on this event.

Literary Analysis Task

In this section, you'll be asked to read a literary passage and then answer questions.

"Mother to Son"
by Langston Hughes

Well, son, I'll tell you:
Life for me ain't been no crystal stair.
It's had tacks in it,
And splinters,
(5) And boards torn up,
And places with no carpet on the floor—Bare.
But all the time
I'se been a-climbin' on,
And reachin' landin's,
(10) And turnin' corners,
And sometimes goin' in the dark
Where there ain't been no light.
So boy, don't you turn back.
Don't you set down on the steps
(15) 'Cause you finds it's kinder hard.
Don't you fall now—
For I'se still goin', honey,
I'se still climbin',
And life for me ain't been no crystal stair.

1. When the son's mother tells him in line 2 that "life for me ain't been no crystal stair," she means that:

    - A. She has lived her life on the ground floor of her house.
    - B. She is someone who has always desired stairs made from crystal.
    - C. She is poor and cannot afford an easy life of luxury.
    - D. She is a maid who is forced to clean up "tacks" and "splinters."

2. Select the words listed below that describe the actions of the mother when she says in lines 8–10 that she's, "a climbin' on,/ And reachin' landin's,/ And turnin' corners" and drag them into the boxes.

   A. Persevering. [   ]

   B. Resigned. [   ]

   C. Incoherent. [   ]

   D. Determined. [   ]

   E. Agnostic [   ]

3. In lines 11–12 when the mother speaks of "sometimes goin' in the dark/Where there ain't been no light," she is speaking of:

   ○ A. Her home without electricity.
   ○ B. Her job in the evening when it is dark.
   ○ C. Her boredom with her life and desire for the excitement that the night life has.
   ○ D. Her being forced to live a difficult life.

4. In lines 14–15 the mother tells her son, "Don't you set down on the steps / 'Cause you finds it's kinder hard." She means that since life is hard, the son should:
   ○ A. Just give up now and avoid the inevitable disappointment.
   ○ B. Keep trying and don't quit.
   ○ C. Life is unpredictable, and there is no formula for success.
   ○ D. Even though you may try your best, there is little hope for success in this cruel world.

5. In lines 16–18 the mother says, "Don't you fall now—/For I'se still goin', honey, / I'se still climbin', And life for me ain't been no crystal stair" because she is trying to _____ her point to her son.

   ☐ A. reinforce
   ☐ B. undermine
   ☐ C. underscore
   ☐ D. intimidate
   ☐ E. improvise

The Ant and the Grasshopper
by Aesop

In a field one summer's day a Grasshopper was hopping about, chirping and singing to its heart's content. An Ant passed by, bearing along with great toil an ear of corn he was taking to the nest.

(5) "Why not come and chat with me," said the Grasshopper, "instead of toiling and moiling in that way?"

"I am helping to lay up food for the winter," said the Ant, "and recommend you to do the same."

"Why bother about winter?" said the Grasshopper; we have plenty of food at present." But the Ant went on its way and continued its toil. When the (10) winter came the Grasshopper had no food and found itself dying of hunger, while it saw the ants distributing every day corn and grain from the stores they had collected in the summer. Then the Grasshopper knew:

It is best to prepare for the days of necessity.

Source: http://www.bartleby.com/17/1/36.html

6. Which of these statements is *not* part of the plot?
   - A. The Grasshopper was hopping in a field.
   - B. The Grasshopper met the Ant.
   - C. The Grasshopper helped the Ant.
   - D. The Ant stored food for the winter.

7. Who are the main characters in the fable?
   - A. The Ant and the Grasshopper.
   - B. The Ant and the other ants.
   - C. The Grasshopper and the other ants.
   - D. The Grasshopper, the Ant, the other ants, and the ear of corn.

8. Which of the following words best describes the traits of the Grasshopper? Select all the correct statements.

- ☐ A. The Grasshopper has exactly the same traits as those of the Ant.
- ☐ B. The Grasshopper has different traits from those of the Ant.
- ☐ C. The Grasshopper is conscientious.
- ☐ D. The Grasshopper is somber and disillusioned.
- ☐ E. The Grasshopper does not agree with the Ant about the actions they both should be taking in the summer.
- ☐ F. The Grasshopper believes throughout the fable that his idea of chirping and singing throughout the summer is a smart one.

9. Part A: Select which of the following are settings in the fable, "The Ant and the Grasshopper."

- ☐ A. A field in the spring
- ☐ B. A barn in the spring
- ☐ C. A field in the summer
- ☐ D. A nest in the summer
- ☐ E. A barn in the summer
- ☐ F. A nest in the fall
- ☐ G. A barn in the fall
- ☐ H. A field in the winter
- ☐ J. A nest in the winter

Part B: Select the following statements that best describe the reason for Aesop's choice of settings in Part A.

- ☐ A. He wanted to add a lot of description, and using more than one setting gave him that opportunity.
- ☐ B. He wanted to develop his characters fully with extensive conflicts.
- ☐ C. He wanted to use humor to clarify his point.
- ☐ D. He wanted to extend the length of his fable.
- ☐ E. He wanted to connect the actions of the main characters to the differences of the seasons.
- ☐ F. He wanted to use the idea of careless behavior to make his point.

10. During the summer, what did the ants store?

- ○ A. bread
- ○ B. milk
- ○ C. corn
- ○ D. hay

11. Which of these would be the best theme for this fable?

    ○ A. Always plan ahead.
    ○ B. Cheaters never prosper.
    ○ C. Take life one day at a time.
    ○ D. Always tell the truth.

12. Which of the following were effects of the Grasshopper not listening to the Ant's advice?

    ☐ A. The Grasshopper and the Ant became bitter enemies.
    ☐ B. The Grasshopper lost its sight.
    ☐ C. The Grasshopper and the Ant became friends.
    ☐ D. The Grasshopper was dying of hunger.
    ☐ E. The Grasshopper declared war on the Ant.
    ☐ F. The Ant stored food for the winter.
    ☐ G. The Grasshopper realized that he was wrong not to store food in the summer.
    ☐ H. The Grasshopper was saved when the Ant invited the Grasshopper to spend the winter with the other ants.

13. Select all of the statements that are true about the point of view in this fable.

    ☐ A. It is told in the first person.
    ☐ B. It is told in the second person.
    ☐ C. It is told in the third person.
    ☐ D. The narrator is the Ant.
    ☐ E. The narrator is the Grasshopper.
    ☐ F. The narrator is omniscient.
    ☐ G. The narrator is antagonistic.
    ☐ H. The narrator is neutral and does not take sides.

Getting Ready for Winter: My Three "Musts"
J.C. Mann

Summertime is a time when the cold temperatures of winter seem like distant memories. The gentle breezes, the warming sun rays, and the temperatures well above freezing serve to provide comfort and a welcomed escape from the harsh realities of winter.

(5) Nonetheless, when the days of summer begin to become shorter and the temperatures begin to fall, the reality of the approach of winter becomes quite clear. At that point in time, it is wise to begin to prepare for the harshness of winter. Not to do so would be a grave mistake. I believe that as winter approaches, there are three "musts" for all my friends and me.

(10) First of all, we must make sure that our winter clothing is prepared to be worn again. Some items like wool sweaters and corduroy jackets usually need to be taken to the cleaners to be refreshed. Other clothing may need to be washed and dried, according to the individual needs of the fabrics or materials. If we wash our clothing, fold it neatly, and put it away in a moth-
(15) proof container, then the amount of ironing and freshening needed before wearing our clothing next summer will be minimal.

Additionally, we must consider the family lawnmower. It is a good idea to drain out all the gasoline before moving the mower to a safe storage place like a shed or garage. The mower should also be run for a short time since
(20) this will ensure that the gasoline in the fuel lines is fully drained. Otherwise, condensation may occur when the gasoline is stored for a long time. The result is usually a gas line that has frozen ice crystals and possibly water in both the gas lines and tank. If the fuel is not going to be drained, then a fuel stabilizer should be added to prevent condensation.

(25) Finally, we need to store all our summer sports equipment properly. Our roller blades need to have the leather cleaned and treated, the laces replaced, and the blades checked for excess wear and maybe repaired. Our baseball gloves need to be cleaned with a gentle leather cleaner and treated with a good preservative. Our basketball should be deflated, cleaned off, and put
(30) away for the following summer. If we plan on using the basketball on an indoor court during the winter, then we should clean it with an appropriate cleaning agent and check it for excess wear. Any other sports equipment, clothing, or footwear should be stored in appropriately as instructed by the manufacturers.

(35)   If we take the time to treat our clothing, our lawnmowers, and our summer sports equipment properly, then we shall get many years of enjoyment from them. Should we choose to take the easy way out and just toss everything into a pile and worry about the items the following summer, then we are designing a plan for disappointment. A little bit of effort can go a long way
(40)   in helping us to keep our seasonal clothing and equipment in great shape.

14. What organizational pattern is used for Mann's essay?

- A. Chronological
- B. Problem/Solution
- C. Cause and Effect
- D. Compare and Contrast

15. **Part A:** Select which statements are true about Mann's essay.

- A. Mann loathes winter.
- B. Mann prefers summer to any season.
- C. Mann is conscientious about his possessions.
- D. Mann takes a laissez-faire attitude toward his possessions.
- E. Mann believes that planning for the future is overrated.
- F. Mann believes that planning ahead is a smart thing to do.

Part B: Given your answers to Part A, with which ones below do Part A's correct answers match with Aesop's fable?

- A. Kindness overcomes all obstacles.
- B. Good planning leads to good results.
- C. Don't wait until the last minute to take action.
- D. Always keep a calendar handy and follow it.
- E. No one should take advantage of another.
- F. If you see someone in need, then lend them a hand.
- G. Honesty is the best policy.

16. Which of the following statements are true of both J.C. Mann and Aesop's Ant? Drag the correct statements and drop them in the boxes below.

    A. They are both careful planners.
    B. They are both respected in their communities.
    C. They both belong to local civic organizations.
    D. They both begin their planning and preparation well in advance.
    E. They both gather a cadre of helpers to assist them with their plans.
    F. They both have doubts that their actions are appropriate, but they overcome these and are successful.

    [ ]

    [ ]

    [ ]

    [ ]

    [ ]

    [ ]

17. The term *condensation* in line 21 refers to:

    ○ A. animal infestation.
    ○ B. dry rotting.
    ○ C. fissures.
    ○ D. moisture build-up.

18. Which of the following statements apply to both passages?

    ☐ A. Aesop and Mann are contemporaries, and the experiences they have written about come from the same era.
    ☐ B. Both Aesop and Mann advocate the benefit of good planning.
    ☐ C. While Aesop's advice deals mainly with nutritional considerations, Mann's advice focuses on possessions.
    ☐ D. Mann has decided not to use a fable to make his point because he believes that writing a fable is equal to "designing a plan for disappointment." (line 39)
    ☐ E. Mann has learned his lesson from his own frivolous behavior and has therefore decided to advise people about the best way to prepare for winter.

19. Select all of the statements that are accurate.

- ☐ A. Aesop and Mann are angry with those who do not take the time to plan.
- ☐ B. Aesop would have written a longer piece if he had known more about the behavior of grasshoppers.
- ☐ C. Mann wrote an informational piece because his audience would not understand fables.
- ☐ D. The advice each author gives is based on evidence from his writing.
- ☐ E. Both Aesop and Mann are advocates with a clearly-stated position.
- ☐ F. Neither Aesop nor Mann has ever taken the advice being given in his passage.

Language Usage Task

Read the following passage and answer the questions by looking at the highlighted text below the corresponding letters.

               A   B   C   D

1. At the *beginning* of *the* school year, *my teachers* met with all of us *students*

     E   F   G

from *the* play we *had* staged during *the* previous school year. 2. *I was hoping* to get

a principal part in the cast this year, and I told my best friend Emma about my wish.

3. *Because she was not interested in the play, she shrugged her shoulders and she wished me luck.* 4. Undaunted, *I became more excited* as the time for rehearsals neared. 5. *Listening carefully, I knew that I was being challenged.* 6. I wanted to make sure that *I didn't miss one thing* that our director Miss Skyler said as she explained the parts. 7. If I tried my best during rehearsals, then I could possibly earn a principal part in the *play.* 8. *Wondering about my chances, I hoped for the best.* 9. When Miss Skyler mentioned that *the* lead role required good dancing skills, I became excited since I have been taking dance lessons for four years.

20. Which of the following phrases are prepositional phrases?

   ☐ A. *At the beginning*
   ☐ B. *of the school year*
   ☐ C. *my teachers met*
   ☐ D. *students*
   ☐ E. *from the play*
   ☐ F. *we had staged*
   ☐ G. *during the previous*

21. Which of the following answers are contained in the phrase "*I was hoping*"?

   ☐ A. Subject verb
   ☐ B. Direct object
   ☐ C. Helping verb
   ☐ D. Indirect object
   ☐ E. Conjunction
   ☐ F. Main verb

22. **Part A:** What type of phrase is the word *play* in the passage a part of?

   ○ A. Object of the preposition
   ○ B. Direct object
   ○ C. Indirect object
   ○ D. Subject

   Part B: Select similar phrase(s) to the one in which *play* is contained to support the answer to Part A.

   ☐ A. "If I tried"
   ☐ B. "I tried my best"
   ☐ C. "during rehearsals"
   ☐ D. "then I could"
   ☐ E. "I could possibly earn"
   ☐ F. "a principal part"

23. Select the two words below that are adjectives in sentence 9. Drag and drop them into the boxes.

- A. "When"
- B. "Miss Skyler"
- C. "the"
- D. "good"
- E. "became"
- F. "dance"

Research Simulation Task

Today you will read the following texts and view the following video: *The Highwayman* by Alfred Noyes, *Highwaymen—Romantic Heroes or Common Criminals?* by Jeremiah Justice, Professional video recording called "The Highway Man." After you read the passages and answer the questions, you will write an essay that compares and contrasts each text.

The Highwayman
By Alfred Noyes
Part One

The wind was a torrent of darkness among the gusty trees.
The moon was a ghostly galleon tossed upon cloudy seas.
The road was a ribbon of moonlight over the purple moor,
And the highwayman came riding—
(5)   Riding—riding—
The highwayman came riding, up to the old inn-door.

He'd a French cocked-hat on his forehead, a bunch of lace at his chin,
A coat of the claret velvet, and breeches of brown doe-skin.
They fitted with never a wrinkle. His boots were up to the thigh.
(10) And he rode with a jewelled twinkle,
    His pistol butts a-twinkle,
His rapier hilt a-twinkle, under the jewelled sky.

Over the cobbles he clattered and clashed in the dark inn-yard.
He tapped with his whip on the shutters, but all was locked and barred.
(15) He whistled a tune to the window, and who should be waiting there
But the landlord's black-eyed daughter,
    Bess, the landlord's daughter,
Plaiting a dark red love-knot into her long black hair.

And dark in the dark old inn-yard a stable-wicket creaked
(20) Where Tim the ostler listened. His face was white and peaked.
His eyes were hollows of madness, his hair like mouldy hay,
But he loved the landlord's daughter,
    The landlord's red-lipped daughter.
Dumb as a dog he listened, and he heard the robber say—

(25) "One kiss, my bonny sweetheart, I'm after a prize to-night,
But I shall be back with the yellow gold before the morning light;
Yet, if they press me sharply, and harry me through the day,
Then look for me by moonlight,
    Watch for me by moonlight,
(30) I'll come to thee by moonlight, though hell should bar the way."

He rose upright in the stirrups. He scarce could reach her hand,
But she loosened her hair in the casement. His face burnt like a brand
As the black cascade of perfume came tumbling over his breast;
And he kissed its waves in the moonlight,
(35)   (O, sweet black waves in the moonlight!)
Then he tugged at his rein in the moonlight, and galloped away to the west.

Part Two

He did not come in the dawning. He did not come at noon;
And out of the tawny sunset, before the rise of the moon,
When the road was a gypsy's ribbon, looping the purple moor,
A red-coat troop came marching—
(40)   Marching—marching—
King George's men came marching, up to the old inn-door.

They said no word to the landlord. They drank his ale instead.
But they gagged his daughter, and bound her, to the foot of her narrow bed.
(45) Two of them knelt at her casement, with muskets at their side!
There was death at every window;
    And hell at one dark window;
For Bess could see, through her casement, the road that *he* would ride.

They had tied her up to attention, with many a sniggering jest.
(50) They had bound a musket beside her, with the muzzle beneath her breast!

"Now, keep good watch!" and they kissed her. She heard the doomed
   man say—
Look for me by moonlight;
    Watch for me by moonlight;
I'll come to thee by moonlight, though hell should bar the way!

(55) She twisted her hands behind her; but all the knots held good!
She writhed her hands till her fingers were wet with sweat or blood!
They stretched and strained in the darkness, and the hours crawled by
   like years
Till, now, on the stroke of midnight,
    Cold, on the stroke of midnight,
(60) The tip of one finger touched it! The trigger at least was hers!

The tip of one finger touched it. She strove no more for the rest.
Up, she stood up to attention, with the muzzle beneath her breast.
She would not risk their hearing; she would not strive again;
For the road lay bare in the moonlight;
(65)   Blank and bare in the moonlight;
And the blood of her veins, in the moonlight, throbbed to her love's refrain.

Tlot-tlot; tlot-tlot! Had they heard it? The horsehoofs ringing clear;
Tlot-tlot; tlot-tlot, in the distance? Were they deaf that they did not hear?
Down the ribbon of moonlight, over the brow of the hill,
(70) The highwayman came riding—
    Riding—riding—
The red coats looked to their priming! She stood up, straight and still.

Tlot-tlot, in the frosty silence! *Tlot-tlot,* in the echoing night!
Nearer he came and nearer. Her face was like a light.
(75) Her eyes grew wide for a moment; she drew one last deep breath,
Then her finger moved in the moonlight,
    Her musket shattered the moonlight,
Shattered her breast in the moonlight and warned him—with her death.

He turned. He spurred to the west; he did not know who stood
(80) Bowed, with her head o'er the musket, drenched with her own blood!
Not till the dawn he heard it, and his face grew grey to hear

How Bess, the landlord's daughter,
    The landlord's black-eyed daughter,
Had watched for her love in the moonlight, and died in the darkness there.

(85) Back, he spurred like a madman, shouting a curse to the sky,
With the white road smoking behind him and his rapier brandished high.
Blood red were his spurs in the golden noon; wine-red was his velvet coat;
When they shot him down on the highway,
    Down like a dog on the highway,
(90) And he lay in his blood on the highway, with a bunch of lace at his throat.

. . .

And still of a winter's night, they say, when the wind is in the trees,
When the moon is a ghostly galleon tossed upon cloudy seas,
When the road is a ribbon of moonlight over the purple moor,
A highwayman comes riding—
    Riding—riding—
(95) *A highwayman comes riding, up to the old inn-door.*

Over the cobbles he clatters and clangs in the dark inn-yard.
He taps with his whip on the shutters, but all is locked and barred.
He whistles a tune to the window, and who should be waiting there
(100) *But the landlord's black-eyed daughter,*
    Bess, the landlord's daughter,
Plaiting a dark red love-knot into her long black hair.

24. **Part A:** In line 2, Alfred Noyes mentions a "ghostly galleon." The use of this phrase indicates which of the literary devices listed below?

   ○ A. Onomatopoeia
   ○ B. Alliteration
   ○ C. Hyperbole
   ○ D. Compositional Risk

Part B: Which of the following choices is also an example of the literary device correctly mentioned in Part A?

- A. "His rapier hilt a-twinkle" (line 12)
- B. "Plaiting a dark red love-knot" (line 18)
- C. "His eyes were hollows of madness" (line 21)
- D. "his hair like mouldy hay" (line 21)

25. **Part A:** In line 20, "Tim the ostler listened" to the conversation between the highwayman and Bess, the landlord's daughter. Why did Tim's face become "white and peaked"?

    - A. Tim always wanted to be a highwayman, and this was his chance to make his dream come true.
    - B. Tim was Bess's cousin, and he had promised his aunt to keep her out of danger.
    - C. Tim was also in love with Bess, but he didn't have the flair that the highwayman had.
    - D. Tim was a member of the king's army, and he was preparing to arrest the highwayman.

    Part B: Select the phrase that supports the response from Part A.

    - A. "Tim the ostler listened." (line 20)
    - B. "His eyes were hollows of madness" (line 21)
    - C. "his hair like mouldy hay" (line 21)
    - D. "he heard the robber say" (line 24)

26. **Part A:** Which one of the following could serve as an alternate title to "The Highwayman"?

    - A. "True Love Never Ends Well"
    - B. "Never Be Kind to Strangers"
    - C. "True Love Knows No Boundaries"
    - D. "Every Man for Himself

Part B: Which of the following lines supports the alternative title?

- A. "Over the cobbles he clattered and clashed in the dark inn-yard." (line 13)
- B. "Then he tugged at his rein in the moonlight, and galloped away to the west. (line 36)
- C. "The tip of one finger touched it! The trigger at least was hers!" (line 60)
- D. "Back, he spurred like a madman, shouting a curse to the sky." (line 85)

Highwaymen—Romantic Heroes or Common Criminals?

Jeremiah Justice

Overview

Much has been written over the years about the highwaymen of the past. Some were portrayed as free-spirited rogues who were the anti-heroes of their times. They rode on horses and robbed from travelers, who were mostly on foot. These disadvantaged travelers had no choice but to succumb to the (5) will of the swift and unprovoked attacks of these scoundrels on horseback.

Historical Eras

When did these highwaymen parlay their "talents" into unearned riches? Highwaymen were said to be roaming the countryside and wreaking their havoc on unsuspecting travelers from Elizabethan times until the beginning of the 1800s. Sometimes known as common thieves and brigands, (10) these scoundrels were also known by more euphemistic names including "knights of the road" and "gentlemen of the road." Phrases used by these highwaymen included "Stand and deliver" and "Your money or your life." Although some worked alone, many highwaymen worked in gangs so it was easier to intimidate their victims. The highwaymen would prowl the less-(15) travelled areas of roads leading from London since those negotiating these roads were often men of means. Most importantly, the king's soldiers, who served the same role as today's police forces, did not patrol these roads often since they themselves would be in danger of an attack.

Du Vall—A Gentleman or a Thief?

Not all highwaymen approached their position in the same manner. A (20) highwayman who was truly a gentleman as well as a thief was Claude Du Vall. The son of a miller who worked as a stable boy and a footman, he learned his manners by being around nobility. Du Vall was famous not only for his skill as a highwayman, but also for his gentlemanly manners. He

was such a charmer that when he was captured and sent to trial, the ladies
(25) of the Court pleaded for his release. When Judge Sir William Morton found
Du Vall to be guilty of his crimes, even Charles II attempted to have Du Vall
pardoned. Only Morton's threat to resign made Charles II rescind his request
for clemency.

Highwaymen—Common Criminals?

Many of these highwaymen were gentlemen themselves. Often, wealthy
(30) gentlemen would surround themselves with a group of thieves and criminals
who would rob from the general public and then share the wealth with the
particular gentleman who "commanded" them. Should these criminals run
afoul of the law, the gentleman for whom they worked would "influence"
the local law enforcers through bribery and other unseemly means. The lure
(35) of the criminal life seemed to be far too enticing for both the gentlemen and
the highwaymen.

A Place for a Woman?

It is interesting to note that women also masqueraded as highwaymen. It
was not considered to be ladylike for a woman to be a criminal of any sort.
However, the women could hide their identities under their clothing, their
(40) hats, and their masks. These women had to be sure that the fashionably long
hair that helped to define their beauty in polite society was hidden artfully
under their hats. Moreover, they knew that they could not speak much since
the lightness of their voices would indicate their femininity.

27. Part A: When Justice in lines 4–5 speaks of the travelers having "*no choice but to succumb to the will*" of the highwaymen, he uses the word *succumb* to mean:

○ A. Defy
○ B. Define
○ C. Surrender
○ D. Challenge

Part B: The word in the first section that supports the correct response in Part A is:

○ A. Disadvantaged (line 4)
○ B. Choice (line 4)
○ C. Will (line 5)
○ D. Swift (line 5)

28. **Part A:** Claude Du Vall was unique as a highwayman because:

　○　A.　He was a foreigner living in England.
　○　B.　He gave back the money he had stolen.
　○　C.　He never robbed from poor people but only from the rich.
　○　D.　He was considered to be a true gentleman who was well-liked by different classes.

Part B: Select the lines from the text that support the correct answer from Part A.

　☐　A.　"…many highwaymen worked in gangs so it was easier to intimidate their victims." (lines 13–14)
　☐　B.　"…he learned his manners by being around nobility." (line 21–22)
　☐　C.　"…he was captured and sent to trial." (line 24)
　☐　D.　"…the ladies of the Court pleaded for his release." (lines 24–25)

29. Which of the following statements is accurate?

　○　A.　Many women wanted to be highwaymen, but they just weren't strong enough.
　○　B.　Women were better highwaymen than the men themselves and admired for it.
　○	C.　A woman who was a highwayman was praised by society.
　○　D.　Women who were highwaymen had to hide their femininity.

30. Choose the statement that supports how women highwaymen had to hide their femininity.

　○　A.　Women who were highwaymen actually outnumbered the men.
　○　B.　Women never disguised themselves when they became highwaymen because they were admired as heroes.
　○　C.　Women were forced to disguise themselves as men if they wanted to be highwaymen.
　○　D.　Women weren't interested in being highwaymen so the question is irrelevant.

> **Please note:** A video based on a similar topic or theme is often added to the paired passages on the NJ PARCC. You may wish to view a video of one of the professional singers who has recorded "The Highwayman" and use that in your response.

Prose Constructed Response—Research Simulation Task

Highwaymen are viewed in different ways by different authors. Compare and contrast the point of view of Alfred Noyes and Jeremiah Justice as they write about highwaymen. Moreover, consider the structure of each text and the manner in which it affects the way the highwaymen are portrayed.

PERFORMANCE-BASED ASSESSMENT ANSWERS

Argumentative Writing Task (Analysis of Argument)

Possible student response:

May 2, 2014

Dear Dr. Byrnes,

    I am writing this letter to you to share my opinion about the state department of education's proposal to make us an online school. I think that having an online school may seem to be a great idea, but I myself have some reservations. Classes on the Internet might be interesting, but there would be less focus on the lesson, less direct contact with the teachers and students, and less opportunity for our school to function as classes and teams.

    I think the biggest drawback is the lack of focus in an online school. Teenagers enjoy learning in a classroom where they can be with their friends. It is not the same to watch a monitor and "experience" a class without any friends around to help them to pay attention to the lesson. A virtual classroom that can be held anywhere holds a potential for distraction with music videos, instant messages, phone calls, Internet "surfing," and even parents and siblings providing distraction. In a classroom, we students have both the teacher and our friends to remind us to pay attention. In an online classroom, we have to rely on our own self-discipline. Remember, we are teenagers. It would be very easy for us to "tune out" the lesson that's being broadcast to our homes.

    The next problem is similar to the first one. By reducing the contact between students and the teacher, there are few opportunities for a personal education. Rather, the lessons are pre-made and completely student-directed. This may be fine for the students who don't get along well in school, but it would be a disaster for those of us who enjoy having heated discussions about issues that matter. In fact, how can an online school know that we students may be having a problem on a particular day, and we really need to have a caring teacher listen to us and give us some feedback? No Internet search can provide us with that personal touch.

There are those who believe that an online school fosters independent learners. These proponents contend that today's students rely too much on teamwork and not enough on individual effort and initiative. While that point of view may be accurate in a limited number of circumstances, an online school actually disregards the importance of teams. Many of the projects that we do in our classes are team projects. I have learned to plan my work in advance, cooperate with my teammates, help a teammate who may be struggling, and even go to my team if I'm having a problem. These core skills are the ones we will need when we grow up and live in a society that values teamwork, cooperation, good planning, support, and the need for close relationships with families and friends. Throughout my eight years in our schools, I have made three best friends as a direct result of being a teammate in my classes. Moreover, Mrs. Antonini has been one of my greatest supporters since I became a member of her debate team in fifth grade.

Dr. Brynes, please reconsider the state department of education's offer to have our school become an online school. I am sure that the state department of education is trying to improve our learning opportunities, but I think they are mistaken with their well-intentioned attempt. They are creating a system that will challenge us to focus on our lessons in an impersonal setting. In addition, they are giving us less contact with our valued teachers and friends while preventing us from acquiring team building skills that are so important for our future success.

Thank you for your time and consideration. I will gladly meet with you if you wish to discuss my letter further.

Sincerely,

Jennifer Marie Cromartie

Explanation to Student Response

This letter is probably going to receive a higher score on the PARCC. The question has been answered thoroughly. The author Jennifer begins by stating the main point clearly at the beginning of the letter: "I am writing this letter to you to share my opinion about the state department of education's proposal to make us an online school." She makes two strong points and develops each in its own paragraph.

She supports her first point ("the lack of focus in an online school") with statements about not having "friends around" to help her friends and her "to pay attention," using "A virtual classroom" that "holds a potential for distraction," and needing "to rely on our own self-discipline." Jennifer supports her second point that "reducing the contact between students and the teacher" will provide for "few opportunities for a personal education." A strong emotional appeal is made on behalf of the students who "may be having a problem on a particular day, and… need to have a caring teacher listen to us and give us some feedback." She further reinforces her argument by asserting that "No Internet search can provide us with that personal touch." The counter argument that "an online school fosters independent learners" is stated succinctly. The necessary support follows with the mention of the support "These proponents contend that today's students rely too much on teamwork and not enough on individual effort and initiative." Directly, statements made to disprove the validity of this counter argument are made. Simply, the proponents of the online school disregard "the importance of teams." The benefits of working in teams are stated as the opportunity to "plan my work in advance, cooperate with my teammates, help a teammate who may be struggling, and even go to my team if I'm having a problem." Furthermore, the importance of an on-site school is supported by the importance of the "core skills," but also the benefits of the friendships made with peers and the teacher. Finally, the closing avoids an aggressive defense of Jennifer's position. Rather, she is direct while being polite. She asks Dr. Byrnes to "please reconsider the state department of education's offer to have our school become an online school." She recognizes the good intention that "the state department of education is trying to improve our learning opportunities, yet she counters this by stating that this department is "mistaken with their well-intentioned attempt" while creating "an impersonal setting" in which the students would learn." She then reminds Dr. Byrnes that the students will have "less contact with (their) valued teachers and friends" while being prevented "from acquiring team building skills that are so important for…future success."

  Not only is the letter well-written, but it is also cognizant of the appropriate rules of grammar. The phrase "not only" is accompanied by the accompanying phrase "but also." The sentences are varied both in length and structure. Academic vocabulary is apparent in words and phrases including "potential for distraction," "independent learners," and "struggling." Finally, the letter demonstrates a carefully constructed argument that is based on reason rather than emotion.

Speculative Writing Task (Narrative Writing)

Possible Student Response:

    This picture has a roller coaster in it. Two people was sitting in the front, and two people was sitting behind them. The kids look happy. So does the adults.

    The two kids went to go to the amusement park, but the boy was afraid to go on the roller coaster. His sister axed him to go on with her, but he says he was sick and wanted to go home. She says that he didn't look sick when they were on the spinning tea cups ride, but he says he was sick. So he wanted to go home. Now.

    His sister says "OK." He said "OK" too. But then she says what's wrong and he didn't answer. So she asked him again and he says he was afraid. So she said she would go on the ride with him. He said "OK."

    So they went on the ride. And they had a good time.

Explanation to Student Response

This answer would probably receive a lower score. The writer did use paragraphs and even attempted to use dialogue. There is a plot, but it is not very well developed. There is no title for the story. The characters are not given an age or a personality. In fact, they're not even given a name. Audiences relate better to characters that are named and have an identity that the audience can understand. The response is very short in length. There are also grammar errors. In the first paragraph, "was" should be "were" and "does" should be "do." In the second paragraph, "axed" should be "asked." In the second and third paragraphs, "says" should be "said." The word "Now" is not a sentence. In the third paragraph, "But" and "So" should not begin sentences. In the third and fourth sentences, there should be a comma before "and" since the sentences would be compound if they didn't start with "But" and "So." In the fourth paragraph, "So" and "And" should not begin sentences. A good story builds to a climax, and this particular piece does not so. It resembles a poor attempt at an overview rather than an effective attempt at a story that has conflict, character development, a solid plot line, characters whose feelings, actions, and reactions supplement the message (theme) of the story, a resolution that underscores the entire piece, and a strong academic vocabulary supported by transitional words and phrases.

    The author needs to add more details to the story. The characters should have names, and their personalities and feelings should be mentioned (nervous, frustrated, and courageous, for example). The plot needs more details, which can be found in the conflict. The reader can easily give the young boy in the story a reason for being afraid of the roller coaster ride. Maybe the boy had a bad experience on the ride the last time he visited the amusement park. Some meaningful dialogue could help the reader to understand the young boy's fear of the roller coaster. These facts bring the reader closer to understanding the characters while also giving the readers reasons to empathize with the characters. Furthermore, the reader is more likely to invest interest in the characters when the author is showing, rather than telling, the details and emotions being developed.

To conclude the story, the author should do two things. First of all, (s)he should describe the actual ride so the reader will be able to see that the brother's fears are going away. Second, (s)he should have the brother and sister both reflect on the change in attitude that has occurred. The brother's conquering of his fear has taught him a lesson: It may be difficult, but it is always necessary to face one's fears.

Literary Task Analysis

"Mother to Son"
1. The correct response is C. "She is poor and cannot afford an easy life of luxury." The "crystal stair" represents wealth, which the mother does not have. Answers A. "She has lived her life on the ground floor of her house," B. "She is someone who has always desired stairs made from crystal," D. "She is a maid who is forced to clean up "tacks" and "splinters."
2. The correct responses are A. "Persevering" and D. "Determined" since they represent the mother's strong desire to succeed in her quest for a better life. Response B. "Resigned" means that the mother has given up, which is incorrect. Response C. "Incoherent" would mean that the mother is not making any sense at all. Response E. "Agnostic" is wrong because an agnostic is one who is unsure about an established position.
3. The correct response is E. "Her being forced to live a difficult life." Responses A. "Her home without electricity," B. "Her job in the evening when it is dark," and C. "Her boredom with her life and desire for the excitement that the night life has" have no basis in the text.
4. The correct response is B. "Keep trying and don't quit." Response A. "Just give up now and avoid the inevitable disappointment" is the opposite of the correct answer and is therefore wrong. Responses C. "Life is unpredictable, and there is not a formula for success" and D. "Even though you may try your best, there is little hope for success in this cruel world" have no basis in the text.

5. The correct responses are A. "reinforce" and C. "underscore" because they both demonstrate the mother's desire to emphasize her point strongly to her son. Response B. "undermine" means the opposite of the mother's intention. Response D. "intimidate" represents a much more aggressive action while response E. "improvise" indicates an action that is unplanned.

"The Ant and the Grasshopper"

6. C. The Grasshopper helped the Ant. The grasshopper wanted the Ant to stop and chat with him instead of finding food for the winter.
7. A. The Ant and the Grasshopper.
8. F. The Grasshopper believes that his idea of chirping and singing throughout the summer is a smart one. He asks the Ant why be bothered with toiling and moiling away with an ear of corn.
9. **Part A: D and J.** When we meet the Grasshopper and the Ant they are in a field during the summer time. When we catch up with the characters at the end of the fable, it is winter and the Ant is passing food out from the nest.
   Part B: E and F. The author wanted to connect the actions of the main characters with the seasons to show the idea of what careless behavior does over time and to make his point.
10. C. Corn. The Ant was toiling and moiling with an ear of corn.
11. A. Always plan ahead. The Grasshopper ended up starving during the winter.
12. D and G. The Grasshopper was dying of hunger during the winter realizing that he was wrong to not store food during the summer months for the winter.
13. C and H. It is told in the third person by a narrator who is neutral and does not take sides.

Getting Ready for Winter: My Three "Musts"

14. A. The organizational pattern of this essay is chronological. The author uses language, such as, first of all, additionally, and finally.
15. **Part A: B and F.** Mann prefers the summer months and believes that planning ahead is a smart thing to do. Then Mann proceeds to explain how best to prepare from the summer months for the winter months ahead.
    Part B: B and C. Good planning leads to good results and not waiting until the last minute to take an action is best. The Ant did not wait for the cold weather to start preparing for the winter. When winter came, he had enough food and was not starving like the Grasshopper. Mann states that "it is wise to begin to prepare for the harshness of winter."
16. A and E. They are both careful planners and believe in preparing and planning for events in advance. The Ant prepared to have food before the winter and Mann describes a plan on how to prepare yourself and your belongings for the harsh winter months.

17. D. Condensation is a moisture build-up.
18. The correct responses are B and C. Both Aesop and Mann advocate the benefit of good planning. While Aesop's advice deals mainly with nutritional considerations, Mann's advice focuses on possessions. Aesop has The Ant advise The Grasshopper "to lay up food for the winter." Mann advises his reader that "it is wise to begin to prepare for the harshness of winter."
19. The correct responses are D and E. The advice each author gives is based on evidence from his writing. Both Aesop and Mann are advocates with a clearly-stated position. Aesop supports his position with The Grasshopper's frivolousness and the change of the seasons while Mann speaks of the "three musts."

Language Usage Task

20. A and G are prepositional phrases.
21. The correct answers are A, C, and F.
22. Part A: The correct answer is A. Object of a preposition.
    Part B: The correct answer is F. A principal part.
23. The correct answers are D, "good" and F, "dance."

Research Simulation Task

"The Highwayman"

24. Part A: The correct response is B. "Alliteration" since the initial "g" sound in "ghostly galleon" is repeated.
    Part B: The correct response is D. "his hair like mouldy hay" since the initial "h" sound in "hair" and "hay" is repeated.
25. Part A: The correct response is C. "Tim was also in love with Bess, but he didn't have the flair that the highwayman had." Tim was jealous of the highwayman, who was more handsome, dynamic, and daring. Being an ostler was an honest profession for Tim, but his mundane job of stableman paled in comparison to the highwayman, whose success was shown by his "French cocked-hat on his forehead, a bunch of lace at his chin, / A coat of the claret velvet, and breeches of brown doe-skin. / They fitted with never a wrinkle." (lines 7–9) Response A. "Tim always wanted to be a highwayman, and this was his chance to make his dream come true." is incorrect since Tim's actions mainly demonstrated jealousy. Responses B. "Tim was Bess's cousin, and he had promised his aunt to

keep her out of danger," D. "Tim was a member of the king's army, and he was preparing to arrest the highwayman."

Part B: The correct responses are B. "His eyes were hollows of madness" (line 21) and C. "his hair like mouldy hay," (line 21) since these traits are not attractive like the highwayman. Responses A. "Tim the ostler listened" (line 20) and D. "he heard the robber say" (line 24) are events in the story, not traits.

26. **Part A:** The correct answer is C. "True Love Knows No Boundaries" because Bess gave up her own life to save the highwayman. Response A. "True Love Never Ends Well" is not correct because the word never is an "absolute." The statement can be true in many instances. Response B. "Never Be Kind to Strangers" has no basis in the text. Response D. "Every Man for Himself" is the opposite of the correct answer since Bess dies to save the highwayman, who dies to avenge her death.

    Part B: The correct responses are C. "The tip of one finger touched it! The trigger at least was hers" (line 60) and D. "Back, he spurred like a madman, shouting a curse to the sky" (line 85). These responses tell of Bess's preparation to warn the highwayman by killing herself and the highwayman's blind rage when he learns of Bess's death. Response A. "Over the cobbles he clattered and clashed in the dark inn-yard" (line 13) simply refers to an earlier visit by the highwayman while response B. "Then he tugged at his rein in the moonlight, and galloped away to the west." (line 46) refers to the highwayman galloping away after visiting Bess.

"Highwaymen—Romantic Heroes or Common Criminals?"

27. **Part A:** The correct response is C. "Surrender" since it is a synonym for "succumb." Response A. "Defy" is an antonym, B. "Define" refers to clarifying, and D. "Challenge" is an antonym.

    Part B: The correct response is A. "Disadvantaged" since one who succumbs is indeed at a disadvantage. Response B. "Choice" is more general than "Disadvantaged" and therefore not as good a word to use. Response C. "Will" indicated the opposite of being willing to "succumb." Response D. "Swift" deals with speed.

28. **Part A:** The correct response is D. "He was considered to a true gentleman who was well-liked by different classes." This is proven by the fact that "the ladies of the Court pleaded for his release" (lines 24–25), as did Charles II (lines 26–27) Response A. "He was a foreigner living in England." is inaccurate. Response B. "He gave back the money he had stolen." refers to Robin Hood, not Claude Du Vall. Response C. "He never robbed from poor people but only from the rich." has no basis in the text.

Part B: The correct responses are B. "...he learned his manners by being around nobility." (lines 21–22) and D. "...the ladies of the Court pleaded for his release." (lines 24–25) Neither response A. "...many highwaymen worked in gangs so it was easier to intimidate their victims" (lines 13–14) nor response C. "...he was captured and sent to trial" (line 23) support the statement. In fact, response "A." is from the paragraph prior to the one about Du Vall.

29. The correct response is D. "Women who were highwaymen had to hide their femininity." This is supported in lines 39–40: "However, the women could hide their identities under their clothing, their hats, and their masks." Responses A. "Many women wanted to be highwaymen, but they just weren't strong enough." and "Women were better highwaymen than the men themselves and admired for it." Have no support in the text. Response C. "A woman who was a highwayman was praised by society." is a completely false statement.

30. Response C. "Women were forced to disguise themselves as men if they wanted to be highwaymen." Is correct. Response A. "Women who were highwaymen actually outnumbered the men." Has no basis in the text. Response B. "Women never disguised themselves when they became highwaymen because they were admired as heroes." Is the opposite of the correct answer. Response D. "Women weren't interested in being highwaymen so the question is irrelevant," has no basis in the text.

Prose Constructed Response—Research Simulation Task

Possible Student Response:

Noyes vs. Justice Differing Opinions

Two different people with two different purposes may be likely to view either something or someone in two different ways. These two authors do indeed see criminals through completely different lenses.

In "The Highwayman," Alfred Noyes portrays the character in a romantic fashion. Even before he appears to Bess, the landlord's daughter, the setting is described romantically. In the opening of the poem, Noyes uses the setting to entice the reader with details including "The wind was a torrent of darkness among the gusty trees. / The moon was a ghostly galleon tossed upon cloudy seas. / The road was a ribbon of moonlight over the purple moor." (lines 1-3) Before the highwayman even appears, the setting creates a mood of intrigue, darkness, and suspense—all traits of the highwayman who wreaks havoc across the countryside while maintaining an air of elegance and mystery. This masked "intruder" who wishes to "steal" the heart of the smitten Bess approaches her while wearing "a French cocked-hat on his forehead, a bunch of lace at his chin, / A coat of the claret velvet, and breeches of brown doe-skin. / They fitted with never a wrinkle." (lines 7-9) Moreover, he wore "boots (that) were up to the thigh. / And he rode with a jewelled twinkle, / His pistol butts a-twinkle, / His rapier hilt a-twinkle, under the jewelled sky." (lines 9-12)

Jeremiah Justice does not condone this romance of thieves, however. Rather than praise the highwaymen for their daring feats and dashing personalities, Justice notes the highwaymen's reputations "as free-spirited rogues who were the anti-heroes of their times." (line 2) Unlike Noyes, Justice spends little time with elevating the highwaymen to a praiseworthy status. Instead, he immediately refers to the fact that "They rode on horses and robbed from travelers, who were mostly on foot." (lines 2-3) He reinforces this point by stating in simple, non-romantic terms that "These disadvantaged travelers had no choice but to succumb to the will of the swift and unprovoked attacks of these scoundrels on horseback." (lines 3-5)

Noyes focuses on the romance of Bess and the highwayman while Justice exhibits disdain for those who "were said to be roaming the countryside and wreaking their havoc on unsuspecting travelers." (lines 7-8) Noyes portrays the highwayman in most admirable terms as he describes the playful scoundrel who "clattered and clashed in the dark inn-yard," and who "whistled a tune" to call to Bess, who was waiting for his arrival while "Plaiting a dark red love-knot into her long black hair." (lines 13, 15, and 18) Tim the Ostler, whose "hair like mouldy hay" and eyes that "were hollows of madness" is forced to watch the highwayman kiss Bess and listen to the highwayman's plans to avoid any pursuers and return "by moonlight, though hell should bar the way." (lines 21 and 30)

Justice takes a different approach, describing highwaymen as "common thieves and brigands," as well as "scoundrels." (line 9) Furthermore, he speaks unflatteringly of these criminals who used phrases such as "Stand and deliver (your possessions)" and "Your money or your life." (lines 11-12) In addition, Justice illustrates his point further by explaining that "many highwaymen worked in gangs so it was easier to intimidate their victims" and "The highwaymen would prowl the less-travelled areas of roads leading from London since those negotiating these roads were often men of means." (lines 12-15)

Noyes describes Bess's "noble" act when "Her musket shattered the moonlight, / Shattered her breast in the moonlight and warned him— with her death." He further makes the highwayman a sympathetic character by having him killed in an attempt to avenge Bess's death "With the white road smoking behind him and his rapier brandished high." (line 86) Justice, on the other hand, portrays the "gentlemanly" Claude Du Vall as "such a charmer that when he was captured and sent to trial, the ladies of the Court pleaded for his release." (lines 22-23) Even Charles II pleaded for his release.

Finally, using a poem to tell the tall of the highwayman gives his story a sense of romance and a musical tone. In fact, the poem ends with the image of Bess "Plaiting a dark red love-knot into her long black hair. (line 102) Justice, on the other hand, uses paragraphs, headings, and phrases including "thieves," "brigands," and "criminals" to demonstrate his disdain. One can easily infer that Justice believes there is no romance for those who are the victims of these criminal charmers.

Noyes romanticizes the highwayman while Justice feels disdain for all highwaymen, even the charming Claude Du Vall. Need more proof? Just look at the two titles. Noyes' work is entitled "The Highwayman" while Justice's is entitled "Highwaymen—Romantic Heroes or Common Criminals?"

Explanation of Student Repsonse:

This begins with a compositional risk to engage the interest of the reader by making a statement that relates directly to the "Differing Opinions" stated in the title. The author then proceeds to methodically diagnose the differences in the two author's philosophies by first demonstrating Noyes romanticizing of the highwayman by using a mood of "intrigue, darkness, and suspense." He furthers the point by citing provocative details of the highwayman including descriptions of his clothing and the "twinkle" reflecting off his pistol and rapier. Justice's opposing point of view in introduced in the next paragraph to contrast Noyes' romanticizing. Justice uses terms including "free-spirited rogues" and "anti-heroes (who) rode on horses and robbed from travelers, who were mostly on foot." The third and fourth paragraphs continue this diametrical opposition as "Noyes focuses on the romance of Bess and the highwayman while Justice exhibits disdain for those who 'were said to be roaming the countryside and wreaking their havoc on unsuspecting travelers.'" Furthermore, the "music" of Noyes" poetry of praise is contrasted directly with the matter-of-fact approach of Justice's unemotional textbook style. The author adds insight at the end by contrasting the titles that each author uses. There is thorough development of the topic, and academic vocabulary is evident with words including "elegance," "praiseworthy," and "sympathetic."

Practice Test— End-of-Year Assessment

CHAPTER 7

> **Please note:** We have included additional questions to the End-of-Year Assessment for extra practice.

Literature Passage

Read *The New Colossus*. Then answer the questions.

The New Colossus
By Emma Lazarus (1883)

(5)
Not like the brazen giant of Greek fame,
With conquering limbs astride from land to land;
Here at our sea-washed, sunset gates shall stand
A mighty woman with a torch, whose flame
Is the imprisoned lightning, and her name

(10)
Mother of Exiles. From her beacon-hand
Glows world-wide welcome; her mild eyes command
The air-bridged harbor that twin cities frame.
"Keep, ancient lands, your storied pomp!" cries she
With silent lips. "Give me your tired, your poor,
Your huddled masses yearning to breathe free,
The wretched refuse of your teeming shore.
Send these, the homeless, tempest-tost to me,
I lift my lamp beside the golden door!"

1. What is the rhyme scheme of the first four lines of the poem?

- A. aaab
- B. aabb
- C. abab
- D. abba

2. In line 1 of the poem a reference is made to "the brazen giant of Greek fame," which is a huge Greek statue of the sun god Helios. This type of reference is an example of:

   ○ A. Alliteration
   ○ B. Irony
   ○ C. Foreshadowing
   ○ D. Allusion

3. Part A: Select the word that best describes the mood of this poem.

   ○ A. Anger
   ○ B. Encouragement
   ○ C. Presumption
   ○ D. Confusion

   Part B: Select the following parts of the poem that reflect the mood described in Part A.

   ☐ A. "the brazen giant"
   ☐ B. "With conquering limbs"
   ☐ C. "A mighty woman"
   ☐ D. "world-wide welcome"
   ☐ E. "Give me your tired, your poor"
   ☐ F. "I lift my lamp beside the golden door!"

4. From the phrase "From her beacon-hand glows world-wide welcome," select the literary devices that are represented.

   ☐ A. comparison/contrast
   ☐ B. denouement
   ☐ C. personification
   ☐ D. simile
   ☐ E. alliteration
   ☐ F. suspense

5. Which one of the following titles must be a good alternative title?

   ○ A. "Welcome to Our Shores"
   ○ B. "The Talking Statue"
   ○ C. "Come to Greece"
   ○ D. "Imagine a World Without Freedom"

Read the poem below and answer the questions.

If

by Rudyard Kipling

If you can keep your head when all about you
Are losing theirs and blaming it on you,
If you can trust yourself when all men doubt you,
But make allowance for their doubting too;
(5) If you can wait and not be tired by waiting,
Or being lied about, don't deal in lies,
Or being hated don't give way to hating,
And yet don't look too good, nor talk too wise;

If you can dream—and not make dreams your master;
(10) If you can think—and not make thoughts your aim;
If you can meet with Triumph and Disaster
And treat those two impostors just the same:
If you can bear to hear the truth you've spoken
Twisted by knaves to make a trap for fools,
(15) Or watch the things you gave your life to, broken,
And stoop and build 'em up with worn-out tools:

If you can make one heap of all your winnings
And risk it on one turn of pitch-and-toss,
And lose, and start again at your beginnings,
(20) And never breathe a word about your loss;
If you can force your heart and nerve and sinew
To serve your turn long after they are gone,
And so hold on when there is nothing in you
Except the Will which says to them: "Hold on!"

(25) If you can talk with crowds and keep your virtue,
Or walk with Kings—nor lose the common touch,
If neither foes nor loving friends can hurt you,
If all men count with you, but none too much;
If you can fill the unforgiving minute
(30) With sixty seconds' worth of distance run,

Yours is the Earth and everything that's in it,
And—which is more—you'll be a Man, my son!

Source: http://www.emule.com/poetry/?page=poem;poem=2937

6. **Part A:** Which sentence best captures the meaning of the phrase "If you can keep your head when all about you / Are losing theirs"?

   ○ A. Being able to think clearly.
   ○ B. Avoiding being deported from the country.
   ○ C. Keeping all your money while others are not.
   ○ D. Keeping calm.

   Part B: What poetic devices are being used in lines 1–4: "If you can keep your head when all about you / Are losing theirs and blaming it on you, If you can trust yourself when all men doubt you, But make allowance for their doubting too." Drag and drop the two correct answers into the boxes.

   A. Simile
   B. Personification
   C. Onomatopoeia
   D. Rhyme
   E. Metaphor
   F. Alliteration

7. Select the word that fits the advice given in this poem.
   ○ A. Persistent
   ○ B. Humility
   ○ C. Great fame
   ○ D. Fortitude

8. What literary device is used in the line "If you can dream—and not make dreams your master"?
   ○ A. Onomatopoeia
   ○ B. Setting
   ○ C. Simile
   ○ D. Personification

9. **Part A:** In the first four lines of the second stanza (lines 9–12) "If you can dream—and not make dreams your master; / If you can think—and not make thoughts your aim, / If you can meet with Triumph and Disaster / And treat those two impostors just the same," which lines rhyme?

   - A. Lines 1 and 4 and lines 2 and 3
   - B. Lines 2 and 3
   - C. Lines 1 and 3 and lines 2 and 4
   - D. Lines 1, 2, and 3

   Part B: What is the rhyme scheme for lines 9–12 mentioned in Part A?

   - A. abba
   - B. aabb
   - C. aaba
   - D. abab

Success in Baseball

Geri Spencer

Everyone has to face a challenge at times in their lives, but how does one do so successfully? Is there a set formula for facing challenges in baseball the correct way? Is this correct way that is being referred to, a correct way for all players? Can these challenges be met with the same strategy every time?
(5) Is there a formula to be followed when seeking success in facing a challenge on the field of play, or does the formula contain certain elements that in combination can enhance the desired success?

As an aspiring pro athlete in baseball, I tend to think of myself as one whose success relies on a basic set of fundamentals which I shall adapt
(10) as the situation dictates. The first component in my striving for success is staying in good physical shape. That means I must exercise certain muscle groups to strengthen them while monitoring my regimen to enhance muscle tone, strength, agility, and flexibility while minimizing the risk of injury. I must work out certain muscle groups according to the schedule established
(15) by my team's trainer. Since I mostly play centerfield, I primarily train for

speed rather than for strength. As a contributing member of a team, I must report any soreness or injury to the trainer immediately since neglecting a developing problem will only exacerbate the problem and impact my teammates in a negative way.

(20) The second consideration I must have is maintaining a good diet. I must eat from a variety of food groups and colors each day to increase my chances of naturally supplementing my daily vitamin and mineral requirements. I cannot eat an excessive amount of red meat. Rather, I eat a reasonably-sized portion of red meat (8 ounces or less) and supplement my need for protein (25) with grains, legumes, and cheese. I also avoid ingesting large amounts of carbohydrates and sugars since these combine to have a negative impact on my blood sugar. Since I suffer from diabetes, I must monitor my sugar levels carefully.

My third consideration is mental. I must practice picturing myself (30) accomplishing the tasks that await me on the ball field. Whether I am ideating the perfect way to swing at a low, outside fast ball or handle a curve that's boring in on my hands, mentally going through the steps to accomplish these moves successfully is beneficial in helping me to program my mind to cue my body to take the appropriate action when the situation arises. Keeping a (35) strong mental edge also helps me to face adversity and challenges during a game.

If an opposing pitcher is making hitting difficult for my teammates and me, I should not be depressed. Rather, I should keep a mental toughness and take the pitcher's effectiveness as a challenge that I shall try my best (40) to overcome. Just as a lack of enthusiasm is infectious, so is the power of positive thinking (as Norman Vincent Peale so deftly pointed out).

To meet the challenges on the ball field, I have found that I must be cognizant of three aspects: staying in good physical shape, maintaining a well-balanced diet, and maintaining mental toughness and acuity. When I (45) use these three components together in an appropriate manner, I find that my chances for success dramatically increase. The synergy of these three elements working closely together provides me with a sound basis upon which to build my success on the playing field. Furthermore, a commitment to excellence must be maintained on a daily basis. In the words of Baltimore (50) Oriole's great third baseman Brooks Robinson, "If you're not practicing, somebody else is, somewhere, and he'll be ready to take your job."

10. **Part A**: Which of the following statements best describes the key message that Geri Spencer is raising in the opening paragraph of "Success in Baseball"?
    - ○ A. Everyone faces challenges during their lifetime.
    - ○ B. There are no challenges that one cannot overcome.
    - ○ C. Challenges are really nothing to worry about.
    - ○ D. There is a set of elements that can enhance one's chances to succeed.

    Part B: Select the sentences from the essay that best prove Spencer's key message from Part A.
    - ☐ A. There are certain elements that when joined together raise the chances for success to be reached.
    - ☐ B. All challenges can be met with the same strategy every time.
    - ☐ C. Success is more the result of luck than it is strategy.
    - ☐ D. Success and failure are similar in their basic structure.
    - ☐ E. People, not strategies make the difference.
    - ☐ F. Successes and failures have a lot in common.

11. When comparing "If" to "Success in Baseball," the statement(s) relevant only to "Success in Baseball" is/are:
    - ☐ A. You must have faith in yourself when others doubt you.
    - ☐ B. Picturing yourself as completing a task successfully is a great aid to help yourself to succeed.
    - ☐ C. Share your disappointment with others.
    - ☐ D. You should handle wins and losses the same way.
    - ☐ E. Don't give your opponent a chance to win—ever!
    - ☐ F. There are three areas to work on for success and when these three things are combined, the effectiveness increases exponentially.

12. What do "If" and "Success in Baseball" have in common?
    - ○ A. text structure
    - ○ B. theme
    - ○ C. rhyme scheme
    - ○ D. hyperbole

Prose Constructed Response

Compare and contrast the poem Rudyard Kipling's "If" with Geri Spencer's informational piece "Success in Baseball." Focus on content, structure, author's purpose, and main idea (theme).

Informational Text

Read the following excerpt from Geri Spencer's "Success in Baseball" and answer the questions that follow.

> As an aspiring pro athlete in baseball, I tend to think of myself as one whose success relies on a basic set of fundamentals which I shall adapt as the situation dictates. The first component in my striving for success is staying in good physical shape. That means I must exercise certain muscle groups to strengthen them while monitoring my regimen to enhance muscle tone, strength, agility, and flexibility while minimizing the risk of injury. I must work out certain muscle groups according to the schedule established by my team's trainer. Since I mostly play centerfield, I primarily train for speed rather than for strength. As a contributing member of a team, I must report any soreness or injury to the trainer immediately since neglecting a developing problem will only exacerbate the problem and impact my teammates in a negative way.

13. **Part A:** In the opening sentence "As an aspiring pro athlete in baseball, I tend to think of myself as one whose success relies on a basic set of fundamentals which I shall adapt as the situation dictates," what is the function of the word *pro*?

    - A. Noun
    - B. Pronoun
    - C. Main Verb
    - D. Adjective

    Part B: Which of the other choices listed in this question has/have the same function as the correct answer for Part A?

    - A. "myself"
    - B. "the"
    - C. "shall"
    - D. "baseball" and "set"

14. In the sentence "The first component in my striving for success is staying in good physical shape," which of the following words is used as a helping verb?

    ○ A. "first"
    ○ B. "component"
    ○ C. "striving"
    ○ D. "is"

15. In the phrase "to enhance muscle tone, strength, agility, and flexibility while minimizing the risk of injury," the word "minimizing" is an example of a

    ○ A. Participle
    ○ B. Direct Object
    ○ C. Linking Verb
    ○ D. Possessive Noun

16. The sentence "Since I mostly play centerfield, I primarily train for speed rather than for strength" is an example of what type of sentence?

    ○ A. Simple
    ○ B. Compound
    ○ C. Complex
    ○ D. Compound-complex

17. In the following sentence "As a contributing member of a team, I must report any soreness or injury to the trainer immediately since neglecting a developing problem will only exacerbate the problem and impact my teammates in a negative way," select the words that are adverbs.

    ☐ A. "contributing"
    ☐ B. "must"
    ☐ C. "to"
    ☐ D. "immediately"
    ☐ E. "developing"
    ☐ F. "only"
    ☐ G. "impact"

Read the passage below about skateboarding. Then answer the questions.

A Brief History of Skateboarding

It is believed that skateboarding began in California. Sometime during the 1950s, California surfers began to "surf" on the streets with wheeled boards. The sport became very popular on the west coast, but the popularity began to fade after a few years. When the popularity began to soar again, the sport began to spread across the United States. Today, it is a very popular sport among teenagers and young adults.

The Era of the 1900s

The first skateboards are made by kids. These look like scooters with handles sticking out of a milk crate. Roller skate wheels are added to the base, usually a "two by four" piece of wood. The practice is limited to one of a neighborhood activity, not a sport.

The Era of the 1950s

Surfing becomes very popular in California. Skateboarding is "born" when California surfers decide to surf outside the water. The surfers fashion skateboards in the same way that kids have been doing. These surfers take small wooden boxes or pieces of wood and attach wheels from roller skates. Companies soon create laminated wood boards. Clay wheels begin to replace those made from steel, but the clay wheels break down quickly and don't have the proper grip. Skateboarding is first known as sidewalk surfing.

The Era of the 1960s

Makaha, Hobie, and other companies begin to stage competitions to raise the popularity of the sport. The sport becomes a fad like the hula hoop. Jan and Dean record "Sidewalk Surfin'" in 1964. (By the way, the sport once known as "sidewalk surfing" is known in the modern era as "longboarding.")

Safety becomes an issue. Injuries are common. Communities begin to ban sidewalk surfing because of many safety issues. The popularity of the sport drops in the later part of the decade.

The Era of the 1970s

Clay wheels are replaced by urethane ones. With increased control, the boards are easier to ride on the sidewalk. Frank Nasworthy designs the smooth-running "Cadillac" wheel. The boards' decks increase in width, giving skaters more control and maneuverability.

The Zephyr team is impressive at the Ocean Festival in Del Mar, California. Zephyr's precision moves make sidewalk surfing a serious sport. Concrete skate parks become popular, skateboarders are ranked, and magazines and movies featuring skateboarding increase in number.

Skateboarders begin riding low to the ground. Maneuvers become more complex and difficult. The "ollie" is credited to Alan "Ollie" Gelfand, who stomps his foot on his board's tail section causing it to pop up in the air while he's riding. As skaters "take to the air," graphics appear on the undersides of the boards. Punk and new wave music are popular with skaters, and an anti-establishment attitude becomes common.

Skateboarding becomes less popular in the late '70s, especially when skateboarders perform on the walls of empty pools in California. With the amount and difficulty of tricks increasing, the number of accidents also increases. Many skate parks close due to high insurance costs.

The Era of the 1980s

The sport's popularity remains low in the early part of the decade. Contests are not as popular as they once were, contest prizes shrink, and sales of skateboards drop. Skateboard videos become popular. Stacey Peralta and George Powell form the Bones Brigade and make videos featuring skaters like Steve Caballero, Tony Hawk, Lance Mountain, and others.

As "the whole world" becomes "the place to perform," homemade ramps and handrails become popular places for skaters to do their moves. The moves become more freestyle, and vertical ("vert") skating is less popular than street skating in places like parking lots and roads.

The Era of the 1990s

In 1995, ESPN stages the first Extreme Games competition, helping the public to view skateboarding as a mainstream sport. In 1997, ESPN also holds the Winter X Games including in-line skating and snowboarding.

Skateparks become popular in towns once again. The boards are more stable and easier to control, safety equipment is greatly improved thanks to modern technology, and corporations are taking an interest in the sport with skaters' clothing becoming popular in youth culture. The sport begins to move away from its underground style.

The Era of the 2000s (The Modern Era)

Skateboarding becomes even more mainstream. The decks of most boards are made from seven laminated sheets of Canadian maple wood. Wheels are hard so they slide better, allowing for greater speed and better manueverability. Most professional skateboaders have corporate sponsors. Video skateboarding games are popular with young adults.

Skateboarding is spreading in popularity all over the world. In 2004, the "International Skateboarding Federation" is formed. The ISF begins serious discussion with the International Olympic Committee. The ISF requests that skateboarding become a sanctioned Olympic sport.

Avril Lavigne records "Sk8er (Skater) Boi" in 2002, reaching the top spot on Billboard's Top 40 Mainstream song ratings chart. "Let Go," the album featuring "SK8er Boi," reaches the number two sopt on Billboard's Top 200 songs.

In 2005, Danny Way sets a world record for skateboarding by jumping over the Great Wall of China without using a motor to boost him.

According to the International Gravity Sports Association, Mischo Erban has set the world's speed record on a skateboard on September 31, 2010 when he traveled at a speed of 130.8 kilometers per hour. This speed is equal to almost 81 miles per hour.

18. Which title is the best one for this passage?

    ○ A. Sidewalk Surfing
    ○ B. Skateboarding from the 1900s until the Present
    ○ C. California Surfers Invent a New Sport That's Like Surfing
    ○ D. Sidewalk Surfing for Kids

19. In the 1950s, California surfers make surfboards because ___.

    ○ A. They are bored with surfing.
    ○ B. Surfing is outlawed after a tragic accident.
    ○ C. They want to surf on land, too.
    ○ D. They want to make a lot of money in competitions.

20. When it is said that skaters "take to the air" in the 1970s, it means ___.

- A. The skateboarders need a pilot's license to skate.
- B. The maneuvers are becoming aerial ones.
- C. Skiers are now becoming skaters, too.
- D. Skateboarding is being covered on the radio: "on the air."

21. Part A: Select the statements that appear in the paragraph about the 1980s.

- ☐ A. The sport's popularity is low in the early part of the decade.
- ☐ B. Videos featuring skateboarding become popular.
- ☐ C. Skaters begin performing on homemade ramps and handrails.
- ☐ D. Allan "Ollie" Gelfand invents the "ollie."

Part B: Which of these statements about the 1980s from Part A is **not** an opinion?

- A. Skateboarding contests are not as popular as they should be.
- B. The sales of skateboards are too low.
- C. Freestyle moves are awesome.
- D. The Bones Brigade made videos.

22. Select the resource that would be the least productive one to use to get information about skateboarding moves and techniques.

- A. Professional skateboarders.
- B. Skateboarding magazine.
- C. Skateboard repair manual.
- D. Skateboard shop owner.

END-OF-YEAR ASSESSMENT ANSWERS

Literature Passage

"The New Colossus"

1. The correct response is D. "abba" since "fame" (a) in line one rhymes with "flame" (a) in line four and "land" (b) in line two rhymes with "stand" (b).
2. The correct answer is D. "Allusion" since the term means a reference to a literary or historical figure. Response A. "Alliteration" is incorrect since it represents the repetition of initial sound (Ex. Peter Piper picked a peck of pickled peppers.). Response B. "Irony" is incorrect since the statue represents strength and not weakness. Response C. "Foreshadowing" is incorrect since there are no hints or clues being given.
3. Part A: The word that best describes the mood of this poem is B. "encouragement" since the Statue of Liberty is welcoming the "tired," the "poor," and the "huddled masses yearning to breathe free." Response A. "Anger" is incorrect because the Statue is "Not like the brazen giant of Greek fame." There is nothing significant in the text to support responses C. "Presumption" and D. "Confusion."
   Part B: Responses D. "world-wide welcome," E. "Give me your tired, your poor," and F. "I lift my lamp beside the golden door" all represent "Encouragement." While responses A. "the brazen giant," B. "With conquering limbs," and C. "A mighty woman" refer to the concept of A. "Anger," they do not reflect the mood of the poem.
4. The correct responses are C. "personification" ("her beacon hand") and E. "alliteration" ("world-wide welcome"). Responses A. "comparison/contrast," B. "denouement" (the final outcome), D. "simile" (a comparison using "like" or "as," and F. "suspense" (a state of excitement) have no support in the text.
5. Response A. "Welcome to Our Shores" is supported by many phrases including "world-wide welcome," (line 7) "Give me your tired, your poor," (line 10) and "Your huddled masses yearning to be free." (line 11) Response B. "The Talking Statue" is merely a small aspect of a larger issue. Response C. "Come to Greece" misses the point of inviting the refugees to the shores of the United States. While response D. "Imagine a World Without Freedom" is an interesting concept, it takes the opposite position of the poem's offering of freedom and is therefore incorrect.

Paired Passages

"If"

6. **Part A:** The correct answer is A. Being able to think clearly and keep your wits about you when others around you are not.
   Part B: The correct answers are D and E; Rhyme and Metaphor.
7. The correct answer is D. Fortitude means staying strong and sticking to something.
8. The correct answer is B, personification. Not letting your dreams control you.
9. **Part A:** The correct answer is C. Lines 1 and 3 and lines 2 and 4 rhyme.
   Part B: The correct answer is D. The rhyme scheme is abab because lines 1 and 3 rhyme and lines 2 and 4 rhyme.

"Success in Baseball"

10. **Part A:** The correct answer is D. There is a set of elements that can enhance one's chances to succeed.
    Part B: The correct answers are A and E. There are certain elements that when joined together raise the chances for success but people and how strong they are, are what make the difference.
11. The correct selections are B and F. Picturing yourself as completing a task successfully is a great aid to help yourself succeed and there are areas to work on for success.
12. The correct answer is B. The theme for both "If" and "Success in Baseball" is all about staying focused, growing up, and working hard. Kipling worked hard on becoming a man. In "Success in Baseball" one must be resilient and focused to get where they want to be in life.

Prose Constructed Response

Sample Student Response:

When someone is presenting instructions, there are many ways to present those instructions. Often, the manner in which the instructions are created and subsequently presented will vary according to the content of not only the material, but also of the intended audience. Those with a flair for the poetic beauty of language might find Kipling's "If" to be a haven for advice concerning ways to handle adversity while those who prefer a more direct approach might find themselves enjoying "Success in Baseball" more.

Concerning content and structure, Kipling is dealing with the hypothetical while Spencer goes directly to the point being addressed.

Kipling uses a number of "If . . . then" statements to raise questions about remaining calm and believing in yourself. For example, he waxes eloquently as he ponders these phrases: "If you can trust yourself when all men doubt you, / But make allowance for their doubting too; / If you can wait and not be tired by waiting, / Or being lied about, don't deal in lies." He is tapping into the basest of human emotions as he considers the impact of some of life's most difficult challenges. On the other hand, Spencer suggests a success formula containing three components that can be effective in solving most problems. She believes that her success lies in her ability "to think of myself as one whose success (in baseball) relies on a basic set of fundamentals which I shall adapt as the situation dictates. While Kipling waxes poetically about overcoming adversity, Spencer is keeping her eye on the goal of success on the playing field. Moreover, the use of stanzas in "If" divide each thought segment while Spencer uses the common paragraph division for her non-fictional prose.

While both Kipling and Spencer have a position to assert, Kipling's position is more global. Issues that are addressed include trusting yourself "when all men doubt you, / But (making) allowance for their doubting too" and forcing your "your heart and nerve and sinew / To serve your turn long after they are gone." These are issues that deal directly with courage, strong self-image, and maturity. Kipling's message seems to be that by facing all of life's challenges and doing so with dignity and grace, then "Yours is the Earth and everything that's in it, / And—which is more—you'll be a Man, my son!"

Spencer, on the other hand, is taking a less global view of success by relating it directly to her experiences in baseball. She distills the factors of success to include but three components. The first component is the need to stay in good physical shape while addressing injuries immediately "since neglecting a developing problem will only exacerbate the problem and impact my teammates in a negative way." The second component is "is maintaining a good diet (and eating foods) from a variety of food groups and colors each day to increase my chances of naturally supplementing my daily vitamin and mineral requirements" while positively addressing her diabetes by monitoring "my sugar levels carefully." The third component, mental imaging and toughness, has a positive effect on Spencer's teammates since it is infectious in a manner similar to that of Peale's "power of positive thinking."

In poetic form, Kipling gives advice that is global, reflective of maturity, and impacts on all individuals in a positive way. On the other hand, Spencer speaks of success on the ball field while concluding with the advice, "a commitment to excellence must be maintained on a daily basis." For those searching for poetically-written advice that impact's success in life, Kipling's "If" is an appropriate resource. For those searching for a more narrow approach to success, particularly success on the baseball field, then Spencer's piece, complete with a quote from Hall of Famer Brooks Robinson, is an appropriate choice.

Informational Text

There are 2 passages used here for Informational Text.

"Success in Baseball"
13. **Part A:** The correct answer is D. The function of the word *pro* in the opening sentence is an adjective.
    Part B: The correct answer is B. "The" is an article which is also an adjective.
14. The correct answer is D. "Is" the helping verb for the sentence, "The first component in my striving for success is staying in good physical shape."
15. The correct answer is A. The word *minimizing* is an example of a participle.
16. The correct answer is C. The type of sentence is complex because it contains at least one independent clause and one dependent clause.
17. The correct selections are D and F. The words *immediately* and *only* from the sentence are adverbs.

"Skateboarding"
18. The correct answer is B. The passage talks about skateboarding from the 1900s to the present day.
19. The correct answer is C. Many people in California wanted to surf on land and on water.
20. The correct answer is B. Skiers are taking to the air and becoming skaters too.
21. **Part A:** The correct answer is C. Skaters began performing on homemade ramps and handrails.
    Part B: The correct answer is D. It is a fact that The Bones Brigade made videos.

22. The correct answer is C. A skateboard repair manual is a good resource to use when you have a broken skateboard, but looking into magazines or talking to and watching professional skateboarders is more productive when learning how to master the art of skateboarding.

Sample Graphic Organizer and Organization Chart for Writing

APPENDIX A

Argumentative Essay Flow Chart

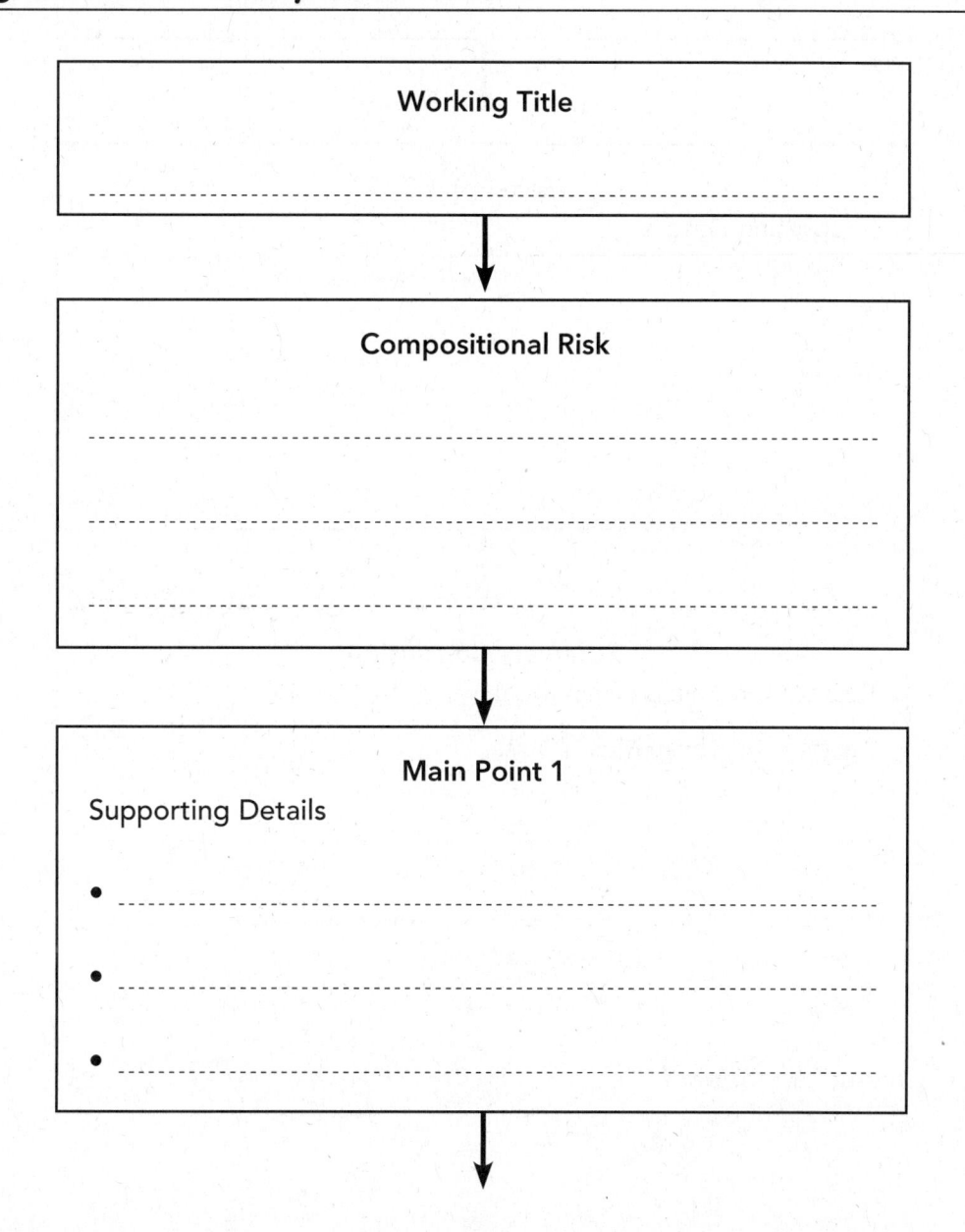

Working Title

↓

Compositional Risk

↓

Main Point 1
Supporting Details

-
-
-

↓

Main Point 2

Supporting Details

- ....
- ....
- ....

Main Point 3

Supporting Details

- ....
- ....
- ....

Summary Conclusion

Restate the Thesis (Main Idea).

Restate the Three Main Points.

- ....
- ....
- ....

Add the Insight.

Speculative Writing Organization Sheet

Step 1—Create the Realistic Main Conflict

Step 2—Create the Plot (Plan of Action)

Step 3—Create the Setting

Step 4—Give Each Main Character a Personality

Step 5—Develop the Story (Plot Line)

Step 6—Write the Solution for the Problem (Resolve the Conflict)

Step 7—Give Your Story a Working Title

Step 8—Write Your First Draft and Include a Compositional Risk in the Opening Paragraph and Insight in the Final Paragraph

Step 9—Add Dialogue

Step 10—Edit and Submit Your Essay

Grade 7 English Language Arts Common Core Standards

APPENDIX B

Reading Literature

Key Ideas and Details:

CCSS.ELA-LITERACY.RL.7.1
Cite several pieces of textual evidence to support analysis of what the text says explicitly as well as inferences drawn from the text.

CCSS.ELA-LITERACY.RL.7.2
Determine a theme or central idea of a text and analyze its development over the course of the text; provide an objective summary of the text.

CCSS.ELA-LITERACY.RL.7.3
Analyze how particular elements of a story or drama interact (e.g., how setting shapes the characters or plot).

Craft and Structure:

CCSS.ELA-LITERACY.RL.7.4
Determine the meaning of words and phrases as they are used in a text, including figurative and connotative meanings; analyze the impact of rhymes and other repetitions of sounds (e.g., alliteration) on a specific verse or stanza of a poem or section of a story or drama.

CCSS.ELA-LITERACY.RL.7.5
Analyze how a drama's or poem's form or structure (e.g., soliloquy, sonnet) contributes to its meaning.

CCSS.ELA-LITERACY.RL.7.6
Analyze how an author develops and contrasts the points of view of different characters or narrators in a text.

Integration of Knowledge and Ideas:

CCSS.ELA-LITERACY.RL.7.7
Compare and contrast a written story, drama, or poem to its audio, filmed, staged, or multimedia version, analyzing the effects of techniques unique to each medium (e.g., lighting, sound, color, or camera focus and angles in a film).

CCSS.ELA-LITERACY.RL.7.8
(RL.7.8 not applicable to literature)

CCSS.ELA-LITERACY.RL.7.9
Compare and contrast a fictional portrayal of a time, place, or character and a historical account of the same period as a means of understanding how authors of fiction use or alter history.

Range of Reading and Level of Text Complexity:

CCSS.ELA-LITERACY.RL.7.10
By the end of the year, read and comprehend literature, including stories, dramas, and poems, in the grades 6–8 text complexity band proficiently, with scaffolding as needed at the high end of the range.

Reading Informational Text

Key Ideas and Details:

CCSS.ELA-LITERACY.RI.7.1
Cite several pieces of textual evidence to support analysis of what the text says explicitly as well as inferences drawn from the text.

CCSS.ELA-LITERACY.RI.7.2
Determine two or more central ideas in a text and analyze their development over the course of the text; provide an objective summary of the text.

CCSS.ELA-LITERACY.RI.7.3
Analyze the interactions between individuals, events, and ideas in a text (e.g., how ideas influence individuals or events, or how individuals influence ideas or events).

Craft and Structure:

CCSS.ELA-LITERACY.RI.7.4
Determine the meaning of words and phrases as they are used in a text, including figurative, connotative, and technical meanings; analyze the impact of a specific word choice on meaning and tone.

CCSS.ELA-LITERACY.RI.7.5
Analyze the structure an author uses to organize a text, including how the major sections contribute to the whole and to the development of the ideas.

CCSS.ELA-LITERACY.RI.7.6
Determine an author's point of view or purpose in a text and analyze how the author distinguishes his or her position from that of others.

Integration of Knowledge and Ideas:

CCSS.ELA-LITERACY.RI.7.7
Compare and contrast a text to an audio, video, or multimedia version of the text, analyzing each medium's portrayal of the subject (e.g., how the delivery of a speech affects the impact of the words).

CCSS.ELA-LITERACY.RI.7.8
Trace and evaluate the argument and specific claims in a text, assessing whether the reasoning is sound and the evidence is relevant and sufficient to support the claims.
CCSS.ELA-LITERACY.RI.7.9
Analyze how two or more authors writing about the same topic shape their presentations of key information by emphasizing different evidence or advancing different interpretations of facts.

Range of Reading and Level of Text Complexity:
CCSS.ELA-LITERACY.RI.7.10
By the end of the year, read and comprehend literary nonfiction in the grades 6–8 text complexity band proficiently, with scaffolding as needed at the high end of the range.

Writing

Text Types and Purposes:
CCSS.ELA-LITERACY.W.7.1
Write arguments to support claims with clear reasons and relevant evidence.
CCSS.ELA-LITERACY.W.7.1.A
Introduce claim(s), acknowledge alternate or opposing claims, and organize the reasons and evidence logically.
CCSS.ELA-LITERACY.W.7.1.B
Support claim(s) with logical reasoning and relevant evidence, using accurate, credible sources and demonstrating an understanding of the topic or text.
CCSS.ELA-LITERACY.W.7.1.C
Use words, phrases, and clauses to create cohesion and clarify the relationships among claim(s), reasons, and evidence.
CCSS.ELA-LITERACY.W.7.1.D
Establish and maintain a formal style.
CCSS.ELA-LITERACY.W.7.1.E
Provide a concluding statement or section that follows from and supports the argument presented.
CCSS.ELA-LITERACY.W.7.2
Write informative/explanatory texts to examine a topic and convey ideas, concepts, and information through the selection, organization, and analysis of relevant content.
CCSS.ELA-LITERACY.W.7.2.A
Introduce a topic clearly, previewing what is to follow; organize ideas, concepts, and information, using strategies such as definition, classification, comparison/contrast, and cause/effect; include formatting (e.g., headings), graphics (e.g., charts, tables), and multimedia when useful to aiding comprehension.

CCSS.ELA-LITERACY.W.7.2.B
Develop the topic with relevant facts, definitions, concrete details, quotations, or other information and examples.

CCSS.ELA-LITERACY.W.7.2.C
Use appropriate transitions to create cohesion and clarify the relationships among ideas and concepts.

CCSS.ELA-LITERACY.W.7.2.D
Use precise language and domain-specific vocabulary to inform about or explain the topic.

CCSS.ELA-LITERACY.W.7.2.E
Establish and maintain a formal style.

CCSS.ELA-LITERACY.W.7.2.F
Provide a concluding statement or section that follows from and supports the information or explanation presented.

CCSS.ELA-LITERACY.W.7.3
Write narratives to develop real or imagined experiences or events using effective technique, relevant descriptive details, and well-structured event sequences.

CCSS.ELA-LITERACY.W.7.3.A
Engage and orient the reader by establishing a context and point of view and introducing a narrator and/or characters; organize an event sequence that unfolds naturally and logically.

CCSS.ELA-LITERACY.W.7.3.B
Use narrative techniques, such as dialogue, pacing, and description, to develop experiences, events, and/or characters.

CCSS.ELA-LITERACY.W.7.3.C
Use a variety of transition words, phrases, and clauses to convey sequence and signal shifts from one time frame or setting to another.

CCSS.ELA-LITERACY.W.7.3.D
Use precise words and phrases, relevant descriptive details, and sensory language to capture the action and convey experiences and events.

CCSS.ELA-LITERACY.W.7.3.E
Provide a conclusion that follows from and reflects on the narrated experiences or events.

Production and Distribution of Writing:

CCSS.ELA-LITERACY.W.7.4
Produce clear and coherent writing in which the development, organization, and style are appropriate to task, purpose, and audience. (Grade-specific expectations for writing types are defined in standards 1–3 above.)

CCSS.ELA-LITERACY.W.7.5
With some guidance and support from peers and adults, develop and strengthen writing as needed by planning, revising, editing, rewriting, or trying a new approach, focusing on how well purpose and audience have been addressed. (Editing for conventions should demonstrate command of language standards 1–3 up to and including grade 7 here.)

CCSS.ELA-LITERACY.W.7.6
Use technology, including the Internet, to produce and publish writing and link to and cite sources as well as to interact and collaborate with others, including linking to and citing sources.

Research to Build and Present Knowledge:

CCSS.ELA-LITERACY.W.7.7
Conduct short research projects to answer a question, drawing on several sources and generating additional related, focused questions for further research and investigation.

CCSS.ELA-LITERACY.W.7.8
Gather relevant information from multiple print and digital sources, using search terms effectively; assess the credibility and accuracy of each source; and quote or paraphrase the data and conclusions of others while avoiding plagiarism and following a standard format for citation.

CCSS.ELA-LITERACY.W.7.9
Draw evidence from literary or informational texts to support analysis, reflection, and research.

CCSS.ELA-LITERACY.W.7.9.A
Apply *grade 7 Reading standards* to literature (e.g., "Compare and contrast a fictional portrayal of a time, place, or character and a historical account of the same period as a means of understanding how authors of fiction use or alter history").

CCSS.ELA-LITERACY.W.7.9.B
Apply *grade 7 Reading standards* to literary nonfiction (e.g., "Trace and evaluate the argument and specific claims in a text, assessing whether the reasoning is sound and the evidence is relevant and sufficient to support the claims").

Range of Writing:

CCSS.ELA-LITERACY.W.7.10
Write routinely over extended time frames (time for research, reflection, and revision) and shorter time frames (a single sitting or a day or two) for a range of discipline-specific tasks, purposes, and audiences.

Speaking and Listening

Comprehension and Collaboration:

CCSS.ELA-Literacy.SL.7.1
Engage effectively in a range of collaborative discussions (one-on-one, in groups, and teacher-led) with diverse partners on grade 7 topics, texts, and issues, building on others' ideas and expressing their own clearly.

CCSS.ELA-Literacy.SL.7.1.A
Come to discussions prepared, having read or researched material under study; explicitly draw on that preparation by referring to evidence on the topic, text, or issue to probe and reflect on ideas under discussion.

CCSS.ELA-Literacy.SL.7.1.B
Follow rules for collegial discussions, track progress toward specific goals and deadlines, and define individual roles as needed.

CCSS.ELA-Literacy.SL.7.1.C
Pose questions that elicit elaboration and respond to others' questions and comments with relevant observations and ideas that bring the discussion back on topic as needed.

CCSS.ELA-Literacy.SL.7.1.D
Acknowledge new information expressed by others and, when warranted, modify their own views.

CCSS.ELA-Literacy.SL.7.2
Analyze the main ideas and supporting details presented in diverse media and formats (e.g., visually, quantitatively, orally) and explain how the ideas clarify a topic, text, or issue under study.

CCSS.ELA-Literacy.SL.7.3
Delineate a speaker's argument and specific claims, evaluating the soundness of the reasoning and the relevance and sufficiency of the evidence.

Presentation of Knowledge and Ideas:

CCSS.ELA-Literacy.SL.7.4
Present claims and findings, emphasizing salient points in a focused, coherent manner with pertinent descriptions, facts, details, and examples; use appropriate eye contact, adequate volume, and clear pronunciation.

CCSS.ELA-Literacy.SL.7.5
Include multimedia components and visual displays in presentations to clarify claims and findings and emphasize salient points.

CCSS.ELA-Literacy.SL.7.6
Adapt speech to a variety of contexts and tasks, demonstrating command of formal English when indicated or appropriate.

Language

Conventions of Standard English:

CCSS.ELA-Literacy.L.7.1
Demonstrate command of the conventions of standard English grammar and usage when writing or speaking.

CCSS.ELA-Literacy.L.7.1.A
Explain the function of phrases and clauses in general and their function in specific sentences.

CCSS.ELA-Literacy.L.7.1.B
Choose among simple, compound, complex, and compound-complex sentences to signal differing relationships among ideas.

CCSS.ELA-Literacy.L.7.1.C
Place phrases and clauses within a sentence, recognizing and correcting misplaced and dangling modifiers.

CCSS.ELA-Literacy.L.7.2
Demonstrate command of the conventions of standard English capitalization, punctuation, and spelling when writing.

CCSS.ELA-Literacy.L.7.2.A
Use a comma to separate coordinate adjectives (e.g., *It was a fascinating, enjoyable movie* but not *He wore an old[,] green shirt*).

CCSS.ELA-Literacy.L.7.2.B
Spell correctly.

Knowledge of Language:

CCSS.ELA-Literacy.L.7.3
Use knowledge of language and its conventions when writing, speaking, reading, or listening.

CCSS.ELA-Literacy.L.7.3.A
Choose language that expresses ideas precisely and concisely, recognizing and eliminating wordiness and redundancy.*

Vocabulary Acquisition and Use:

CCSS.ELA-Literacy.L.7.4
Determine or clarify the meaning of unknown and multiple-meaning words and phrases based on *grade 7 reading and content*, choosing flexibly from a range of strategies.

CCSS.ELA-Literacy.L.7.4.A
Use context (e.g., the overall meaning of a sentence or paragraph; a word's position or function in a sentence) as a clue to the meaning of a word or phrase.

CCSS.ELA-Literacy.L.7.4.B
Use common, grade-appropriate Greek or Latin affixes and roots as clues to the meaning of a word (e.g., *belligerent, bellicose, rebel*).

CCSS.ELA-Literacy.L.7.4.C
Consult general and specialized reference materials (e.g., dictionaries, glossaries, thesauruses), both print and digital, to find the pronunciation of a word or determine or clarify its precise meaning or its part of speech.

CCSS.ELA-Literacy.L.7.4.D
Verify the preliminary determination of the meaning of a word or phrase (e.g., by checking the inferred meaning in context or in a dictionary).

CCSS.ELA-Literacy.L.7.5
Demonstrate understanding of figurative language, word relationships, and nuances in word meanings.

CCSS.ELA-Literacy.L.7.5.A
Interpret figures of speech (e.g., literary, biblical, and mythological allusions) in context.

CCSS.ELA-Literacy.L.7.5.B
Use the relationship between particular words (e.g., synonym/antonym, analogy) to better understand each of the words.

CCSS.ELA-Literacy.L.7.5.C
Distinguish among the connotations (associations) of words with similar denotations (definitions) (e.g., *refined, respectful, polite, diplomatic, condescending*).

CCSS.ELA-Literacy.L.7.6
Acquire and use accurately grade-appropriate general academic and domain-specific words and phrases; gather vocabulary knowledge when considering a word or phrase important to comprehension or expression.

Index

A
Abbreviations, 144
Active voice, 202–204
Adjectives, 60, 218–220
Adverbs, 60, 205, 218–220
Agreement, 189–195
Alliteration, 131–142
Analytical essays, 69
Anecdote, 5
Answering with prior knowledge, 181–187
Appositive, 211
Argumentative essay, 9–16

B
Book references, 7
Brief story, 5–6

C
Case agreement, 189–193
Cause and effect, 87–88, 98–108
Central idea, 151–156
Characters, 50–52, 82–97
Chronological pattern, 86–87
Clarifying, 157–162
Comma, 210–213, 220
"Common sense" check, 22
Compare and contrast, 88
Complex sentence, 196, 205
Compositional risks, 31–34
    description of, 5–9
    interesting fact or observation, 32
    "painting a word picture" for, 6
    rhetorical question, 32
    sample, 32–34
    startling statement, 32
    types of, 5
Compound sentence, 196, 205
Conclusion, summary, 28–29
Conflict, 47–48, 109–118
Conflict resolution, 54

D
Declarative sentence, 211
Descriptive essay, 88
Details, 144–150
Dialogue, 59, 220–221
Directions
    description of, 17
    following, 169–174
Direct object pronouns, 190
Direct quotations, 220–221

E
Editing, 37, 59–64
End marks for sentences, 210–213
Essay
    insight used at end of, 9
    speculative. *See* Speculative essay
Exclamation marks, 211, 220
Exclamatory sentence, 211

F
Fact, 102, 163–168
Finding information, 181–187
First-person narrator, 98
Following directions, 169–174
Foreshadowing, 109
Fragments, 207–210

345

G
Gender agreement, of subject, 193–195
Grammar, 59–60
Graphic organizers, 333–334

H
Homographs, 214–216
Homophones, 214–216
"Hook," 5
Humor, 8
Hyperbole, 33
Hyphenated modifier, 33

I
Imperative sentence, 211
Indirect object pronouns, 190
Indirect quotations, 220–221
Information
  finding of, 181–187
  sources of, 175–180
Informational (everyday) reading
  central idea, 151–156
  clarifying, 157–162
  details, 144–150
  fact, 163–168
  finding information, 181–187
  following directions, 169–174
  information sources, 175–180
  Insight, 9
  literary forms, 175–180
  opinion, 163–168
  overview of, 143
  predicting, 157–162
  prior knowledge used for answering, 181–187
  questioning, 157–162
  sequence of events, 144–150
  theme, 151–156
Interesting fact or observation, 32
Interrogative sentence, 211
Inverted declaratives, 217
Inverted order sentences, 217

L
Linking verbs, 218
Literary allusion, 7
Literary forms, 175–180
Literature
  alliteration, 131–142
  cause and effect, 98–108
  characters, 82–97
  conflict, 109–118
  making predictions, 109–118
  metaphor, 131–142
  mood, 119–130
  personification, 131–142
  plot, 82–97
  point of view, 98–108
  preview techniques for, 71–73
  resolution, 109–118
  rhyme scheme, 131–142
  setting, 82–97
  simile, 131–142
  theme, 98–108
  tone, 119–130

M
Magic threes, 33
Main conflict, 47–48
Main idea, 21–22
Main points, 22–27
Major conflicts, 109
Making predictions, 109–118
Metaphor, 32–33, 131–142
Minor conflicts, 109
Misplaced modifiers, 200–201
Mood, 119–130
Multiple-choice questions, 70
Multiple-meaning words, 70

N
Number agreement, of subject, 190

O
Objective case, 190
Object of the preposition, 192
Object pronouns, 192
Opinion, 102, 163–168

P
"Painting a word picture," 6
Paired passage, 86–87, 89
Passive voice, 202–204
Past tense, 60
Periods, 220
Personification, 131–142
Persuasive essay, 9–10
Play references, 7
Plot, 48–49, 82–97
Plot line, 52–53
Poetic devices, 131–142
Point of view, 98–108
Possessive case, 190
Predicting, 157–162
Predictions, making, 109–118
Prepositional phrase, 205
Preview techniques, 71–73
Prewriting, 10, 15, 45–46
Prior knowledge used for answering, 181–187
Problem/solution, 87
Prompt, 16–17
Pronouns, 189–195
Proofreading, 37
Punctuation, 210–213

Q
Questioning, 157–162
Question marks, 211, 220
Quotation, 7–8, 220–221
Quotation marks, 220–225

R
Research, 71
Resolution, 109–118
Rhetorical question, 32
Rhyme scheme, 131–142
Run-ons, 207–210

S
Second-person narrator, 98
Sentences
   types of, 195–199
   unusual order in, 217–218
Sequence of events, 144–150
Setting, 49–50, 82–97
Simile, 32, 131–142
Slang, 60–61
Speculative essay
   characters, 50–52
   content of, 60–61
   definition of, 45
   dialogue, 59
   editing of, 59–64
   final draft of, 61–63
   first draft of, 56–59
   main conflict, 47–48
   plot, 48–49
   plot line, 52–53
   prewriting of, 45–46
   resolution of conflict, 54
   setting, 49–50
   story plan for, 46
   subject of, 45
   topic of, 64
   working title, 54
   writing practice, 64–67
Spelling, 59–60, 225–228
Stanza, 131
Startling statement, 8, 32
Story plan, 46
Strategic plan
   "common sense" check, 22

directions, 17
   main points, 22–27
   summary conclusion, 28–29
   supporting details, 22–27
   thesis statement, 21–22
   transitions, 29–30
   working title, 19–21, 26
   writing, 36–37
   writing prompt, 16–17
Subjective case study of, 189
Subject pronouns, 192
Summary conclusion, 28–29
Supporting details, 12, 22–27

T
"Teaser," 5
Tense shifts, 60
Theme, 98–108, 151–156
Thesis statement, 21–22
Third-person narrator, 98
Title, working, 19–21, 26, 54
Tone, 119–130
Transitions, 29–30, 144

U
Underlining, 222–225

V
Voice, 202–204

W
"What if?" scenario, 6
Working title, 19–21, 26, 54
Writing
   checklist for, 37–38
   practice in, 40–44
   strategies for, 36–37